CREATING LEGAL WORLDS

Story and Style in a Culture of Argument

Creating Legal Worlds

*Story and Style in a Culture
of Argument*

GREIG HENDERSON

UNIVERSITY OF TORONTO PRESS
Toronto Buffalo London

© University of Toronto Press 2015
Toronto Buffalo London
www.utppublishing.com

ISBN 978-1-4426-3708-5

Library and Archives Canada Cataloguing in Publication

Henderson, Greig Edward, 1952–, author
Creating legal worlds : story and style in a culture of argument /
Greig Henderson.

Includes bibliographical references and index.
ISBN 978-1-4426-3708-5 (bound)

1. Law – Language. 2. Law and literature. 3. Forensic orations. 4. Rhetoric.
I. Title.

K213.H45 2015   340'.14   C2015-901217-1

This book has been published with the help of a grant from the Federation
for the Humanities and Social Sciences, through the Awards to Scholarly
Publications Program, using funds provided by the Social Sciences and
Humanities Research Council of Canada.

University of Toronto Press acknowledges the financial assistance to its
publishing program of the Canada Council for the Arts and the Ontario Arts
Council, an agency of the Government of Ontario.

**Canada Council Conseil des Arts
for the Arts   du Canada**

ONTARIO ARTS COUNCIL
CONSEIL DES ARTS DE L'ONTARIO

an Ontario government agency
un organisme du gouvernement de l'Ontario

University of Toronto Press acknowledges the financial support of the
Government of Canada through the Canada Book Fund for its publishing
activities.

Contents

Foreword vii

Acknowledgments ix

Introduction 3

1 The Cost of Persuasion: Figure, Story, and Eloquence in the Rhetoric of Judicial Discourse 16

2 Pure and Impure Styles: Formalism and Pragmatism in the Language of Decision Writing 38

3 The Perils of Analogy: Legal World-Making and Judicial Self-Fashioning in *Palsgraf v. Long Island Railroad* 58

4 Murder, They Wrote: The Rhetoric of Causation in the Language of the Law 74

5 Narrative Theory and the Art of Judgment: The Anatomy of a Supreme Court Decision 89

6 The Look in His Eyes: *Rusk v. State, State v. Rusk* 119

7 Rhetoric, Philosophy, and Law 144

Postscript: Rhetoric, Postmodernism, and Scepticism 157

Works Cited 169

Index 173

Foreword

Alfred North Whitehead, the mathematician and philosopher, said that nobody can be a good reasoner unless by constant practice he or she has realized the importance of getting hold of the big ideas and hanging on to them like grim death. In *Creating Legal Worlds: Story and Style in a Culture of Argument*, Greig Henderson gets hold of a big idea that is fundamental to good legal reasoning and good judgment writing.

Lawyers and judges have long known the importance of storytelling to persuasion, but they have not often understood how or why it is that stories are so powerful and so effective. In *Creating Legal Worlds*, Professor Henderson gives theory to why stories persuade, and he explains the correctness of the conventional wisdom that the facts are more important than the law in legal reasoning and in legal decision-making. He also shows and explains that a judge's choice of what facts to narrate and how to express those facts as a story says a great deal about legal culture and about the character of the judicial decision-maker and the persuasiveness of his or her judgments.

Legal argument has been long studied. Aristotle theorized that there were three modes of successful persuasion in public speech, including legal argument. First, persuasion depended upon *ethos*, the advocate's success in conveying to the audience the perception that he or she can be trusted. Second, success depended upon *pathos*, the advocate's ability to awaken the emotions of the audience as a way to accept the argument. Third, success depended upon the logical validity or *logos* of what is argued. As revealed by *Creating Legal Worlds*, storytelling plays a prominent role in the construction of *logos, pathos*, and *ethos*.

Reasoning, be it in science, mathematics, philosophy, or jurisprudence, is in pursuit of the truth, and Professor Henderson's big idea about the creation of legal worlds through storytelling is very valuable to judges, who must of necessity be practical reasoners or pragmatists. A judge cannot be a radical sceptic or nihilist. In coming to a judgment, a judge finds what passes for truth, and that truth is found by rhetorical reasoning in the sense described, explained, and ultimately recommended by Professor Henderson.

While not a manual or a handbook for legal writing, *Creating Legal Worlds* offers substantial practical lessons about legal writing, particularly judgment writing. Professor Henderson undertakes a rhetorical analysis of several judgments, some of them quite famous in the development of the law, and others commonplace or routine exercises in judgment writing. His illustrations show the everyday craftsmanship of judges, and his analysis reveals that a judge being oblivious to the effect of storytelling on persuasion leads to a discordant and unsuccessful judgment, where the judgment not only fails to persuade but also produces an untrue and unjust outcome. Professor Henderson shows that a judge cannot be a good reasoner unless by constant study he or she gets hold of the big idea of the importance and power of storytelling to the pursuit of justice.

Paul M. Perell,
Justice, Ontario Superior Court of Justice,
October 2014

Acknowledgments

As Supreme Court Justice Louis LeBel memorably noted more than a decade ago, the duty to make full, fair, and frank disclosure in affidavits does not require the disclosure of "all information":

> So long as the affidavit meets the requisite legal norm, there is no need for it to be as lengthy as *À la recherche du temps perdu,* as lively as the *Kama Sutra,* or as detailed as an automotive repair manual. All that it must do is set out the facts fully and frankly for the authorizing judge in order that he or she can make an assessment of whether these rise to the standard required in the legal test for the authorization. Ideally, an affidavit should be not only full and frank but also clear and concise. (*R. v. Araujo,* [2000] 2 S.C.R. 992)

I am not sure what the standard required for acknowledgments is, but I do aspire to be clear and concise if not full and frank. Since 1985 I have been a faculty member in the judicial writing program sponsored by the Canadian Institute for the Administration of Justice. Over the past few decades, I have also conducted writing seminars for various courts, boards, agencies, tribunals, and law firms. As an interloper in law and literature scholarship, I look at the choices and challenges that beset a judge, adjudicator, or lawyer mainly from the point of view of the writer. The book that has emerged is, I hope, as lengthy, lively, and detailed as the subject demands.

Most of what I have learned about legal writing comes from the friends and colleagues I have had the good fortune to be associated with: Steve Armstrong, Dale Barleben, Victoria Bennett, Ed Berry, Jonathan Butler, George Byrnes, Jim Carnwath, Michael Dixon, Jane Griesdorf,

Nicole Duval Hesler, Christine Huglo Robertson, Henry Hutcheon, John Laskin, Jay Ludwig, Jim Macdonald, Barb Morris, Nick Mount, James O'Reilly, John Ouzas, Paul Perell, Moira Phillips, Jim Raymond, Howard Rubel, Simon Stern, Lisa Surridge, Cheryl Susack, and John Warnock. To them, to the graduate students who participated in my Law as Literature seminar, to the judges, adjudicators, and lawyers I have worked with over the years, to the two anonymous reviewers and their helpful comments, and to my editor, Daniel Quinlan, I owe a great deal. I also owe a great deal to the five most important females in my life: Erica, Kerry, Sarah, Amanda, and Scout. To them I dedicate this book.

CREATING LEGAL WORLDS

Story and Style in a Culture of Argument

Introduction

> We inhabit a *nomos* – a normative universe. We constantly create and maintain a world of right and wrong, of lawful and unlawful, of valid and void ... No set of legal prescriptions exists apart from the narratives that locate it and give it meaning. For every constitution there is an epic, for each decalogue a scripture. Once understood in the context of the narratives that give it meaning, law becomes not merely a system of rules to be observed, but a world in which we live.
>
> Robert Cover, 95

This study is about legal world-making and judicial self-fashioning, about how judges create normative universes for us to live in and fashion ethical images of themselves as judges every time they decide a case. Its enabling assumptions are that judicial writing is a form of narrative and rhetoric, that "storytelling in law is narrative within a culture of argument" (Gewirtz, 5), and that narrative is an integral element of legal argument, not something simply tacked on to humanize the law or authenticate the parties. Especially in the context of cases dealing with liability and homicide, two areas of law in which the concept of causation plays a pivotal role, I try to show that the rhetorical power of hypothetical and factual narratives ends up carrying as much argumentative weight as the logical force of legal distinctions. In a more general sense, I try to show that narrative is crucial to legal decision-making because the primary task of the judge is to make a plausible and coherent story out of the sometimes conflicting and contradictory particulars of a given case. Thus the angle of vision from which the story is told (narrative perspective) and the language and style in which it is couched (narrative voice) have an impact on the decision arrived at. The agents a judge empowers to see and say are often the agents whose arguments prevail. All writing involves making choices, and the rhetorical, narratological, and stylistic choices a judge makes, consciously or unconsciously, create a legal world for others to inhabit and embody the moral character of its creator. *Nomos*, perspective, voice, and *ethos* matter in law just as they matter in literature. And narrative is the cement that binds these two disciplines together.

As rhetorical activities in which narrative plays a formative and foundational role, law and literature have much in common. Both attempt to shape reality through language, both use strategies of persuasion to do so, both require construction and interpretation, and both, as James Boyd White points out, are arts "by which culture and community are established, maintained, and transformed" (*Heracles' Bow*, 28).

Traditionally, law and literature scholarship has focused on law *in* literature, on how legal practice and culture are represented and thematized in literature, film, and television through narratives of, say, law and order, crime and punishment, trial and verdict, censorship and expression. While recognizing the necessity and validity of such studies, current scholarship in the field focuses on law *as* literature, using the methods of literary criticism to understand, interpret, and evaluate legal discourse. As Guyora Binder and Robert Weisberg point out in *Literary Criticisms of Law*, law is "a kind of literary or cultural activity," "a practice of making various kinds of literary artifacts: interpretations, narratives, characters, rhetorical performances, linguistic signs, figurative tropes, and representations of the social world" (ix). "The literary is intrinsic to law insofar as law fashions the characters, personas, sensibilities, identities, myths, and traditions that compose our social world" (18).

To see law as literature opens up exciting avenues of inquiry and allows the full arsenal of criticism and theory to be brought to bear upon legal discourse: rhetoric, narratology, dialogism, stylistics, deconstruction, new historicism, feminism, postcolonialism, reception history, and so on. Important questions emerge. What stories get told? In whose voice? From whose perspective? What stories get suppressed? What voices and perspectives are excluded or marginalized? How do ethnicity, race, national origin, class, religious affiliation, gender, and sexuality factor into such stories?

Although this study plants itself firmly in the interrelated domains of rhetoric, narratology, dialogism, and stylistics, the field of law and literature has expanded into a fully interdisciplinary undertaking. Building on scholarship in legal and literary studies over the past four decades, the emerging field of law, culture, and humanities foregrounds the importance of textual analysis as a means to probe issues such as justice, equality, power, ethics, identity, interpretation, obligation, authority, and speech. Instead of treating law as separate from an everyday life and culture that are somehow outside the institutions of justice, cultural legal studies understands law and literature as mutually constitutive domains.

While not as sweepingly interdisciplinary and unremittingly historicist as recent works in cultural legal studies, this study certainly takes law and literature to be mutually constitutive domains. Its focus is on judicial writing as a form of narrative and rhetoric. From this standpoint, "storytelling in law is narrative within a culture of argument … Storytelling is, or is made to function as, argument" (Gewirtz, 5). The literary aspect of law as literature is not "something extrinsic to law that corrects or redeems or ornaments it" (Binder and Weisberg, 18). It is "a constitutive dimension of law rather than a redemptive supplement" (19). At times storytelling may work to authenticate a voice or humanize the law, but these are not its essential functions. Storytelling in law is not necessarily authentic or humane. And it is never neutral or disinterested. A story is always presented from a certain angle of vision and in a certain voice. Its way of presenting characters and events is also a way of shaping the responses of its audience, of getting them to believe something, feel something, or do something. Storytelling is but a rhetorical resource to be exploited, for good or for ill.

Following James Boyd White, Peter Brooks, Paul Gewirtz, Richard Weisberg, and others, I see law as a branch of rhetoric. By rhetoric I mean the use of language to inform, persuade, or motivate an audience; it involves discovering all available means of persuasion to accomplish a certain purpose in a certain situation for a certain audience and then using the most apt and cogent ones. Like all users of language, writers of judgments inform, persuade, or motivate by deploying three basic strategies: *logos* – the appeal to reason, logic, argument, or example (the substantial); *pathos* – the appeal to passion, sentiment, imagery, or emotion (the motivational); and *ethos* – the appeal to the character, image, or expertise of the writer (the authoritative). In an ideal judgment, all three strategies harmoniously work together: *logos,* the process of reasoning by which a judge interprets the past and brings it to bear on the present; *pathos,* the degree to which his or her court recognizes the legitimacy and humanity of the losing parties and hears their stories; and *ethos,* the character his or her court gives itself, the ethical community it imagines.

Besides identifying these three basic strategies of persuasion, classical rhetoricians identify three parts of discourse: *inventio* – the invention or discovery of arguments, *dispositio* – the arrangement or organization of those arguments, and *elocutio* – the style (florid, forcible, or plain) in which those arguments are expressed.

These persuasive strategies, organizational structures, and expressive styles are important to legal writing because every time judges write decisions, they are faced with rhetorical choices, and by the stories they choose to tell and by the styles in which they choose to tell them, they are creating legal worlds for others to live in as well as fashioning images of themselves as judges. In every case they are called upon to decide, the story can be characterized in a variety of ways. And those choices and characterizations sometimes have momentous consequences. In this regard, storytelling in law is different from storytelling in literature.

So while it is undeniably true that storytelling is inescapable in both law and literature and that narrative and rhetoric not only pervade both disciplines but also constitute them, there are significant differences between how suasive storytelling operates in law and how it operates in literature. For one thing, storytelling in law, as I have said, is narrative within a culture of argument, and what stories are permitted to be told and what stories are doomed to be excluded are governed by laws of evidence and rules of procedure. For another, the interpretations of law's stories matter in a way that those of literature's stories do not. As Robert Cover dramatically puts it in "Violence and the Word": "Legal interpretation takes place in a field of pain and death ... Legal interpretive acts signal and occasion the imposition of violence upon others. A judge articulates her understanding of a text, and as a result, somebody loses his freedom, his property, his children, even his life" (203). Correct or not, judicial interpretations, unlike literary interpretations, are binding; the full coercive power of the state is behind them.

Though such sobering differences must always be kept in mind, so too must the invigorating similarities. As James Boyd White points out, law, like literature, is dialogical and communal.

> To conceive of the law as a rhetorical and social system, as a way in which we use an inherited language to talk to each other and to maintain a community, suggests in a new way that the heart of law is what we always

knew it was: the open hearing in which one point of view, one construction of language and reality, is tested against another. The multiplicity of
readings that the law permits is not its weakness, but its strength, for it is
this that makes room for different voices, and gives a purchase by which
culture may be modified in response to the demands of circumstance. It is
a method at once for the recognition of others, for the acknowledgment of
ignorance, and for cultural change. (*Heracles' Bow*, 104)

In their writings, judges create not only legal worlds but also images
of themselves. And this study is generally concerned with legal world-
making and judicial self-fashioning as well as with an array of other
topics, among them the role the literary function of language plays in
judicial discourse, the sense in which judgments are narratives, the relationship between eloquence and virtue, the rhetoric of causation in
the language of the law, the illuminative power of concepts drawn from
narratology and dialogism, and the function of style as an integral part
of the writing, thinking, and deciding process.

The first chapter looks at figure, story, and eloquence – features of discourse normally associated with literature rather than with law. Nevertheless, the literary function of language is often on display in judicial
writing, which is not to say that such display is always for the better.
This function of language makes itself manifest whenever figuration,
imagery, diction, sentence structure, or any deviation from the linguistic norm make us slow down and take notice of them, thereby forcing
us to become conscious of the words themselves and to prolong and
intensify our concentration. When Justice McClung says it must be
pointed out that the complainant in a sexual assault case did not present herself to the accused "wearing a bonnet and crinolines," he gets
not only our attention but also the attention of the Supreme Court of
Canada; he also gets their rebuke. In this chapter, I try to show that
most of McClung's literary and rhetorical devices are counterproductive: they prolong and intensify our concentration at all the wrong
places, they strikingly give voice to his sexist values and stereotypic
mindset, and they trivialize and attenuate what might be a plausible (if
not ultimately sustainable) argument to acquit, an argument based on
the complainant's "implied consent" to the accused's sexual advances.

In contrast to Justice McClung is Lord Denning, whose vivid writing
provokes sympathy through its concise style, plain language, and mem-
orable imagery: "It was bluebell time in Kent" (*Hinz v. Berry*, 42). This
case involves a woman who was the mother of four children and foster

mother to four others. Having been traumatized by witnessing the in-juries of her children and the death of her husband, victims of an out-of-control Jaguar "that rushed into the lay-by and crashed into [her husband] and the children" (42), she was awarded damages for ner-vous shock as well as for pecuniary loss. Denning, in upholding the decision of the lower court, makes literary devices and evocative story-telling vital to his argument from pathos and equity. Unfortunately for McClung, his devices and storytelling are fatal to his argument from implied consent.

These examples remind us that a judgment is first and foremost a sto-ry, a narrative of found facts about the parties. But there are always at least two kinds of stories. One is a human story, a concrete narrative of who did what to whom, where, when, how, and why. The other is a legal story, an abstract narrative of issue, fact, law, and conclusion, a story that is more a logic of justification than a narrative of events. As I argue in this chapter, the art of persuasion resides in knowing what story to tell.

In the infamous O.J. Simpson trial, Alan Dershowitz knew what sto-ry not to tell and saw his role as thwarting the jury's desire for a tightly plotted human story in which an enraged ex-husband slaughtered his ex-wife and her male companion. In "Life Is Not a Dramatic Narrative," Dershowitz maintains that a jury's desire for plot and purpose often imposes a false coherence on facts that are in reality random and dis-connected. In putting Simpson's case forward in the best light possi-ble, the defence must ensure that its legal story of reasonable doubt prevails over the prosecution's human story of rage and vengeance. For reasons I elaborate on in this chapter, I do not buy into Dershowitz's anti-teleological argument because in constructing his story of reason-able doubt, he is still shaping facts for a purpose even if that purpose is to disrupt the narrative coherence of a compelling melodrama.

Nor do I buy into the argument that there is something intrinsically good about narrative. In *Poethics*, Richard Weisberg claims that the jus-tices in *Brown v. Board of Education* should have told the human story of Linda Brown's victimage under segregation and should have invoked the history of systemic racism that underwrote it. Had they done so, Weisberg argues, they would have written an inspiring emancipation narrative instead of a sterile empirical argument grounded in equal rights under the law to an education of one's choice. Even if it might seem intuitively right to use vivid storytelling to dramatize centuries of racial injustice, a highly poetic description of the facts in *Brown* would have been rhetorically disastrous, as Richard Posner, among others, has pointed out. "Such a narrative," he writes, "would have made it even more difficult for the southern states to accept the decision" (*Law and Literature*, 347).

The overvaluation of concrete detail and poetic description as avatars of morality and humaneness is often allied with a belief that eloquence and virtue are one and the same. The two most eminent progenitors and producers of law and literature scholarship, Richard Weisberg and James Boyd White, affirm this belief. Weisberg claims that "no bad judicial opinion can be 'well written'" (251), while White claims that "the morally vicious cannot be aesthetically great" (*Heracles' Bow*, 132). Using Oliver Wendell Holmes's *Buck v. Bell* as an example, a judgment that endorses the sexual sterilization of inmates who are afflicted with a hereditary form of insanity or imbecility – "three generations of imbeciles are enough" (207) – I contend that Holmes's morally vicious decision, while perhaps not aesthetically great, is well written and aesthetically pleasing. But as the slaughter bench of history attests, an articulate and eloquent style is no guarantor of virtue.

Style also figures in chapter 2, especially as it relates to legal world-making and judicial self-fashioning. The animating assumption of this chapter is that style is not ornament or embellishment but an integral part of the writing, thinking, and deciding process. As Justice Cardozo notes, style "is not something added to substance as mere protuberant adornment. The two are fused in a unity" (5). The chapter focuses on word choice, kinds of sentences, figurative language, and literary devices in the legal writing of two accomplished jurists – Lord Denning, a deceased English appellate judge who was known for his "distinctive style" and "boldly created judgments," and Justice David Watt, an Ontario appellate judge "who writes like a paperback novelist" (Makin, *Globe and Mail*, 11 March 2011).

My argument is simple: In Denning's judgments, most of the time, style and substance "are fused in a unity." In Watt's judgments, at least some of the time, style "is something added to substance as a mere protuberant adornment." Denning's pastoral vision of an England that by the late 1960s had largely disappeared is at once nostalgic and ethnocentric. In *Lloyd's Bank v. Bundy* it is innocuous, the evocation of a family farm going back for generations, but elsewhere, as I argue later in the chapter, it betrays a more disturbing mindset. Conservatism shades into xenophobia; ethnocentrism into racism. Despite its ideological underpinnings, Denning's narrative style is almost always connected to the legal substance of his argument, an argument couched in what Richard

Posner calls an impure or pragmatic style, a style that is as much concerned with equity as with law, a style that aims itself at the general public. Such a style is familiar, conversational, informal, and fresh.[1]

Watt's style is inconsistent. His flamboyant openings are often glaringly incongruent with the rest of his discourse. The introductory paragraphs are terse and fragmented, but as Watt moves into the legal issues before him, the paperback novelist disappears and the traditional judge takes over. These issues are analysed in what Richard Posner calls a pure or formalist style, one that aims itself at a professional audience and sees the law as logical, objective, and constrained. Such a style is impersonal, elevated, technical, and conventional.[2] Justice Watt's openings are dramatically and narratively charged, but the bodies of his decisions are written in a pure or formalist style. The problem is not in his storytelling per se but in its inappropriateness to the issues he is being asked to decide.

Style and storytelling also figure in chapter 3. Exploring the quandaries of *Palsgraf v. Long Island Railroad*, a famous tort case in American legal history, this chapter zeroes in on legal world-making and judicial self-fashioning. Justice Cardozo, writing for the majority in a formal and impersonal style, and Justice Andrews, writing for the minority in a casual and colloquial style, create different legal worlds and fashion different images of themselves as judges. Both use analogical reasoning to deal with the enigmas of liability and proximate cause. Both drown in an ocean of similitude.

In this famous case, two railroad guards help a man with a package board a moving train. The package falls to the ground and explodes. Some distance away, Mrs Palsgraf is hurt by a falling scale. Her injuries

---

1 "Impure stylists," Posner writes in "Judges' Writing Styles," "like to pretend that what they are doing when they write a judicial opinion is explaining to a hypothetical audience of laypersons why the case is being decided in the way that it is. These judges eschew the 'professionalizing' devices of the purist writer – the jargon, the solemnity, the high sheen, the impersonality, the piled-up details conveying an attitude of scrupulous exactness, the fondness for truisms, the unembarrassed repetition of obvious propositions, the long quotations from previous cases to demonstrate fidelity to precedent, the euphemisms, and the exaggerated confidence" (1430).

2 As Posner says in the same article, "Judicial opinions in the pure style tend to be long for what they have to say, solemn, highly polished and artifactual – far removed from the tone of conversation – impersonal … and predictable in the sense of conforming closely to professional expectations about the structure and style of a judicial opinion" (1429).

turn out to be permanent, and she can no longer work as a housekeeper. Writing for the majority, Cardozo finds that she does not have a cause of action for negligence because she was not in a foreseeable zone of danger. Writing for the minority, Justice Andrews disagrees with this finding and sees it as embracing too narrow a concept of negligence. He maintains that Mrs Palsgraf would never have been injured had there been no explosion and that the explosion would not have occurred if not for the negligent actions of the railroad guards.

Cardozo uses many figures of speech for the foreseeable zone of danger, among them orbit of danger, radius of danger, danger zone, range of apprehension, and eye of ordinary vigilance. On the surface, his argument seems to rely on the foundational concept of liability and seems to epitomize the appeal to logic, but in the world of torts, analogy proves to have a fatal attraction. As I try to show in this chapter, Cardozo takes us rapidly through a series of images and analogies, among them a maze of contradictions, a bundle of newspapers that turns out to be a can of dynamite, a guard stumbling over a valise, and a person who jostles his neighbour in a crowd and causes a bomb to fall upon the ground. The images and analogies are themselves a maze of contradictions, and what is intended to bring clarification brings confusion instead.

Dissenting against Cardozo's decision, Andrews construes the issue in terms of proximate cause and proximate consequences, not in terms of what an ordinary person would reasonably perceive as a foreseeable zone of danger. To see through the lens of cause and effect is to direct our attention towards empirical events rather than legal niceties surrounding the issues of negligence and liability. But Andrews too is addicted to analogies, the proliferation of which ends up undermining the concept of proximate cause itself. In attempting to explain the concept of proximate cause, Andrews offers up a plethora of analogies: a boy throwing a stone in a pond and altering the history of that pond to all eternity, causation as a chain or net, causation as a stream mingling with tributaries to form a river that flows into the ocean, a murder in Sarajevo that leads to an assassination in London twenty years later, an overturned lantern that may burn all Chicago, and a negligent chauffeur colliding with another car filled with dynamite. Andrews explores all these scenarios along the way to concluding that neither analogy nor logic can comprehend proximate cause. "What we mean by the word 'proximate' is that because of convenience, of public policy, of a rough sense of justice, the law arbitrarily declines to trace a series of events beyond a certain point" (8).

To multiply so many analogies to arrive at a pragmatic criterion that could have been invoked without advancing any analogy at all seems rather self-defeating. The overall effect of these metastasizing analogies is to deconstruct the very concept of causation Justice Andrews wants to rely on, making everything a question of expediency, practical politics, and common sense.

Chapter 4 is also about causation. In it, I portray causal distinctions in law as self-subverting concepts that perpetually run the risk of sinking into a quicksand of adjectival excess. Thus for murder to be labelled first degree, its cause must be substantial, integral, essential, efficient, effective, real, proximate, direct, decisive, or immediate. For murder to be labelled second degree, its cause must be contributory, beyond *de minimis*, not trivial, significant, not insignificant, occasional, remote, operating, or inducing. (To make things worse, sometimes the same adjectives appear under both categories.) And this is but a selection of the adjectives that populate the case law and inform the causal criteria applied to murder cases. Though no doubt sincerely applied by the courts, these criteria cannot deliver the precision they promise, and the rhetorical power of vivid factual narratives ends up carrying as much argumentative weight as the logical force of erudite causal distinctions.

To illustrate this point I look in detail at two important Canadian murder cases: *R. v. Harbottle* and *R. v. Nette*. I suggest that these cases and their cognates are not so much arguments for particular standards or kinds of causation as they are arguments for relatively more or less serious degrees of criminal responsibility. In such cases, the horrible facts are unfailingly invoked in all their nauseating detail, engendering moral revulsion and justifying the severe stigma and intensified blameworthiness that attach to first degree murder. Deprived of their vivid imagery, grisly narratives, and explanatory examples, these carefully wrought decisions would be far less convincing and effective.

Chapter 5 is also about storytelling and takes its cue from what recent French critics call narratology, the structural study of narrative, and from what Mikhail Bakhtin calls dialogism, the multivoicedness of discourse.

Narratology makes a key distinction between narrative content and narrative presentation, between *what* really or allegedly happened and *how* what really or allegedly happened is related to the reader, between the chronological sequence of events (*l'histoire*) and the textual sequence of events (*le discours*). In a courtroom, of course, the judge and jury are routinely exposed to multiple discourses, multiple versions of what really or allegedly happened. Narrative is crucial to legal decision-making because the primary task of the judge or jury is to make a plausible and coherent story (*une histoire*) out of the chaotic particulars of a case that is often awash in a sea of conflicting evidence, contradictory versions of events, incongruent precedents, unclear controlling laws, incompatible expert reports, ambiguous legal documents, and, in general, at least two opposed and competing discourses.

To encompass what really happened is a complex business because a judgment, like a short story or a novel, must relate events from a particular angle of vision (narrative perspective, how an account is focalized) and in a particular language (narrative voice, how an account is verbalized). On its face, this distinction between focalizer, the agent who sees, and verbalizer, the agent who says, might seem to belong to the arcana of literary criticism, but not much reflection is required to realize that the distinction has profound implications for judicial writing. How does a judge narrate a case? Does he or she focalize the case from the perspective of one of the parties or from the perspective of the law and its institutions? Does he or she speak in an omniscient voice or grant the parties agency and allow them to speak in their own voices?

Useful as these narratological concepts undoubtedly are, they need to be supplemented by the dialogical concepts of Mikhail Bakhtin to furnish a more detailed picture of how language functions in judicial writing. For Bakhtin, language must be understood as social activity, as dialogue. However monological an utterance may seem to be, however much it seems to focus on its own topic, it cannot help but be a response to what has already been said about the topic.

This is especially true of the language of the law, a language that is essentially heteroglot, polyglot, and dialogical, heteroglossia being Bakhtin's term for the multiple social languages that exist within a single national language – languages of social groups, professions, generations, and the like – and polyglossia being his term for different national languages. Judgments embrace both multiple social languages (those of experts, parties, lawyers, and the like) and different national languages (English, Latin, Norman French, and the like). The language of a judgment is actually a *system* of languages that mutually and ideologically interinanimate one another. It is misleading to describe and analyse such discourse as a single unitary language emanating from an omniscient author. Any given judgment is part of the unending legal conversation that both precedes and outlives it. Judges are in dialogue with the precedent decisions of their forbears as well as with statute speech, charter speech, case law speech, appellate speech, Supreme

Court speech, dissent speech, lawyer speech, witness speech, expert speech, party speech, police speech, and so on.

In a judgment that gets the ultimate review, what often emerges is a complex dialogue between the court of first instance, the appellate court, and the Supreme Court, not to mention the sometimes dissenting voices within the last two. The second part of chapter 5 traces the emergence of such dialogue in a controversial Canadian case, *R. v. Ewanchuk,* by examining the crucial yet largely unacknowledged role that verbalization and focalization play in the rhetoric of judgment and by comparing and contrasting how the case is narrativized differently by the participants in the trial and by the various judges who heard the evidence. I conclude that judgments are not monologues. They are instances of what Bakhtin calls living heteroglossia, dialogues composed of many voices.

Chapter 6 deals with standards of consent and resistance. *Edward S. Rusk v. State of Maryland* is a sexual assault case from the late 1970s that features multiple and sometimes conflicting discourses. The case moves from the trial court to the Court of Special Appeals and, finally, to the Court of Appeals of Maryland. Here as elsewhere, factual narratives are seen to have persuasive power. If one side's version of the facts and framing of the issues prevails, that side is likely to win. This is why the law is so scrupulous about what stories get to be told in court. Stories that may prejudice jurors are often excluded – stories, for example, that involve convictions for past crimes similar to the alleged crime currently before the court. In *Rusk v. State,* Judges Thompson and Wilner of the Court of Special Appeals are both working with essentially the same set of facts, the set of facts found by the trial judge, but they put radically different spins on these facts, deploy markedly different strategies of inclusion and exclusion, and create strikingly different portraits of the victim, who, it would seem, is as much on trial as the appellant. These contrasting narrativizations are crucial; they compel the legal reasoning that follows in their wake. The conclusion arrived at is already implicit in the story told, and even though precedents are cited and reasons elaborated, much of the argumentative labour is being done by narrative.

Throughout this study, storytelling, rhetoric, and style are examined in the context of legal argument. The enabling assumption is that every judgment creates its own legal world and embodies the *ethos* of its composer. I try to show that the literary function of language does have a role to play in judicial discourse, as do narrative perspective and narrative voice. Judgments are stories, yes, but stories come in different sizes, shapes, and forms; they may be used or abused, and they are not simply an anodyne for sterility and abstraction. I also try to show that because of the built-in limitations of empirical demonstration and logical proof, storytelling and analogy are integral to the fashioning and application of standards of causation in liability and murder cases. Unlike contiguity and succession, causation cannot be seen. It invites rhetoric, for the realm of the uncertain is the realm of rhetoric, a contingent realm of probability and plausibility, not an apodictic realm of certainty and truth. In this sense, then, the realm of law is also a realm of rhetoric.

The implications of this claim are explored in the final chapter, which looks at law and rhetoric in the context of classical philosophy. Aristotle's strategic innovation, I contend, is to replace Plato's binary opposition between the real and the apparent with his own binary opposition between the necessary and the contingent. Once rhetoric is placed in the realm of the contingent, it can be viewed not as a distorted representation of reality deficient in epistemic substance and ontological truth but as a kind of practical knowledge grounded in common sense and prudential wisdom. Such knowledge and wisdom constitute what Aristotle calls *phronesis,* practical thought. And practical thought is at the core of judicial reasoning.

1 The Cost of Persuasion: Figure, Story, and Eloquence in the Rhetoric of Judicial Discourse

Figure, story, and eloquence – though features of discourse we more readily associate with literature than with law – matter in legal writing as well. The first part of this chapter examines how, for better or for worse, the literary function of language enters into judicial discourse. That function makes its presence felt whenever figures of speech or images make a reader slow down and take notice of them. The second part considers judgments as narratives and examines the relationship between what might be called *human story* – the concrete narrative of who did what to whom, where, when, how, and why – and *legal story* – the abstract narrative of issue, fact, law, and conclusion.[1] I shall argue that the understandable desire to inject humanity and concreteness into judicial writing is sometimes misguided and sometimes impairs rather than enhances its persuasiveness. The third part considers persuasiveness in relation to ethical value, making the seemingly obvious point that eloquence is no guarantor of virtue and that beautifully crafted judgments can be morally vicious. I say "seemingly obvious" because eminent scholars such as Richard Weisberg and James Boyd White argue otherwise.

---

1 These stories, of course, are not mutually exclusive, how (agency) and why (purpose) adding an element of the abstract to the concrete human story, and fact and conclusion adding an element of the concrete to the abstract legal story. As my friend Paul Perell points out, if the conclusion sends one to jail, one will certainly stare at a lot of concrete. I am indebted to Paul for his helpful comments as I am to Michael Dixon, Nick Mount, Dale Barleben, and Ed Berry. I am also indebted to the editors at *The University of Toronto Quarterly*. Under the same title, this chapter originally appeared in vol. 75, no. 4, 2006 (905–24).

The Literary Function

With its reliance on the deductive model of particular issue, relevant fact, controlling law, and entailed conclusion, judicial discourse might seem to be the last place where the literary function of language would have any meaningful work to do. In truth, however, particularly during the invention phase, every kind of discourse relies on metaphor and analogy for the discovery of arguments, comparison and contrast being at the core of all discursive reasoning. Judicial discourse, as James Boyd White points out, incorporates and transforms "the kind of thought that works not by argument from general premises to conclusion, but by a process of analogy and disanalogy, perceived similarities and differences" (*Heracles' Bow*, 130).

Though the similarities and differences that undergird legal reasoning are most visible in the invention phase and animate the topics that generate arguments, analogy and metaphor also have a key part to play in the communication phase, for the literary function of language is a working component of all linguistic action. This function is apparent, as Roman Jakobson points out, whenever signs become palpable.[2] Whether using pun, alliteration, parallelism, or any other rhetorical device, any piece of language that calls attention to itself is drawing upon the literary function by making us conscious of the words themselves and thereby forcing us to prolong and intensify our concentration.[3] Something unexpected has happened, and the more our conventional expectations are violated, the more literary and the less expository a text is. The spectrum goes from expository at the one end to literary at the other, from the formulaic to the experimental, from the boredom of the transparently predictable to the overstrain of the opaquely unintelligible. Expository writing tries to eliminate the unexpected and to be predictable if not formulaic. Except perhaps in dissent, judicial writing is normally more expository than literary, but there is always room for

---

2 The literary "function, by promoting the palpability of signs, deepens the fundamental dichotomy of signs and objects" (Jakobson, 33).

3 It must nevertheless be admitted that the grammatically incoherent and syntactically distorted language of an incompetent writer makes us conscious of the words themselves and thereby forces us to prolong and intensify our concentration. Most of the time, however, we can distinguish intended literary effect from unintended linguistic muddle, though with some *avant-garde* writing, such a distinction is not always self-evident.

constructive eloquence. When the American jurist Richard Posner notes that "the unnecessary details and truisms that stud most judicial opinions create a soothing facade of facticity" ("Judges' Writing Styles," 1441), he is drawing upon the literary function through a vivid and emphatic verb (stud), through sibilance (the *es* sounds of soothing, facade, and facticity), and through alliteration (facade, facticity). His artful language makes us pause and prolong our attention as we admire his felicitous turn of phrase, and more importantly, feel the force of his argument.[4]

The literary function of language often enters into legal discourse when the cost of persuasion is high.[5] The cost of persuasion is a concept devised by Posner to measure the extent and intensity of an audience's preconceptions and the rhetorical investment required to overcome

---

4 Here is the remark in its context. Note how brilliantly the final line clinches the argument. "Padding is an important part of most judicial opinions. Judges are not comfortable writing opinions to the effect that 'We have very little sense of what is going on in this case. The record is poorly developed, and the lawyers are lousy. We have no confidence that we have got it right. We know we're groping in the dark. But we're paid to decide cases, and here goes.' Nevertheless, this is the actual character of many appellate cases that are decided in published opinions. The simplest cases are not brought, or not appealed, or are decided in unpublished opinions (sometimes with no opinion – just with the word 'affirmed'). A substantial fraction of published opinions are in close cases, and another substantial fraction are in cases that do not seem close but that are in a muddle of one sort or another. The unnecessary details and truisms that stud most judicial opinions create a soothing façade of facticity" (1441).

5 The eloquence of artful language, it would seem, can burst into discourse at almost any point, sometimes with fatal consequences, as we shall later see, for where writers are eloquent, there reside their true passions. In *Literary Criticisms of Law*, where the consequences of eloquence are reasonably benign if one does not have an idealistic conception of lawyers, the authors, two professors of law, Guyora Binder and Robert Weisberg, lament the decline of a noble, if tragic, legal tradition and display their contempt for practitioners of law after Lincoln. "The Whig hope that the lawyer's craft could cabin these fundamental conflicts [between abolition and union, individual independence and material equality] was doomed before the Civil War's first shot, as was the promise of a coherent republican culture integrated by legal interpretation. Lawyers have mourned their loss of cultural identity ever since. Useful they might be in an unheroic, parasitic sort of way; but as cultural icons they have had only their stuffy propriety – their desiccated husk of their aspiration to civility – to offer a nation yearning for redemption. Lincoln, it is said, exuded a funereal gloom that impressed his contemporaries as nobly tragic. By contrast, his ghoulish epigones at the bar bestir all the affection and authority accorded undertakers: formally attired, complimenting the corpse, and counting the fee" (56). Here the language calls attention to itself and draws upon the literary function. Whether it protests too much is a matter of taste.

those preconceptions. Extent refers to how far one has to move readers from their everyday beliefs and values in order to convince them to accept one's argument. Intensity refers to how tenaciously they hold to those beliefs and values. If a murderer is to go free because of a technicality, the cost of persuasion is high indeed for the judge who must rationalize this result.

A literary example of high-cost persuasion is seen in the dilemma that presents itself to Marc Antony when he confronts the mob after the murder of Caesar. Antony knows that the ultimate cost of inciting vengeance may be his own life, and he intuits correctly that understatement and irony have a lower cost of persuasion than hyperbole and truth. He thus begins his famous speech to the mob by using the expression "honourable men" as a seemingly benign epithet for the killers of Caesar. Only gradually, by using the ambiguities of irony to bridge the transition, does he dare convert "honourable men" into a malignant epithet. He most certainly does not say: "Be angry, citizens of Rome. These traitors, butchers, and cowards have slain in cold blood our noble leader." Instead, by metonymic displacement, he makes the people contemplate the dagger-pierced and blood-drenched mantle that Caesar wore the day he was killed, whipping them up slowly into a frenzy of vindictive anger by using the mantle as a vehicle for making provocative comments on the brutality and ingratitude of the assassins:

> You all do know this mantle, I remember
> The first time ever Caesar put it on.
> 'Twas on a summer's evening in his tent,
> That day he overcame the Nervii.
> Look, in this place ran Cassius' dagger through.
> See what a rent the envious Casca made.
> Through this the well-beloved Brutus stabbed,
> And as he plucked his cursed steel away,
> Mark how the blood of Caesar followed it,
> As rushing out of doors, to be resolved
> If Brutus so unkindly knocked, or no.
> For Brutus, as you know, was Caesar's angel.
> Judge, O you gods, how dearly Caesar loved him!
> This was the most unkindest cut of all,
> For when the noble Caesar saw him stab,
> Ingratitude, more strong than traitors' arms,
> Quite vanquished him. Then burst his mighty heart,

And, in his mantle muffling up his face,
Even at the base of Pompey's statue,
Which all the while ran blood, great Caesar fell.   (3.2.171–90)

Evident throughout this speech is what the classical rhetoricians call *enargeia* – palpability and vividness – a use of imagery that is at the heart of the appeal to *pathos*, an appeal that is amply exemplified in many of the judgments of the well-known British appellate judge Lord Denning, whose openings provoke sympathy through terse sentences, simple diction, and unforgettable images.

It happened on April 19, 1964. It was bluebell time in Kent. Mr. and Mrs. Hinz, the plaintiff, had been married some ten years, and they had four children, all aged nine and under. The youngest was one. The plaintiff was a remarkable woman. In addition to her own four, she was foster mother to four other children. To add to it, she was two months pregnant with her fifth child.

    On this day they drove out in a Bedford Dormobile van from Tonbridge to Canvey Island. They took all eight children with them. As they were coming back they turned into a lay-by at Thurnham to have a picnic tea. The plaintiff had taken Stephanie, her third child, across the road to pick bluebells on the opposite side. There came along a Jaguar out of control driven by Mr. Berry, the defendant. A tyre had burst. The Jaguar rushed into the lay-by and crashed into Mr. Hinz and the children. Mr. Hinz was frightfully injured and died a little later. Nearly all the children were hurt. Blood was streaming from their heads. The plaintiff, hearing the crash, turned round and saw the disaster. She ran across the road and did all she could. Her husband was beyond recall, but the children recovered. (*Hinz v. Berry*, 42)

In terms of *enargeia* this is vivid and palpable writing that makes a devastatingly effective appeal to *pathos*, the innocence of picking bluebells being brutally juxtaposed to the carnage wrought by the careening Jaguar. Here the wrenchingly concrete narrative is an essential element of the argument that the morbid depression suffered by the plaintiff as the result of witnessing this terrible accident merited damages of four thousand pounds for nervous shock in addition to fifteen thousand pounds for pecuniary loss. One could go so far as to say that the evocative narrative *is* the argument. Refusing to strike down on appeal the award for nervous shock and making an argument more from equity than from law, Denning strategically relies on imagery and narrative, knowing that the literary function of language is best equipped to drive home the exceptional circumstances that justified damages for nervous shock.

The literary function, however, has its attendant dangers. What language is rhetorically doing on the figurative level can undermine and subvert what it is referentially saying on the literal level. In the 1998 sexual assault case between Her Majesty the Queen and Steven Brian Ewanchuk, the Honourable Mr Justice McClung uttered a sentence that followed him to his grave – "It must be pointed out that the complainant did not present herself to Ewanchuk or enter his trailer in a bonnet and crinolines."[6] Mr Ewanchuk had been charged with sexual assault and acquitted by the lower court, an acquittal that Justice McClung, writing for the majority, upheld. Since the trial judge found as fact that the Crown did not prove beyond reasonable doubt that there was a lack of consent on the part of the woman and that Ewanchuk had knowledge of her lack of consent, McClung felt "there is simply no jurisdiction in an appellate court to upset trial findings of fact that have evidentiary support." He goes on to say that

> [t]he facts revealed by the record establish that the accused had no proven intention of forcibly pursuing his way with the complainant during the two and one-half hours they were alone in his trailer. The Crown tried to prove that what occurred did so against her apparent consent, but did not succeed. Whether or not the sexual activity took place with or without consent is a question of fact and the absence of consent was a finding that was refused at this trial. (para. 3)

Ultimately, the Supreme Court found an error in law and reversed the decision, saying that the trial judge erred in his understanding of

---

6 Although most judges learn early in their careers to interpret and write in a way that avoids crisis and reduces social tension, McClung would seem to be an exception. In a *National Post* interview, 27 February 1999, he defended his decision in the *Ewanchuk* case, adding fuel to the fire in noting that the victim "was not lost on her way home from the nunnery," and in a letter to the same paper two days before, he characterized Madame Justice L'Heureux-Dubé's ruling as a "graceless slide into personal invective." He also suggested that the judge's feminism contributed to the high suicide rate of Quebec males, either knowing or not knowing that her husband had committed suicide in 1978.

proof of consent in sexual assault as well as in his conclusion that the defence of "implied consent" exists in Canadian law.

The alleged assault happened on 3 June 1994. It was a hot summer day in Edmonton. Both parties were wearing shorts and T-shirts. They ended up in Ewanchuk's trailer to discuss an employment opportunity for the woman with his custom cabinet and woodworking business. As the trial judge puts it:

> During this time of two and one half hours, A [Ewanchuk] did three things which B [the woman] did not like. When A was giving B a body massage, his hands got close to B's breasts. B said "no," and A immediately stopped. When B and A were lying on the floor, A rubbed his pelvic bone area against B's pelvic area. B said "no," and A immediately stopped. Later on A took his soft penis out of his shorts and placed it on the outside of B's clothes in her pelvic area. B said "no," and A immediately stopped. During all of the two and one half hours that A and B were together, she never told A that she wanted to leave. When B finally told A that she wanted to leave, she and A simply walked out of the trailer. (2)

That the trial and appellate judges were found to be mistaken in their understanding of the concept of consent is not relevant here. What is relevant is that Justice McClung's endorsement of the trial judge's reasons had surface plausibility, and his seeing no error in law was a defensible finding that a rational appellate judge might have come to. But his finding was vitiated by his wanton use of imagery and figuration – imagery and figuration that proved to have a radioactive half-life of their own:

> It must be pointed out that the complainant did not present herself to Ewanchuk or enter his trailer in a bonnet and crinolines. She told Ewanchuk that she was the mother of a six-month old baby and that, along with her boyfriend, she shared an apartment with another couple. (I point out these aspects of the trial record, but with no intention of denigrating her or lessening the legal protection to which she was entitled.) (4)

This is a classic deconstructive moment wherein rhetoric undermines and subverts reference. The archaic imagery of bonnet and crinolines reveals how archaic and stereotypic the judge's attitudes towards woman are. The implication not only that the unmarried complainant is not a virgin but also that she and her boyfriend may indulge in dalliances with another unmarried couple is hardly mitigated by the paraliptic parenthesis saying that the judge intends neither to denigrate the complainant nor to lessen the legal protection to which she is entitled. Paralipsis, the trope of feigned omission, allows one to say what one has to say under the guise of not saying it. The denigrating and lessening are accomplished by a positive statement masquerading as a negative intent. After referring to "three clumsy passes by Ewanchuk," as if the lovable oaf lacked skill in the art of prosecuting what the judge inaptly calls "his romantic intentions," McClung goes further:

> Three overtures were made by Ewanchuk. The first two were marginally identifiable, if at all, as sexual in nature. They involved mutual body massages which, while they neared her sexual organs, were not in contact with them. Nonetheless, the last was clearly a sexual activity; a deliberate exposure of his sexual anatomy as he rubbed himself against her clothed pelvic area. This performance, if viewed in isolation ... would hardly raise Ewanchuk's stature in the pantheon of chivalric behaviour, but it did take place in private and following her protest – "No!" – led to nothing. The record would indicate that the one clearly sexual activity in the case ended swiftly with her injunctive "No!" (11)

> It is right that we be constantly reminded that sexual assault can intractably erode the present and future integrity of its victims. Clearly this is so. Yet we must also remain aware that nothing can destroy a life so utterly as an extended term of imprisonment following a precipitately decided sexual assault conviction. In the search for proof of guilt, sloganeering such as "No means No!," "Zero Tolerance!," and "Take back the night!" which, while they marshall desired social ideals, are no safe substitute for the orderly and objective judicial application of Canada's criminal statutes. (12)

Such forcible writing calls attention to itself and makes one take note of infelicities that might otherwise slip by. "Pantheon" – either a temple dedicated to the gods, or a group of gods or important people – does not quite fit with "chivalric behaviour"; chivalric heroes would be better. "Intractably," in its literal sense, does not quite fit with "erode." Furthermore, a sexual assault conviction, even if not "precipitately decided," could still destroy a life. (In this case, the Chief Justice's dissent and the Supreme Court's reversal are dense with detailed analyses of the legal meaning of consent; they are anything but precipitate.) Even "marshall" is not quite *le mot juste*, while the pejorative term "sloganeering" detracts from the *ethos* of the writer. And despite the elevated language, the integrity of the victims is not really being enshrined; nor are the desired social ideals. Literary devices – diction, imagery, figuration – make us read more slowly, and the more slowly we read this judgment, the more problematic it becomes.

> There was no trial finding that [Ewanchuk] employed willful blindness or was reckless or drunk. There was no trial finding that he pursued a sexual touching in the face of an obvious lack of consent from his *partner*. No appellate retrial of this exercise in fact can *strip* an acquitted respondent of these findings. No beguiling or emotive restatement of the evidence can convert that fact finding to an error of law in order to *erect* a Crown appeal which otherwise does not lie. (18, emphasis added)

Notwithstanding the awkwardness of the phrase "employed willful blindness," "partner" is an entirely inappropriate term for a person known for a mere two-and-a-half hours. Also, the wordplay on "strip" and "erect" brings the "soft penis" back into view and is used by McClung to reinforce what he sees as the lack of hard evidence in the Crown's submissions and the concomitant softness of its case against Ewanchuk, who, like the complainant, remained clothed during the incident, save for his moment of flaccid penile exposure. Moreover, it is not clear why a restatement of the evidence would have to be beguiling or emotive to discover an error of law. Neither the Court of Appeal dissent nor the Supreme Court reversal is especially beguiling or emotive.

Unsurprisingly, McClung declines to take the high road in his peroration:

> In my reading of the trial record, this Crown appeal must be dismissed. Beyond the error of law issue, the sum of the evidence indicates that Ewanchuk's advances to the complainant were far less criminal than hormonal. In a less litigious age going too far in the boyfriend's car was better dealt with on site – a well-chosen expletive, a slap in the face or, if necessary, a well-directed knee. What this accused tried to initiate hardly qualifies him for the lasting stigma of a conviction for sexual assault and Alberta's current bullet-train removal to the penitentiary for prolonged shrift. (21)

> The appeal must be dismissed. (22)

To characterize the accused's advances as hormonal, to recommend verbal or physical assault as a method for dealing with unwanted sexual advances – these rightly provoked the ire of feminists and non-feminists alike. But the religious language – *stigma, shrift* – is just as provocative. Whether innocent or not in this case, the accused, with two previous convictions for sexual assault, is not a convincing Christ-figure, and he is unlikely to be riding the bullet train to prison in order to obtain absolution for himself by confessing and doing penance. The archaic language underscores the archaic values of its user.[7]

Most of McClung's literary devices are counterproductive. They prolong and intensify our concentration at all the wrong places, they strikingly give voice to his sexist values and stereotypic mindset, and they trivialize and attenuate what might be a plausible, if not ultimately sustainable, argument. The message the judge performs is at odds with the one he states. Whereas Denning's literary devices and narrative immediacy are part and parcel of his argument from *pathos* and equity, McClung's are fatal to his argument from implied consent. Even granting that McClung's upholding of the trial judge's decision raises real issues about the meaning and implications of Parliament's 1992 efforts to reform the law of sexual assault, one cannot help but wonder whether a neutrally written decision – a decision devoid of the myths and stereotypes that several of the justices' commentaries dwell upon – would have ended up being reviewed by the highest court. According to Benjamin Cardozo, if a judgment is to have a lasting impact, it needs "persuasive force, or the impressive virtue of sincerity and fire, or the mnemonic power of alliteration or antithesis, or the terseness and tang of the proverb and maxim. Neglect the help of these allies and it will never win its way" (cited by Richard Weisberg, 7). True enough, but abuse the help of these allies, it would seem, and the opinion risks wending its way to the Supreme Court.

---

7 Sometimes, however, McClung's unusual language is effective. Earlier in the judgment, he notes that the 1992 parliamentary changes to proof of consent in sexual assault do not "re-define the right of appellate courts to fossick guilt from fact-driven acquittals." If one is familiar with "fossick," a term of Australian origin that means to search for gold, especially by reworking washings or waste piles, or, more generally, to rummage or search around, one can appreciate its metaphoric aptness for this context.

For the sake of pleasing finality, it would be nice to pretend nothing more need be said, but rhetorical analysis, if it aspires to any sort of honesty, must always factor in the issue of decorum, the appropriateness of a discourse for its subject, occasion, purpose, and audience.[8] If McClung's intended audience comprises those who share his frustration with feminism and political correctness, then his sexist language, extravagant figuration, and religious overtones are a fitting appeal to exactly that audience. But if his purpose is to prevent "a precipitately decided sexual assault conviction" against Mr Ewanchuk, then his alienation of the mainstream lay and legal audience of a generally liberal Canadian society is an ill-conceived strategy, a strategy that invites judicial review, and gets it. Too dark to contemplate is the possibility that McClung's purpose may be little more than to luxuriate in the sheer syllables of vituperation and that his concern for Mr Ewanchuk's fate is more rhetorical than real.

Judgments as Narratives

The examples from Denning and McClung remind us that a judgment is first and foremost a story, a narrative of found facts about the parties.[9] But a moving and coherent story does not make an argument true and valid any more than Denning's adroit use of literary and narrative devices makes his decisions true and valid. There are always at least two kinds of stories. One is a human story of who did what to whom, where, when, how, and why, a story that incorporates the dramatistic pentad of act, agent, scene, agency, and purpose. This human story involves what Kenneth Burke calls a temporizing of essence, a story of past, present, and future wherein purpose or motive emerges from a sequence of

---

8 My colleague Nick Mount enforced this honesty upon me by pointing out that McClung may have simply done what he intended to do – namely, attack political correctness and rile feminists.

9 One must remember, of course, that "storytelling in law is narrative within a culture of argument" and that what stories can be told are governed by rules contained in the law of evidence and procedure. In addition, the parties always generate at least two competing and opposing stories. "Neither story, neither language, is the sole source of authority; at some point choices will have to be made that favor one over the other. And both must yield, in much if not in all, to the voice of the law that governs the process as a whole" (White, *Justice as Translation*, 262).

events and their consequences, from chronology plus causation.[10] The other is a legal story of rules, principles, procedures, and laws. The legal story involves what we might call an essentializing of temporality, a story of premises and conclusions wherein a logic of justification reveals a deductive structure of issue, fact, law, and conclusion. The art of persuasion resides in knowing which story to foreground. Narrative thinking in law is simply a pragmatic attempt to discover a plausible coherence in the disparate and chaotic particulars of a case that is often awash in a sea of diametrically opposed stories, conflicting eyewitness accounts, contradictory evidence, incongruous precedents, unclear controlling laws, incompatible expert reports, ambiguous legal documents, and so forth.[11] And sometimes, for one side or the other, the concrete human story is fraught with peril.

Consider the infamous O.J. Simpson trial. There the defendant had obvious motive and opportunity, and Alan Dershowitz saw his role as thwarting the jury's desire for a tightly plotted story with a riveting and powerful climax: the bloody murder of a previously assaulted wife and her supposed paramour by an enraged and jealous ex-husband. Believing that "a rule of teleology has little resonance in real life" (100),

---

10 In *A Rhetoric of Motives*, Kenneth Burke defines temporizing of essence as spinning out into narrative a series of logical relationships. Through such temporizing, "the logical idea of a thing's essence can be translated into a temporal or narrative equivalent by statement in terms of the thing's source or beginning" (13). The biblical myth has Eve created from Adam's rib, a beginning which narratively says that women in the logic of this social order are derivative of and inferior to men. One can also define essence in terms of the end, as, for example, equating someone's criminal nature with his or her likelihood of ending up on the gallows. Essence is revealed through a sequence of actions, actual or potential. By telling a story of the emergence of order out of chaos, mythical concepts such as Hobbes's state of nature or Freud's primal horde – regardless of whether one regards them as genetic fallacies, ontological models, or heuristic models – are narrative devices for explaining, justifying, and naturalizing the logic of a given civil order. What I call the essentializing of temporality reverses the process, translating yesterday/today/tomorrow into major premise/minor premise/conclusion. In law, it is a logic of justification that moves deductively from issue to fact to law to conclusion.

11 "In short, a trial consists of fragmented narratives and narrative multiplicity ... In addition, one side's narrative is constantly being met by the other side's counter-narrative ... so that 'reality' is always being disassembled with multiple, conflicting, and partly overlapping versions, each version presented as true, each fighting to be declared 'what really happened' – with very high stakes riding on that ultimate declaration" (Gewirtz, 8).

Dershowitz maintains that in this case our natural craving for narrative symmetry and purposive explanation imposes a false coherence on facts that are in reality random and disconnected. The human story of rage and vengeance, which insists on plot and revels in melodrama, must be superseded by a legal story of reasonable doubt, which insists on chance and coincidence. For Dershowitz, "life does not imitate art. Life is not a purposive narrative that follows Chekhov's canon [that we are part of a purposive universe]. Events are often simply meaningless, irrelevant to what comes next; events can be out of sequence, random, purely accidental, without purpose ... This desperate attempt to derive purpose from purposelessness will often distort reality" (100). He maintains that "this critical dichotomy between the teleological rules of drama and interpretation, on the one hand, and the mostly random rules of real life, on the other, has profoundly important implications for our legal system" (101), especially insofar as teleological rules inculcate in us a desire to see virtue rewarded, vice punished, and justice achieved.

It is strange, however, that Dershowitz cites Anton Chekhov as a dramatist exemplifying teleological rules, for Chekhov's is a drama that is resolutely anti-Aristotelian, a drama that has no discernible pattern of beginning, middle, and end, a drama that exhibits no purposeful flow of cause and effect, a drama that leaves audience and characters alike perpetually in the middle of things, a drama in which neither insight nor epiphany emerges save for the audience's recognition of the ineluctable tragicomic disparity between world view and world. Chekhov's conception of drama is as unremittingly anti-teleological as it gets, and his dramaturgy would seem, at first blush, to make him more of a weapon than a target. In Chekhov's plays, seldom if ever is virtue rewarded, vice punished, and justice achieved.

Though Dershowitz repeatedly insists that the "desperate attempt to derive purpose from purposelessness will often distort reality" (100), his own anti-teleological argument is itself a desperate attempt to distort reality – indeed, almost a metaphysical ploy. One may agree that the craving for unity that besets the human mind is deplorable, but teleology – whether imposed or discovered – has tremendous resonance in real life. It is no accident that the evangelist's first words to the potential convert are "God has a plan for your life" or that a psychotherapeutic narrative, in its movement from repression to expression, aims to convert a life story that is punitive and incomprehensible into one that is consoling and coherent. Life may or may not imitate art, but our ways of understanding and explaining life do. Our first hearing of "once upon a time" and "they lived happily ever after" begins the process whereby a grammar of narrative is embedded in our psyches along with a storehouse of images, archetypes, stereotypes, myths, formulas, plots, and so forth.

Narrativity, the innate capacity to generate and comprehend stories, is at the core of human signification. Story is inescapable. "Our minds," Wayne Booth notes, "are unable to resist making sense of whatever data we encounter, even if they are in fact random" (62). "We treat 'formless' stories just as we treat the *un*storied world that meets us daily: we turn it into a story" (192). In a similar vein, Gerard Genette points out that simply "to *name* contingency is already to assign it a function, to give it a meaning" (268), to make it part of a story.

In constructing his legal story of reasonable doubt to rebut the human story of rage and vengeance, Dershowitz is consistently searching out inconsistencies; he is shaping facts for a purpose, deliberately substituting casualty for causality. It does not matter whether one consistently searches out consistencies or consistently searches out inconsistencies; the principle of consistency remains intact. The story advocating conviction and the story advocating acquittal are equally purposive. They may even depend on the same evidence, though the former seeks to affirm coherence while the latter seeks to disrupt it. The first story, however, foregrounds the concrete realities of suffering and death, whereas the second story foregrounds the abstract ideals of due process, constitutional rights, presumption of innocence, burden of proof, and so forth, which is not to say that the Simpson team of lawyers was at all averse to exploiting when necessary the emotively suasive racialist stratagem. So even though Dershowitz avers that "human experience cannot be cabined into the structure of narrative" (105), that is precisely what his argument is doing. All writing is genre-bound. The genre in this instance may be more akin to the Chekhovian play, the existentialist novel, or *le nouveau roman* than to the classic realist novel, but the very positing of the category of contingency cabins human experience into the structure of a carefully constructed though putatively random sequence of events.

Even if story is inescapable, Dershowitz has a point. Narrative is sometimes dangerously persuasive, and the judge who feels impelled to let a vicious criminal go free is well advised to avoid any narrative description of the heinous crime, and to focus instead on the supreme importance of due process and constitutional rights. In such a case, abstract principle and technical detail should be embraced with the same fervour as concrete story is rejected. Citizens have to be moved a great distance from their tenaciously held beliefs that vicious criminals should be severely punished and not let off because of mere technicalities, and any rhetorical strategy for dealing with such high-cost issues has to be deftly executed, as in the case below:

> The defendant stands charged with a series of burglary, kidnapping, rape, and battery incidents which allegedly occurred in 1976 and 1978. In the majority of the cases, the assailant was masked, gloved, and wore a hooded covering over his head, preventing the victims from visually observing the facial features of the assailant. Only the eyes of the assailant were uncovered. Following the arrest of the defendant on November 11, 1978, several lineup confrontations were arranged by the police for the victims, using a number of subjects including the defendant for the purpose of identifying the assailant.
>
> The defendant has moved for suppression of the evidence of line-up identification mainly upon three grounds ... (1) that one or more of the line-ups were conducted without the defendant's counsel being present; (2) that people in the line-up wore clothing that had been illegally seized from the defendant's automobile; and (3) that the lineups were suggestive. (cited by Goldfarb and Raymond, 71)

Knowing that there are more bad facts than good facts, the Honorable Jesse R. Walters of the Idaho Court of Appeals, in composing his argument to suppress the evidence, wisely deploys an issue-driven structure, making "Absence of Counsel," "Clothing," and "Lineup Suggestibility" his essentializing headings. At no point does he provide a chronology of facts, his discussion of facts being limited to those that are determinative of the three issues he identifies. The human story of who did what to whom is mostly bypassed, and the legal story of issue, fact, law, and conclusion is given centre stage.

If a judge were to deny the defendant's appeal, he or she might take a different approach:

> The defendant stands charged with a series of burglary, kidnapping, rape, and battery incidents. On four different occasions, he mugged elderly women, dragged them to a desolate site, held them captive for several hours, raped them repeatedly at knife point, beat them senseless – breaking arms, ribs, noses, and jaws in the process – and eventually, after his sick pleasure had been taken, he dumped the unconscious victims in a ditch and left them for dead.

If the appeal is to be denied, the concrete human story of who did what to whom has manifest persuasive value. The chronology of facts

essentializes the defendant by using a temporal series of perverse purposes and despicable acts to reveal his character. Though to privilege
the concrete human story makes sense in this context, I believe that
Guyora Binder and Robert Weisberg are correct in their contention that
the current trend in law-and-literature scholarship gives too much
weight to the concrete human story as if the purpose of literary devices
were to rejuvenate the law, to add spirit to the letter. As they rightly
suggest, we should not view "'the literary' as something extrinsic to
law that corrects or redeems or ornaments it. We should recognize that
the literary is intrinsic to law insofar as law fashions the characters,
personas, sensibilities, identities, myths, and traditions that compose
our social world" (18). We should see "the literary as a constitutive dimension of law rather than a redemptive supplement" (19).

In *Poethics*, for example, a different Weisberg, Richard, claims that
judges are more likely to capture the compassionate spirit of the law if
they privilege the concrete human story over the abstract legal story. Had
the justices in *Brown v. Board of Education* been able to give literary expression to Linda Brown's victimage under segregation and the history
of systemic racism that underwrote it, Weisberg argues, they would have
written an inspiring emancipation narrative instead of a sterile empirical
argument grounded in social science. Only narrative, Weisberg maintains, has the power to instantiate the suffering of children denied equal
rights under the law to an education of their choice and to expose the
horrors of the racist history of the South. On the one hand, he contends,
there is the frigid facticity of social science; on the other, the authentic
voice of the victim. The dominant but inauthentic discourse of the law, he
avers, stymies and mutes the authentic narrative of the oppressed.

Surely, however, Weisberg overstates the case considerably. Nothing
authenticates any narrative voice, and though it may seem intuitively
right to align concrete detail with moral resonance, and abstract gener-
alization with rational chill, a highly poetic description of the facts in
Brown v. Board of Education would have been rhetorically disastrous, as
Richard Posner, among others, has pointed out. "The Supreme Court,"
he writes, "was right to forgo a narrative of the history of the oppres-
sions of black people in the South, even though that history is essential
background to understand the harm of segregated schooling. Such a
narrative would have made it even more difficult for the southern states
to accept the decision" (*Law and Literature*, 347). The argument from
social science rather than from lived experience and national history
allowed for a unanimous decision, making it possible for the southern
judges to concur.

Persuasion, however, always exacts a price, for as Sanford Levinson points out, Chief Justice Warren's opinion is "remarkably unilluminating about the history of American racial relations" and "the ravages of racial segregation," nor does it "arouse a truly righteous anger against the oppression that had characterized, at that time, well over three centuries of American history" (197–8). Levinson, however, recognizes the necessity of these omissions and notes that it was a conscious decision on the judge's part, Warren himself having said to his colleagues that the opinion "should be short, readable by the lay public, non-rhetorical and, above all, non-accusatory" (cited by Levinson, 198). The decision to eschew the human story was the right rhetorical strategy for the socio-historical context in which Warren wrote. It meant that the decision to outlaw segregation would have some chance of being implemented in a region where citizens had to be moved a great distance from traditional beliefs and values intensely held. Warren had no illusions as to the cost of persuasion.

Thus Richard Weisberg's statement that "*Brown*'s strange reliance on social scientific data robbed the opinion of the poignant focus on the historical and legal fate of individual black people, a focus that might have prevented so much of current affirmative-action backlash" (10) is true but irrelevant, since Warren was well aware that such an accusatory focus, however poignant, had to be sacrificed for sake of pragmatic exigencies, and he was clearly not in a position to have foreseen the affirmative-action backlash that would arise in the wake of *Brown*. Weisberg, however, goes even further, making the improbable claim that "no bad judicial opinion can be 'well written.' No seemingly just opinion will endure unless its discursive form matches its quest for fairness" (251).

Justice and Eloquence

Even if one agrees with Cardozo, whom Weisberg cites, that "the strength that is born of form and the feebleness that is born of the lack of form are in truth qualities of the substance" (4), there is no reason why moral substance is likely to be better formed than immoral or amoral substance. In insisting that "no opinion with a misguided outcome has ever in fact been 'well crafted'" (7), Weisberg affirms his membership in what Posner calls "the edifying school of legal scholarship" (*Law and Literature*, 305), a school whose equivalent in literary scholarship is epitomized by James Boyd White's proclamation that "the morally vicious cannot be aesthetically great" (*Heracles' Bow*, 132).[12] Although this ancient argument about the relationship between ethics and aesthetics cannot be won by the edifying school except through the quasi-tautological strategy of equating virtue with eloquence, to treat sophisticated works of art and jurisprudence as stimulants or vomitives for the ethical sensibility of self and society is anathema to those who appreciate the rich complexity of motives realized and implied by any nuanced piece of writing. Eloquence is at least double-edged, and, in Joseph Conrad's novel *Heart of Darkness*, the essential duplicity of the rhetorical motive is summed up beautifully by the protagonist, Marlow, speaking of Kurtz:

> The point was in his being a gifted creature, and that of his gifts the one that stood out pre-eminently, that carried with it a real sense of presence, was his ability to talk, his words – the gift of expression, the bewildering, the illuminating, the most exalted and the most contemptible, the pulsating stream of light, or the deceitful flow from the heart of an impenetrable darkness. (86–7)

The gifted creatures who compose the most exalted and the most contemptible judicial opinions are susceptible to the same duplicity of motive, and if Oliver Wendell Holmes's *Buck v. Bell, Superintendent* seems more the deceitful flow from the heart of an impenetrable darkness than a pulsating stream of light, especially when read with knowledge of the enormity of subsequent historical events, it is nonetheless a well-crafted judgment that has endured as a rhetorical specimen despite the wrongness of its outcome. As the headnote to the case indicates, Holmes makes two findings in this 1927 judgment:

1 The Virginia statute providing for the sexual sterilization of inmates of institutions supported by the State who shall be found to be afflicted with an hereditary form of insanity or imbecility, is within the power of the State under the Fourteenth Amendment. ["No state

---

12 Despite its questionable premises, the edifying school has produced some wonderful works of criticism and philosophy, works such as Martha Nussbaum's *Poetic Justice: The Literary Imagination and Public Life*, Wayne Booth's *The Company We Keep: An Ethics of Fiction*, and those that compose the entire oeuvre of James Boyd White.

shall make or enforce any law which shall abridge the privileges
or immunities of citizens of the United States; nor shall any state
deprive any person of life, liberty, or property, without due process
of law; nor deny to any person within its jurisdiction the equal
protection of the laws."]
2 Failure to extend the provisions to persons outside the institutions
named does not render it obnoxious to the Equal Protection Clause.
(200)

Advocating for Carrie Buck, a mentally defective young woman slat-
ed to be neutered, I.P. Whitehead contends that the operation of salpin-
gectomy, which sterilizes a woman by opening her abdominal cavity
and cutting the Fallopian tubes, "violates her constitutional right of
bodily integrity and is therefore repugnant to the due process of law
clause of the Fourteenth Amendment" (201). He further contends that
even if the object of the Virginia statute is to prevent the reproduction
of mentally defective people, and even if procedures have been followed and hearings held, the test of due process has not been met, for
"the limits of the power of the State (which in the end is nothing more
than the faction in control of the government) to rid itself of those citizens deemed undesirable according to its standards, by means of surgical sterilization, have not been set" (202). Whitehead's concluding
dystopian projection is chilling in its unwitting prophecy of the Nazi
horrors to come:

> A new reign of doctors will be inaugurated and in the name of science new
> classes will be added, even races may be brought within the scope of such
> regulation, and the worst forms of tyranny practiced. In the place of con-
> stitutional government of the fathers we shall have set up Plato's Republic.
> (202–3)

Advocating for Superintendent Bell, Aubrey E. Strode argues that the
statute neither imposes cruel and unusual punishment nor fails to af-
ford due process of law. "An exercise of the police power analogous to
that of the statute here in question," he maintains, "may be found in the
compulsory vaccination statutes; for there, as here, a surgical operation
is required for the protection of the individual and society" (203). The
dubious analogy between sterilization and vaccination as comparable
"surgical" procedures is revisited by Holmes in his decision.

Holmes commences by laying out the issue as to whether the steril-ization of Carrie Buck – "a feeble-minded white woman ... the daugh-ter of a feeble-minded woman in the same institution, and the mother of an illegitimate feeble-minded child" (205) – denies her due process of law and the equal protection of the laws. He then lays out the rationale for the Virginia statute – heredity plays an important part in the trans-mission of insanity and imbecility, and sterilization not only poses no significant risk to a feeble-minded woman's health but also serves the best interests of both patient and society. He next elaborates the pro-cedure of the case from the superintendent's initial presentation of a petition to the special board of directors at the hospital to, with many steps in between, the ultimate presentation of the case for review by the Supreme Court of Appeals. "There can be no doubt," he concludes, "that so far as procedure is concerned the rights of the patient are most carefully considered, and as every step in the case was taken in scrupu-lous compliance with the statute and after months of observation, there is no doubt that in that respect the plaintiff ... has had due process of law" (207).

Richard Weisberg notwithstanding, the opinion to this point, how-ever misguided its outcome, is well crafted – the issue is up front and drives the analysis, the facts and law are laid out succinctly, and the conclusion follows logically from the premises enunciated. Moreover, the penultimate paragraph attains no mean measure of perverse eloquence.[13]

> We have seen more than once that the public welfare may call upon the best citizens for their lives. It would be strange if it could not call upon those who already sap the strength of the State for these lesser sacrifices, often not felt to be such by those concerned, in order to prevent our being swamped with incompetence. It is better for all the world, if instead of waiting to execute degenerate offspring for crime, or to let them starve for imbecility, society can prevent those who are manifestly unfit from con-tinuing their kind. The principle that sustains compulsory vaccination is broad enough to cover cutting the Fallopian tubes. Three generations of imbeciles are enough. (207)

---

13 Posner discusses this paragraph in *Law and Literature*, 273. I have built on his succinct and cogent analysis.

Even if one is aware that "imbecile" belongs to a scientific classification system no longer in use – a system that defines an imbecile as a person of moderate to severe mental retardation having a mental age from three to seven years – this is, to most of us, a morally repugnant paragraph whose eloquence bespeaks an ugly but intense passion for eugenics, not to mention capital punishment of degenerate offspring, a passion that reveals all too clearly the elitist values of its author. Nevertheless, it is aesthetically pleasing if not aesthetically great prose – vividly wrought, deeply felt, and aphoristically resonant. Deconstructed, its analogical reasoning breaks down, but for a 1927 audience, whose cost of persuasion was no doubt very much lower than our own, the flow of analogy might well overwhelm the flaw in logic. The rhetorically effective and rationally consistent are not necessarily one and the same.

The first analogy is drawn between the sacrifice of dead soldiers and that of sterilized mental defectives, but the impact of each on public welfare is decidedly different. Soldiers prevent our being swamped with enemy forces; sterilizations, our being swamped with incompetence. The distinction between the orders of magnitude underscores the incommensurability of the comparators – the paramount concern for national security as opposed to the paranoid fear of being overwhelmed with the degenerative offspring of the feeble-minded. The second analogy is drawn between compulsory vaccination and sterilization, but it can only hold if it can be empirically proven that feeble-mindedness really does cause crime. And even if it does, are the only alternatives for dealing with the so-called criminals execution or starvation? Moreover, the degree of invasiveness in what Strode calls "surgical operations" is radically different, the term "surgical operation" being something of an overstatement for the description of a vaccination.

Buck v. Bell is a morally vicious opinion, yet if it does not approach aesthetic greatness, it does approach rhetorical greatness. Good rhetoric, as the grisly slaughter bench of history attests, is not the same as goodness. But something quintessentially human is lost if judicial discourse seeks to purge itself of eloquence by enshrining fact and law above all else. Analogy and figure, image and story, *pathos* and *ethos* – these too have vital parts to play in the art of legal writing. Not for nothing does Aristotle insist that rhetoric is the counterpart of logic, its necessary partner in the dance of reason.

To give rhetoric its due, however, is not to imply that there is some restorative fountain of literariness available to assuage the desiccation of conventional judicial prose. There is just a repertoire of literary and rhetorical devices to be well or poorly used. And there is nothing intrinsically good about narrative. It can be accurate moral description, authentic self-expression, mendacious ploy, myth of the dominant social group dressed in the ideological garb of fact, or any other number of things in any given discourse. This is why rhetoric in the popular mind is such a suspect term – the thinking that accompanies it has a measure of amoral calculation that makes many people feel uncomfortable, and understandably so. Though the strategies of rhetoric are neither good nor evil in themselves, they may be directed towards noble or ignoble ends, with just or unjust results. Eloquence, as *Buck v. Bell* illustrates, is no guarantor of virtue.

2 Pure and Impure Styles: Formalism and Pragmatism in the Language of Decision Writing

According to Fred Rodell, "there are two things wrong with almost all legal writing. One is its style. The other is its content" (38). Although I am hesitant to disagree with such an eminent professor of law, I would say there is only one thing wrong with almost all legal writing, not to mention almost all professional writing, and that one thing is style and content taken together. How we say something is just as important as what we say, and failures to communicate often stem from the false belief that style and form can be separated from content and substance. Style is functional. It is not ornament or embellishment but an integral part of the writing, thinking, and deciding process. As Justice Cardozo famously puts it:

> We are merely wasting our time, so many will inform us, if we bother about form when only substance is important. I suppose this might be true if only one could tell us where substance ends and form begins ... [But] form is not something added to substance as a mere protuberant adornment. The two are fused in a unity ... There is absolutely no substance without [form] ... The argument strongly put is not the same as the argument put feebly ... The strength that is born of form and the feebleness that is born of the lack of form are in truth qualities of the substance. They are the tokens of the thing's identity. They make it what it is. (5–6)

This is not to say that there is only one strong form or one good style. There are as many styles as there are writers, and all writers use different styles in different contexts. The problem is finding the right style for the right context. What classical rhetoricians call decorum is the difficult art of matching style to subject, occasion, purpose, genre, and audience. In this chapter I will address the issue of decorum in the legal writing of two accomplished jurists – Lord Denning and Justice David Watt.

Lord Denning was an English appellate judge made famous by his vivid narratives, plain words, and unforgettable images: "It happened on April 19, 1964. It was bluebell time in Kent" (*Hinz v. Berry*, 42). David Watt is an Ontario appellate judge who was characterized by Kirk Makin as "the judge who writes like a paperback novelist" (*Globe and Mail*, 11 March 2011). Makin goes on to say that "the Ontario bar is split over whether judicial rulings that read like an Elmore Leonard novel offer welcome relief from legal jargon or 'trivialize' murder." Whereas Makin mentions Denning in passing, identifying him as a judge known for his "distinctive style" and "bold, creatively crafted judgments," he does not identify him as a formative influence on Justice Watt. Nevertheless, it seems to me that the judgments of Lord Denning, not the novels of Elmore Leonard, are the real inspiration for Justice Watt's stylistic adventures.

My argument is simple: in Denning's judgments, most of the time, style and substance "are fused in a unity"; in Watt's judgments, at least some of the time, style is "something added to substance as a mere protuberant adornment."

Denning's introductions are justly celebrated. They grab our attention, create sympathy for the focal character, and leave little doubt as to how the case is going to be resolved. Denning was blessed by good fortune. The names and circumstances he inherited by chance appear as if they were invented by a Dickensian novelist: Broadchalke, Old Herbert Bundy, Yew Tree Farm, Old Peter Beswick (a coal merchant), Mr Harry Hook (a urinating street trader), Mr Plenty (a milk roundsman), a venerable cricket club in conflict with an avaricious housing development, not to mention a barmaid who trespassed in a junkyard and was badly bitten by a big dog. Even the cars cooperate:

> There came along a Jaguar out of control driven by Mr. Berry, the defendant. A tyre had burst. The Jaguar rushed into the lay-by and crashed into Mr. Hinz and the children. Mr. Hinz was frightfully injured and died a little later. Nearly all the children were hurt. Blood was streaming from their heads. The plaintiff, hearing the crash, turned round and saw the disaster. She ran across the road and did all she could. Her husband was beyond recall, but the children recovered. (*Hinz v. Berry*, 42)

With its connotations of animalistic ferocity, especially in contrast to the image of an innocent child picking bluebells by the roadside, a Jaguar is *la voiture juste*. An Austin Mini Minor, literally and figuratively, would not have had the same impact.

Lloyd's Bank v. Bundy

Lloyd's Bank v. Bundy does not open as dramatically as *Hinz v. Berry*, but it makes the same appeal to *pathos*. Denning's pastoral vision of a merry old England that by 1975, the date of the judgment, had largely disappeared, is at once nostalgic and ethnocentric. Here that vision is innocuous, the evocation of a family farm going back for generations, but elsewhere, as I shall later argue, it betrays a more disturbing mindset:

> Broadchalke is one of the most pleasing villages in England. Old Herbert Bundy, the defendant, was a farmer there. His home was at Yew Tree Farm. It went back for three hundred years. His family had been there for generations. It was his only asset. But he did a very foolish thing. He mortgaged it to the bank. Up to the very hilt. Not to borrow money for himself, but for the sake of his son. Now the bank have come down on him. They have foreclosed. They want to get him out of Yew Tree Farm and to sell it. They have brought this action against him for possession. Going out means ruin for him. He was granted legal aid. His lawyers put in a defence. They said that when he executed the charge to the bank he did not know what he was doing: or at any rate the circumstances were such that he ought not to be bound by it. At the trial his plight was plain. The judge was sorry for him. He said he was a "poor old gentleman." He was so obviously incapacitated that the judge admitted his proof in evidence. He had a heart attack in the witness-box. Yet the judge felt he could do nothing for him. "There is nothing," he said, "which takes this out of the vast range of commercial transactions." He ordered Herbert Bundy to give up possession of Yew Tree Farm to the bank. Now there is an appeal to this court. The ground is that the circumstances were so exceptional that Herbert Bundy should not be held bound. (*Lloyds Bank Ltd. v. Bundy*, 334)

Though verbalized by Lord Denning – his is the narrative voice – the first paragraph is focalized through Old Herbert Bundy – his is the narrative perspective. There is little doubt the "poor old gentleman" is going to be vindicated.

The style in this paragraph is deceptively plain and simple. I say "deceptively" because it is rhetorically contrived. An art to conceal art, it seems to be the language of the street, but it is clearly the product of a highly sophisticated writer assuming the voice of a common and reasonable person. Almost all of the sentences are simple, short, and declarative. The style is paratactic; conjunctions are rare. Even when conjunctions do appear, the compound sentences are written as if they were simple sentences. "It was his only asset. But he did a very foolish thing." Normally, a comma would follow "asset," and the coordinate conjunction "but" would link the two independent clauses together to make a compound sentence. The sentence fragment that follows – "Up to the very hilt" – is brilliantly emphatic and accentuates Bundy's plight. Another fragment follows in its wake – "Not for the sake of himself, but for his son" – again concealing what is really a compound sentence and drawing attention to Bundy's selflessness as a caring and devoted parent. "Now the bank have come down on him" violates the rule of subject/verb agreement, but in doing so, turns the bank into an anonymous and sinister "they," a pronoun that heads the next three sentences.

The terse sentences in this opening paragraph, two-thirds of which contain fewer than ten words, create a staccato effect and imitate the confusion of Old Herbert Bundy, who is being assailed by short jabs from all sides. From his perspective, events are happening too quickly to be processed, and the speedy, jerky language reflects his befuddled psychological state. Appropriately enough, the longest sentence – thirty-six words – is given to Bundy's lawyers. "They said that when he executed the charge to the bank he did not know what he was doing: or at any rate the circumstances were such that he ought not to be bound to it." With its use of the subordinate conjunction "when," this is the one complex sentence in the paragraph. Another longish sentence, the final one in the paragraph, describes the nature of the appeal: "The ground is that the circumstances were so exceptional that Herbert Bundy should not be held bound." Of the twenty-two sentences in this paragraph, only seven are longer than ten words.

One does not spontaneously write this way. The choppy sentences and emphatic fragments are designed to mirror the Kafkaesque world into which Herbert Bundy feels he has entered. The diction is everyday for the most part, and Anglo-Saxon words predominate. Though manifestly referential and denotative, the language is latently emotive and connotative. Bundy's plight and the legal issue are clearly laid out in what seems to be neutral and descriptive language, but the appeal to *pathos* lurks in almost every sentence – the pastoral connotations of Broadchalke, Yew Tree Farm, and traditional English rural life, not to mention the sympathy generated for "a poor old gentleman" who lost his farm for the sake of his son and who had a heart attack in the witness box.

In just a few lines, Denning pits the innocent, old, and virtuous Herbert Bundy against the nameless and sinister "they" of the bank. Bundy hails from good English stock, hardworking folk who have run the family farm for generations. As a farmer, he is a productive and respectable member of Broadchalke, one of the most pleasing villages in England. The bank has no such pedigree. The name of Bundy's farm is English and picturesque – Yew Tree Farm – and Bundy's occupation as a farmer is solidly English. By contrast, it is uncertain where the mean-spirited bank has come from, but they have brought this action, they have foreclosed, they have come down on Old Herbert Bundy. They are violent invaders of the peace of the English pastoral setting. And what was the only failing of Old Herbert Bundy? He was foolish. He mortgaged his farm to the hilt for the sake of his son. Because of this, he now faces ruin. The poor old gentleman is to be evicted from his ancestral home.

This, I believe, is what the paragraph connotes, though it does so without resorting to emotive language. Denning is remarkably sparing in his use of emotively charged words – "pleasing" and "old" are the only two in this paragraph. He lets narrative description do the work instead. He is also sparing in his use of figurative language. "Up to the very hilt" would be a tired trope in most contexts, but Denning defamiliarizes and revivifies it by making it an emphatic fragment. "At the trial his plight was plain" uses the scheme of alliteration and might be perceived by some as an instance of art to display art. Unlike in the earlier phrase "but for the sake of his son," the conspicuous repetition of consonants in this clause feels obtrusive and draws attention to itself.

This raises an important point. Denning's style is not for everyone. For some, the short sentences also draw attention to themselves and become an annoying mannerism. And his habitually long paragraphs are often unfriendly to the eye. But whatever we might feel about the aesthetic merits of Denning's style, there is no denying its rhetorical efficacy. It is part and parcel of his argument that this incapacitated old man should not be held bound to his word in the exceptional circumstances the rest of the judgment delineates. For that argument to be convincing, it is necessary to establish Bundy's infirmity and the magnitude of his loss, a loss that for him is nothing less than everything, the family farm that was his only asset.

The first time Bundy signed a guarantee for his son he had independent legal advice. "The solicitor told the father that £5000 was the utmost that he could sink into his son's affairs. The house was worth about £10,000 and this was half his assets" (334–5). The second guarantee he signed was for £11,000 pounds, an amount that "[swept] up all that the father had" (335). Mr Head, the new assistant bank manager, "produced the forms that had already been filled in. The father signed them and Mr. Head witnessed them then and there. On this occasion, Mr. Head ... did not leave the forms with the father: nor did the father have any independent advice" (335). Five months later the son's business collapsed. "In due course the bank insisted on the sale of the house ... The sale has not been completed because Herbert Bundy is still in possession. The bank have brought these proceedings to evict Herbert Bundy" (336).

Having furnished the factual context, Denning turns to the legal context. First, there is "the general rule."

> Now let me say at once that in the vast majority of cases a customer who signs a bank guarantee or a charge cannot get out of it. No bargain will be upset which is the result of the ordinary interplay of forces. There are many hard cases which are caught by this rule. Take the case of a poor man who is homeless. He agrees to pay a high rent to a landlord just to get a roof over his head. The common law will not interfere. It is left to Parliament. Next take the case of a borrower in urgent need of money. He borrows it from the bank at high interest and it is guaranteed by a friend. The guarantor gives his bond and gets nothing in return. The common law will not interfere. Parliament has intervened to prevent moneylenders charging excessive interest. But it has never interfered with banks. (336)

It is tempting to view this paragraph as the quintessence of the plain style in legal writing, but closer scrutiny reveals a compositional shaping that betrays the mark of a consummate rhetorician. Denning begins with a gruff, no-nonsense imperative. "Now let me say at once that in the vast majority of cases a customer who signs a bank guarantee or a charge cannot get out of it." The colloquial predicate – "cannot get out of it" – would seem to emanate from an experienced man of the street who knows how things work in this world. At twenty-eight words, it is the longest sentence in the paragraph, a paragraph that has much more variety in sentence length than the opening one. Only a third of its sentences are under ten words. The second and third sentences set up the examples that take up the bulk of the paragraph. In effect, these examples are two stanzas in a choreographed set piece, as Edward Berry has pointed out in *Writing Reasons* (143–4).

a. Take the case of a poor man who is homeless. (10 words)
b. He agrees to pay a high rent to a landlord just to get a roof over his head. (18)
c. The common law will not interfere. (6)
d. It is left to Parliament. (5)

a. Next take the case of a borrower in urgent need of money. (12)
b. He borrows it from the bank at high interest and it is guaranteed by a friend. (16)
    The guarantor gives his bond and gets nothing in return. (10)
c. The common law will not interfere. (6)
d. Parliament has intervened to prevent moneylenders charging excessive interest. (9)
    But it has never interfered with banks. (7)

The parallelism is not exact – the second stanza has two extra sentences – but the sentences rise climactically to the tersely emphatic final line: "But it has never interfered with banks." As in the opening paragraph, a compound structure is disguised by starting the sentence with a coordinate conjunction.

Each stanza begins with an imperative "take the case" and follows with simple declarative sentences. The (c) sentences are identical. The (d) sentences are the only two that are strikingly different. The (d) sentence in the first stanza begins with a dummy subject (the expletive "it is") and is an ellipsis: "It is left to Parliament [to interfere]." The (d) sentence in the second stanza is a simple declarative sentence: "Parliament has intervened to prevent moneylenders charging excessive interest." Of its nine words, however, only two are monosyllables, a much lower ratio than that of the other sentences. The first part of a *de facto* compound sentence, it sets up the strong conclusion: "But it has never interfered with banks."

I would say that this paragraph is the quintessence of art to conceal art. Unobtrusive as the style may be, it effectively sets out the general rule and paves the way for Denning to elaborate the exceptions. "There are cases in our books in which the courts will set aside a contract, or a transfer of property, when the parties have not met on equal terms – when one is so strong in bargaining power and the other so weak – that as a matter of common fairness, it is not right that the strong should be allowed to push the weak to the wall" (336–7). When he moves into his legal analysis, his sentences become more grammatically and syntactically complex, but not so complex as to eschew concrete images and alliteration – "it is not right that the strong should be allowed to push the weak to the wall." As Denning sees it, the issue before him is to determine whether "there has been inequality of bargaining power, such as to merit the intervention of the court" (337).

His logic of exposition is transparent and inevitable. He goes through the specific categories – duress of goods, unconscionable transaction, undue influence, undue pressure, salvage agreements – and concludes that "through all these instances there runs a single thread … inequality of bargaining power" (339). And that general category applies to the case at bar. First, the bank knew "the son's company was in serious difficulty" and gave the overdraft for its own benefit. "All that the company gained was a short respite from the impending doom" (339). Second, "the relationship between the bank and father was one of trust and confidence." The father trusted the bank, and "the bank failed in that trust. It allowed the father to charge the house to his ruin" (339). Third, the son had a powerful influence on his father. Bundy loved and trusted his son. He would do anything to help him. He would put his farm at risk. Fourth, "there was a conflict of interest between the bank and father" (340). He was never told to get independent advice. "If the father had gone to his solicitor – or to any man of business – there is no doubt any one of them would say: 'You must not enter into this transaction. You are giving up your house, your sole remaining asset, for no benefit to you. The company is in such a parlous state that you must not do it'" (340).

Lord Denning is admired for his style and rightly so, but his legal reasoning – lucid, concise, and cogent – is just as impressive. There are few wasted words in this six-page judgment. Justice Watt, by contrast, is somewhat more prolix.

Ontario (Ministry of Labour) v. Enbridge Gas Distribution Inc.

On 24 April 2003, three stores and five residential apartments were destroyed by an explosion in an Etobicoke strip mall, a blast that also tore a hole in the side of a nearby home. Seven people were killed. Workers of a construction company, Warren Bitulithic Limited, had ruptured a gas line, sparking the explosion. The company was ordered to pay a fine of nearly $300,000 for digging without determining the exact location of an underground gas line and for damaging an underground natural gas pipeline.

Warren Bitulithic was one of three companies charged in the explosion. Enbridge Gas and a subcontractor, Precision Utility, were charged with failing to provide accurate information about the location of the natural gas pipelines. The trial judge dismissed the charges against Enbridge and Precision. On appeal, the acquittals entered at trial by way of this directed verdict were set aside. The appellate judge found that the trial judge had erred in finding that neither company was an "employer." As employers, the companies had a duty to ensure the health and safety of the employees under contract as well as a duty to provide accurate information about the location of the pipeline. A subcontracting relationship does not allow a company to shirk its obligations. A new trial was ordered. The companies sought leave to appeal. Their application was dismissed by the Honourable Justice David Watt of the Ontario Court of Appeal.

Justice Watt's version of the events goes like this:

> Explosions damage and destroy things. Sometimes, their victims are people. Like here. An explosion damaged and destroyed several buildings. Hurt some people too. And killed others. This explosion was preventable. If only ...
>
> A contractor using a backhoe displaced a natural gas pipeline. Natural gas crept into the basement of a two-storey commercial plaza. A source of ignition entered the mix. An explosion and fire followed. Buildings were damaged and destroyed. People were injured. And seven people were killed. (paras. 1–2)

This case was heard on 26 August 2010, more than seven years after the tragic accident. The need for dramatic immediacy is not apparent. Watt's is a style that draws attention to itself. The fragments in the first paragraph – "Like here," "Hurt some people too," "And killed others," "If only" – are protuberant and indecorous. That seven people have died is a fact that does not emerge until the end of the second paragraph. Moreover, the first paragraph is devoid of vivid concrete images. Explosions, things, buildings, and people are nouns so nondescript as to almost seem abstract.

"A contractor using a backhoe displaced a natural gas line" is not very dramatic. "Displaced" is a weak verb. And "A source of ignition entered the mix" is a backhanded way of saying the rupture sparked a massive explosion. Moreover, the "and" before "seven people were killed" enfeebles the sentence. The judge's motives in these first two paragraphs are not clear, but if his intent is to create dramatic immediacy, then the first paragraph should be omitted and the second one should be moved up and intensified.

> A contractor using a backhoe ruptured a natural gas pipeline, sparking a massive explosion that leveled a two-storey commercial plaza and pounded three stores into the basement. Five apartments were destroyed. A nearby home was left with a gaping hole. Seven people died.
>
> The contractor was fined and paid out almost $300,000 for digging without determining the exact location of the pipeline. The utility, Enbridge Gas, and its locator, Precision Utility, paid nothing. Charges against them were dismissed by the trial judge but reinstated by the appellate judge. A new trial was ordered. The utility and locator now want leave to appeal against that order.

If the issue were otherwise, the overview could be intensified even more by inserting the real names of the victims and businesses.

> Etobicoke has one of the most pleasing strip malls in Ontario. Irene Miyama was an esthetician there. She ran the Grecian Hair Salon. On Thursday afternoon, as always, she met with her elderly clients and did their hair and nails. Adele Brown (73), Elizabeth Roy (74), and Lillian Guglieth (73) were regulars. They enjoyed the atmosphere and conversation. They enjoyed being tended to. But their enjoyment ended abruptly and fatally. A massive gas explosion obliterated the Grecian Hair Salon and killed its proprietor and patrons. It also obliterated Elegant Cleaners, Milano's Pizza, and five apartments, killing Dora Carambelas (60), Tina Kirkimtzis (32), and long-time resident Robert Fairley (50). Four others were injured.

Obviously, in this case, it would be in extremely bad taste to parody the opening of *Lloyd's Bank v. Bundy*. People have died. But imitating Denning at all is fraught with danger, and the degree to which a judge should personalize a tragedy depends on the nature of the case. If the families of the victims are suing for damages, then personalizing the victims makes sense. But even in such a situation, a Denningesque opening runs the risk of drawing attention to the stylistic aptness of the imitation rather than to the horrible fate of the victims.

The problem with Watt's opening is its incongruence with the rest of the judgment. The first three paragraphs are terse and fragmented. In the fourth paragraph, however, the paperback novelist disappears and the traditional judge takes over. The voice of the latter is appropriate to the subject matter. This is a highly technical decision, as its complicated headnote suggests:

> HELD: Application dismissed. It was not clear that the Crown had changed the basis of liability advanced at trial and appeal. In any event, the shifting prosecution ground of appeal did not raise a question of law in the strict sense and was unlikely to have an impact on firmly established jurisprudence. There was no basis to grant leave on the issue of whether the companies were employers for the purpose of the [Occupational Health and Safety Act] regulation which imputed liability. The regulation was no longer in force and thus there was no public interest aspect to the appeal. The new provision did not apply to the prosecution. The interpretation imposed on the former provision by the appellate judge was neither obviously wrong nor of doubtful correctness. For similar reasons, there was no basis to grant leave to appeal on the issue regarding the interpretation of the companies' duties under the [Technical Standards and Safety Act] regulation. The limitations ground of appeal did not raise a question of law alone and did not have a public interest component or resonance for the general administration of justice. The interpretation rendered by both the trial judge and appellate judge was consistent with the underlying legislation. Leave to appeal was accordingly denied.

Elmore Leonard would be hard pressed to find a compelling plot in this headnote. The precipitating accident is dramatic. The legal issues are not. The issues before Justice Watt comprise Enbridge and Utility's fourfold claim that the charge against them was not entered within the required time, that there was no duty upon them to provide an accurate "locate," that neither was an "employer" under the Occupational Health and Safety Act, and that the appellate judge "erred in law in permitting the prosecutors to resile on appeal from positions they had taken at trial and to advance a new basis of liability upon which to obtain a new trial." In no way does Watt's narrative opening and overview make these four issues clear. It is not until the end of paragraph 30 that the reader knows what the leave to appeal involves. Denning, by contrast, gets to the issue by end of his first paragraph. With Watt, the overview and background facts (paras. 1–30) present a great deal of information that is not determinative of the issues. The problem is not in his storytelling but in its irrelevance to the issues he is being asked to decide.

These issues would seem to require what Richard Posner calls a pure style, and after the third paragraph, Watt proffers such a style for the preponderance of his judgment. Aimed at a professional audience, a pure or formalist style sees the law as logical, objective, and constrained. Such a style is impersonal, elevated, technical, and conventional. This style appears to come naturally to Justice Watt. By contrast, an impure or pragmatic style is as much concerned with equity as with law and aims itself at the general public. It is familiar, conversational, informal, and fresh. This style appears to come naturally to Lord Denning.

Obviously, this distinction is not categorical or absolute. Denning has his formalist moments, just as Watt has his pragmatist moments. Nevertheless, Watt aims his words at the general public in his openings but writes for a legal audience the rest of the way. Denning writes for the public all the way. He does not condescend to his readers but works hard to make his legal reasoning accessible and intelligible to them. Watt makes his readers work hard – his point-last style keeps governing principles and their application separate, thus creating a gap between exposition and analysis – but his reasoning in the end is cogent and convincing. He is an impressively thorough jurist. Denning's point-first style is issue-driven. The facts, the positions of the parties, the law, and the analysis are for the most part integrated under the issues, not given long discrete sections. Principle and application are proximate. The law is explained and cited at the point of its analysis. Though not practicable in every case, a point-first style and issue-driven structure often cut opinions in half because only those facts that are determinative of the issues make it into the final draft. *R. v. Simon* is another of Watt's judgments that showcases storytelling at the outset but eventually devolves into a point-last style and submission-driven structure.

R. v. Simon

This case is about the propriety of the trial judge's instructions to the jury. Mr Simon is appealing his conviction for second degree murder. The four grounds of appeal involve the issue of liability, the fault element in murder, the need for a judge to make clear that a juror does not have to choose between competing versions of events, and the exclusion of Mr Simon from a pre-charge conference. Justice Watt finds that the judge properly instructed the jury that Simon could be convicted either as a shooter in a failed drug transaction, that is to say as the principal in an unlawful killing, or as a party to a plan to buy drugs or rob the dealer, that is to say as a party to an unlawful killing. The judge also properly explained the fault element: Simon's being armed with a gun supports the assertion that the robbery was planned, that Simon intended to cause bodily harm if necessary, that he knew that such bodily harm would likely be fatal, and that he was thus reckless as to whether the victim lived or died. Although the judge initially made a mistake in explaining recklessness, he quickly and adequately corrected his erroneous instruction to the jury. He also made it clear that jurors do not have to choose between competing versions of events and that an accused's lack of credibility does not relieve a prosecutor from meeting his or her burden of proof beyond a reasonable doubt. And, finally, there was nothing unfair about Simon's exclusion from the in-chambers meeting about the charge. Nothing that took place in the meeting affected his vital interests.

Justice Watts begins:

> Handguns and drug deals are frequent companions, but not good friends. Rip-offs happen. Shootings do too. *Caveat emptor. Caveat venditor.* People get hurt. People get killed. Sometimes, the buyer. Other times, the seller. That happened here.
>
> Jason Porter was a drug dealer. Everton Cribb and Allister Simon came to Porter's house to buy one-half pound of marijuana. Cribb and Simon brought handguns with them. During a struggle, Cribb or Simon shot Porter once in the chest. Porter died.
>
> Cribb pleaded guilty to manslaughter, then testified for the Crown at Simon's trial. A jury convicted Simon of second degree murder.
>
> Simon appeals his conviction. He says that the trial judge made mistakes in his final instructions to the jury, by leaving some things out and getting other things wrong. Simon also argues that he was improperly excluded

from some discussions about the judge's final instructions because those discussions took place in the judge's chambers, rather than in open court. (paras. 1–4)

This is a powerful opening. Even though the Latin phrases are not likely to be found in a crime novel, they have a pleasing rhythm. Nevertheless, it is arguable that the first paragraph should be eliminated entirely in favour of a Denningesque beginning. Just as Herbert Bundy was a farmer, Peter Beswick was a coal merchant, and Mr Plenty was a milkman, Jason Porter was a drug dealer. Here the allusion to Denning works, and the opening four paragraphs make effective use of storytelling even if the three other grounds of appeal should have been specified in the fourth paragraph. The crucial difference between this case and *Enbridge* is that here the narrative is relevant to the issues before Justice Watt. Nevertheless, the reader needs to know the nature of these issues to process the story intelligently. The key questions need to be up front. Was Crib a principal in or party to an unlawful killing? Did he intend to cause bodily harm and know that such bodily harm would likely prove to be fatal? Was he reckless as to whether the victim would live or die? Knowing what the issues are not only makes us informed readers but also enhances the impact of Watt's dramatic conclusion to his introductory section.

The Confrontation
A scuffle began in the kitchen. Porter and Cribb were wrestling over some marijuana. Porter yelled out to Joe MacIntosh for help. MacIntosh, who lived on the second floor, headed downstairs. According to some witnesses, the appellant had a handgun trained on both the combatants, Porter and Cribb.

Evidence about who shot Jason Porter varied. Montreuil [a witness to the crime] believed that Cribb was the shooter. The basis for her conclusion seemed to be that Cribb was the taller of the two men (Cribb and the appellant), at least taller than the man who was fighting with Porter. Cieplucha [another witness] saw the appellant point a chrome-plated handgun at Porter, then at Cieplucha himself. Cieplucha did not see who shot Porter. Garcia also saw a silver-coloured gun, but could not recall whether it was in the hand of the appellant or that of Cribb.

Everton Cribb said that both he and the appellant had handguns with them because they were buying drugs from strangers.

When police searched the house after responding to a 911 call, they found no weapons, drugs or cash. The gun that fired the fatal bullet, a 380 mm. semi-automatic weapon, has never been found.

Cause of Death
Jason Porter died from a gunshot wound to the chest. The gun was fired from a distance of about six or seven feet, although the weapon could have been as close as one foot from the deceased. (paras. 14–18)

The narrative details – the scuffle, the uncertainty as to who was the shooter, the fact that the gun was fired at almost point-blank range – are vividly presented. Here the storytelling is apt and functional. The narrative details, however, only assume their full significance in the context of the issues of liability, fault, and recklessness, as Watt makes clear with respect to recklessness some fifty-five paragraphs later.

In addition to the subservient role of recklessness in the fault element in s. 229(a)(ii), we should not lose sight of the evidence in this case. A gunshot from a handgun of significant calibre, fired from a distance of not more than six or seven feet, perhaps as close as one foot from the deceased. A wound to a vital part of the deceased. And no suggestion of any incapacitating elements, such as intoxication, whether the shooter was Cribb or the appellant. Nothing more need be said. (73)

For each of the grounds of appeal, Watt goes through the Instructions of the Trial Judge, the Positions of the Counsel at Trial, the Arguments on Appeal, the Governing Principles, and the Principles Applied, thus separating exposition and analysis. This is a thorough and comprehensive way of structuring a decision, and one that comes naturally to the formalist style. It moves inductively from the particular to the general and reflects the way most of us think – point-last, not point-first. But however natural, a point-last style is not reader-friendly. Even if it is exemplary in the logic of its unfolding, it is highly redundant. The same information appears in different sections, and if it does not, the reader is forced to backtrack. Because of its inclusiveness, this is an ideal structure for an advanced draft; it functions as a sophisticated checklist.

A final draft, however, is about the communication of reasons, not about their discovery. It should be oriented towards the needs of the reader, not those of the writer. Opposing arguments should be dealt with in tandem and analysed in the context of the issues to be resolved.

They should not be rehearsed in their own separate sections. They should dialectically engage each other so that the judge can mediate between them and arrive at his or her own determination. Principles should be enunciated at the point of application, not explained in isolation from argument and analysis. If *R. v. Simon* were written in a point-first style using an issue-driven structure, its length would be reduced by half. Whereas Denning's decisions are usually written in such a style and structure, he sometimes goes overboard in his introductions.

Miller v. Jackson

The narrative excess of the introduction to this judgment is Denning at his worst or best, depending on your taste. To be fair, the judgment is a dissent based on the court's right to exercise its equitable jurisdiction, and arguments from equity are far more dependent on storytelling than arguments from law. Where there is no controlling law, a judge in some sense is making it up as he or she goes along. In *Miller,* there is no dispute about the issue of liability. Balls launched from a cricket pitch have damaged residential property and represent a potential danger to the occupants. The householders seek an injunction against playing cricket on that pitch. The majority decision grants the injunction. Denning believes that the use of the ground for cricket is reasonable and does not become a nuisance just because somebody buys a house in a new development. The court, he maintains, has a duty to regard the public interest. An injunction brings seventy years of cricket to an end. The greater interest of the public should prevail over the hardship of householders subjected to occasionally errant balls. The injunction, he says, should be discharged, and damages for four hundred pounds should be substituted for past and future inconvenience. His introductory paragraph to his dissenting opinion pulls out all the stops:

> In summertime village cricket is the delight of everyone. Nearly every village has its own cricket field where the young men play and the old men watch. In the village of Lintz in County Durham they have their own ground, where they have played these last 70 years. They tend it well. The wicket area is well rolled and mown. The outfield is kept short. It has a good club house for the players and seats for the onlookers. The village team play there on Saturdays and Sundays. They belong to a league, competing with the neighbouring villages. On other evenings after work they practise while the light lasts. Yet now after these 70 years a judge of the

High Court has ordered that they must not play there any more. He has issued an injunction to stop them. He has done it at the instance of a newcomer who is no lover of cricket. This newcomer has built, or has had built for him, a house on the edge of the cricket ground which four years ago was a field where cattle grazed. The animals did not mind the cricket. But now this adjoining field has been turned into a housing estate. The newcomer bought one of the houses on the edge of the cricket ground. No doubt the open space was a selling point. Now he complains that when a batsman hits a six the ball has been known to land in his garden or on or near his house. His wife has got so upset about it that they always go out at week-ends. They do not go into the garden when cricket is being played. They say that this is intolerable. So they asked the judge to stop the cricket being played. And the judge, much against his will, has felt that he must order the cricket to be stopped: with the consequence, I suppose, that the Lintz Cricket Club will disappear. The cricket ground will be turned to some other use. I expect for more houses or a factory. The young men will turn to other things instead of cricket. The whole village will be much the poorer. And all this because of a newcomer who has just bought a house there next to the cricket ground. (976)

The narrative continues for another five paragraphs, developing in even more detail a nostalgic pastoral vision of an England that is disappearing before Denning's very eyes. What could be more English than cricket or football? The young men play and the old men watch. Presumably, the village lasses bat their eyelashes and throw their handkerchiefs.

Like the sexism, the xenophobia is mild. The cause of the club's eviction is a newcomer who, unlike the grazing cows, is no lover of cricket. The animals do not mind the cricket, but he and his neurotic if not hysterical wife do. "His wife," Denning writes, "has got so upset about it that they always go out at week-ends" (976). She is later described as "a very sensitive lady who has worked herself up into such a state that she exclaimed to the judge: 'I just want to be allowed to live in peace ... Have I got to wait until someone is killed before anything can be done?'" (982). One might pass over this mildly misogynist portraiture were it not for Denning's later and infamous remarks about the unfitness of certain black people as jurors and the people of colour who are overrunning England.

In 1982, seven years after *Miller*, Denning published *What Next in the Law*; in it, he seemed to suggest that some members of the black community were unsuitable to serve on juries and that immigrant groups may have different moral standards than those of native English citizens. His remarks followed a trial over the St Paul's riot in Bristol; two jurors on the case threatened to sue him, and the Society of Black Lawyers wrote to the Lord Chancellor to request that Denning "politely and firmly" be made to retire. Denning apologized for his remarks on 21 May and handed a letter to the Lord Chancellor detailing his resignation, effective as of 29 September.

It would seem that the very intensity of *Miller's* pastoral vision paves the way for the later indiscretions of a man who lived for over a hundred years, from January 1899 to March 1999, years in which the forces of industry, technology, and urbanization achieved hegemony in modern England. In *Miller,* the enemies of the English village are clearly identified – real estate developers, householders, industrialists, and newcomers. And what is being lost is nothing less than an Anglo-Saxon culture that has prevailed for centuries. Houses and factories will inevitably supplant cricket grounds, and Denning on some level knows this to be true, even if, for him, "the *public* interest lies in protecting the environment by preserving our playing fields in the face of mounting development, and by enabling our youth to enjoy all the benefits of outdoor games, such as cricket and football. The *private* interest lies in securing the privacy of [an individual's] home and garden without intrusion or interference by anyone" (981). Either the cricket club must move or the Millers must move, and the writing is not only on the wall; it is in the majority judgment.

Cummings v. Granger

Five years before his forced retirement, Denning wrote a judgment that, by his standards, is curiously devoid of *pathos,* though not of alliteration. "This is the case of the barmaid who was badly bitten by a big dog." The unchained dog was kept in a gated scrapyard, and "the big gates had a warning on them in huge letters "Beware of the Dog." The owner "said that the dog took particular objection to coloured people" (106). After closing time, the barmaid's friend Mr Hobson wanted to get some tools out of his car, which was in the yard.

> He knew where to find the key of the yard. He got the key. He unlocked the padlock and went in by the wicket gate. The plaintiff says that she stayed outside on the pavement, but the judge did not believe her. The

judge found that she followed her companion in. She got nearly to the middle of the yard when the dog attacked her.

A neighbour in the house opposite saw what was happening. He had just got into bed when he heard the dog barking. He jumped out of bed and looked. He saw the dog in the yard attacking the plaintiff. She was in the middle of the yard. Her man friend was trying to get the dog away by beating it with a piece of wood or iron. He saw him helping the plaintiff to the car to drive her to hospital.

Her cheek was torn open and she was badly injured. She has had plastic surgery, but she has a very severe scar still remaining on her cheek. She now claims damages against the owner of the dog.

After the accident the plaintiff's handbag and shoe were found in the middle of the yard. She had to explain how this came to be. She did it this way. She said she was standing outside on the pavement waiting for her friend to come out. Then she heard a noise. She turned round and there was the dog. She was terrified of it, but she says that she tried to make friends with it. She patted it on the head. This seemed to infuriate the dog. It went at her and dragged her from the pavement through the gate and then back into the yard. That is why she was seen to be in the yard and that is why her handbag and shoe were there in the middle of the yard.

The judge did not believe that the plaintiff stayed outside. He found that she had gone inside. She had followed her companion without any authority at all. She was a trespasser in the yard. That must be accepted. Mr. Irvine took us through the evidence. He asked us to find that the plaintiff's story was correct, but I am quite clear that we cannot interfere with the judge's finding. She was a trespasser.

Nevertheless, the judge held that the plaintiff had a good cause of action against the defendant, the keeper of the dog under the *Animals Act* 1971. He held that that Act imposed a strict liability on the defendant; but that it was partly the plaintiff's own fault. He said that the parties were both equally to blame. He found the total damages to be £2,892.95 and awarded the plaintiff one half, that is, £1,446.46.

The barmaid remains unnamed throughout the judgment. She is the defendant, the lady, the plaintiff. Her severe injuries provoke no sympathy even though her cheek was torn open and she now has a very severe scar. She knew the dog was there. She voluntarily took the risk. And, as we are told twice in these opening paragraphs, she was a trespasser. She is not entitled to the damages awarded to her by the trial judge.

Nevertheless, there is a lingering sense of dissonance. Even though Denning has no sympathy for the scarred barmaid, his vivid narrative, unintentionally no doubt, creates sympathy for the victim. The infuriated dog's "attacking the plaintiff," Mr Hobson's "trying to get the dog away by beating it with a piece of wood or iron," the barmaid's severed cheek, the permanent scar she is left with – these and other concrete details play up the horror and violence of the event. In this case at least, Denning's characteristic flair for dramatic immediacy and evocative imagery is incongruent with his cold and blunt conclusion.

The Alsatian's "particular objection to coloured people" is mentioned more than once, implying that the barmaid herself is a woman of colour. I am not saying that Denning should have decided in her favour, but, like poor Mrs Palsgraf, she has suffered grievously, and that suffering ought to be given some sympathetic recognition.

Denning's pastoral nostalgia for merry old England goes in hand in hand with an ethnocentric if not racist rejection of multiculturalism. Insofar as his vivid storytelling champions the causes of ordinary folk like Herbert Bundy, it is uplifting. Insofar as it demonizes the other, it is troubling. Compelling style cannot atone for offensive content.

Throughout this study, I stress the formative role story and style play in the rhetoric of legal argument, especially as story and style pertain to legal world-making and judicial self-portraiture. In Lord Denning's final writings, an ethnocentric and nostalgic world is created by an intolerant and unsympathetic judge. It is sad to end this chapter with a low point in the career of one of the most lively and talented judicial rhetors, a rhetor whose life spanned almost the entirety of the twentieth century. Whatever his philosophical shortcomings may have been, old Tom Denning was a writer.

3 The Perils of Analogy: Legal World-Making and Judicial Self-Fashioning in *Palsgraf v. Long Island Railroad*

This chapter looks at law as a branch of rhetoric. By rhetoric I mean the use of language to inform, persuade, or motivate an audience. Like all users of language, writers of judgments inform, persuade, or motivate by deploying three basic strategies: *logos* – the appeal to reason, logic, or example; *pathos* – the appeal to passion, sentiment, or emotion; and *ethos* – the appeal to the character, image, or expertise of the writer. In an ideal judgment, all three strategies harmoniously work together: *logos*, the process of reasoning by which a judge interprets the past and brings it to bear on the present; *pathos*, the degree to which his or her court recognizes the legitimacy and humanity of the losing parties and hears their stories; and *ethos*, the character his or her court gives itself, the ethical community it imagines.

Every time judges write decisions, they are faced with rhetorical choices, and by the stories they choose to tell and by the styles in which they choose to tell them, they are creating legal worlds for others to live in as well as fashioning images of themselves as judges. In every case they are called upon to decide, the story can be characterized in a variety of ways. Sometimes those characterizations create impoverished worlds.

Osterlind v. Hill deals with a vexing issue in the tort law of its time – namely, is there an affirmative duty to rescue?[1] Hill rented a canoe to Osterlind and another man, both of whom were drunk. The canoe overturned, and Osterlind clung to it for half an hour screaming for help.

---

1 This case is discussed (12–14) and reproduced (22–4) in Richard Weisberg's *Poethics and Other Strategies of Law and Literature*.

Hill was an expert swimmer and had a rope available, but he sat on the dock smoking cigarettes while Osterlind drowned before his eyes.

Osterlind's relatives sued on the intestate's behalf. Believing himself to be irrevocably bound by precedent, Justice Braley affirmed the lower court's ruling in favour of Hill. For the relatives to prevail, he writes, they "must set forth facts, which, if proved, establish the breach of a legal duty owed by the defendant to the intestate" (23). In the case they rely on as a precedent, the plaintiff was "so intoxicated as to be incapable of standing or walking or caring for himself in any way" (23). But in the case at bar,

> after the canoe was overturned the intestate hung to the canoe for approximately one-half hour and made loud calls for assistance. On the facts stated in the declaration the intestate was not in a helpless condition ... In view of the absence of any duty to refrain from renting a canoe to a person in the condition of the intestate ... the failure of the defendant to respond to the intestate's outcries is immaterial. (23–4)

Because Osterlind screamed for help for thirty minutes while desperately clinging to the overturned canoe, Justice Braley finds that he was not drunk enough to have placed the defendant on notice at the time of rental. In so portraying the facts of the case, Braley is neither fashioning a humane judicial self nor imagining a compassionate legal world. This is not to say that he should have decided otherwise. But even if he had no legal options, he did have rhetorical options. To pave the way for a future alteration of a cold and callous rule, Braley could have dramatized the facts vividly, empathized with the victim and his family, and anguished over the moral dilemma the precedent imposed upon him. Even if the defendant's failure to rescue a drowning man is legally immaterial, it is morally deplorable. And even if Braley felt powerless to change the legal world he inherited, he could have imagined a world to come in which what is morally right tempers what is legally required.

A similar dilemma arises in *Palsgraf v. Long Island Railroad*, perhaps the most famous case in American tort law. Here, too, human suffering is eclipsed by legal nicety. Mrs Palsgraf is on the railroad platform, waiting for a train with her two daughters. Another train pulls in; two passengers run to catch it; one of them has a package under his arm. As the train begins to leave the platform, two railroad guards attempt to help the two passengers get on board while the train is moving. As they assist the passengers to get on to the train, a package falls to the platform. Unbeknown to the guards, the package contains powerful fireworks and explodes. The explosion is heard several blocks away, a stampede erupts, ambulances arrive, and more than a dozen people suffer burns and abrasions.

Some distance away, Palsgraf is hurt by a falling scale that strikes her in the arm, hip, and thigh. Afterwards, she can walk with great difficulty but cannot continue her job as a housekeeper; she also suffers from shock-related symptoms including stuttering.

At the first trial, the jury awards Palsgraf six thousand dollars, a huge sum of money in 1927. But when the railroad's appeal reaches New York's highest court, the jury's decision is overturned by a 4–3 vote. The majority finds that negligence is not actionable unless it involves the invasion of a legally protected interest, the violation of a right. The conduct of the railroad's guards, if a wrong in relation to the holder of the package, was not a wrong in relation to the plaintiff, who was standing many feet away. Only the package holder might be said to have a legally protected interest. This is a very narrow interpretation of the law. It does not imagine a very expansive legal world for people to live in. A reckless man running with a package of explosives has a legally protected interest in the safety of his package. An innocent victim permanently injured by an explosion, despite her interest in her own bodily security, has no cause for action, because she is deemed to be too far away from the scene of the blast.

Writing for the majority, Justice Cardozo finds that a person has to be within a foreseeable zone of danger in order to have a cause of action for negligence. Agents cannot be given a duty to watch out for people not in their range of apprehension. Range of apprehension is the first of several figures of speech for the foreseeable zone of danger, itself a figure of speech.[2]

Writing for the minority, Justice Andrews disagrees with this standard and sees it as embracing too narrow a concept of negligence. For him, due care is a duty imposed on everyone. "Everyone owes to the world at large," he writes, "the duty of refraining from those acts that

---

2 Among these figures of speech are orbit of danger, range of apprehension, radius of danger, danger zone, and eye of ordinary vigilance.

may unreasonably threaten the safety of others" (7). The world at large Andrews envisages is much more expansive than the constricted legal space envisaged by Cardozo. In this case, Andrews maintains, Palsgraf would never have been injured had there been no explosion, and the explosion would not have occurred if not for the negligent actions of the railroad's guards.

Cardozo won the day and made Palsgraf pay the railroad's legal expenses, an award of costs that provoked criticism. He also presented the facts inaccurately, simplifying the circumstances by not even mentioning the pandemonium and multiple injuries that followed in the wake of the explosion and by noticeably exaggerating Palsgraf's distance from the train. He reduces her to her legal status only – that of plaintiff; he never mentions her by name, and he utterly silences her concrete human story. The narrative he unfolds distorts what really happened and occupies but a single paragraph. The physical and psychological consequences of Palsgraf's injuries receive no mention whatsoever. Even though her injuries are irrelevant to Cardozo's reasons for decision, there is no need for him to deny her legitimacy and humanity as a losing litigant. Nor is there any need to exclude *pathos* from the legal world created by his judgment, the opening paragraph of which tells the story vividly, finally zeroing in on the guards' act of helping the man board the train:

> In this act, the package was dislodged, and fell upon the rails. It was a package of small size, about fifteen inches long, and was covered by a newspaper. In fact it contained fireworks, but there was nothing in its appearance to give notice of its contents. The fireworks when they fell exploded. The shock of the explosion threw down some scales at the other end of the platform, many feet away. The scales struck the plaintiff, causing the injuries for which she sues. (2)

From Cardozo's point of view, this is a persuasive way of relating the story. To say in the passive voice that the package was dislodged is to overlook the agent who dislodged it. Size, too, apparently matters. That the package was small and concealed by a newspaper underscores its seeming innocuousness. Cardozo's writing style in this opening paragraph is, for the most part, exemplary in its lucidity: sentences are short, diction is everyday, syntax is simple, and figurative language is avoided. In the next paragraph, however, his style shifts into what will be the dominant mode for the rest of the decision, the mode of writing for which Cardozo is famous:

> The conduct of the defendant's guard, if a wrong in relation to the holder of the package, was not a wrong in its relation to the plaintiff, standing far away. Relatively to her it was not negligence at all. Nothing in the situation gave notice that the falling package had in it the potency of peril to persons thus removed. Negligence is not actionable unless it involves the invasion of a legally protected interest. "Proof of negligence in the air so to speak, will not do" [Pollock]. (2)

As this passage indicates, Cardozo's characteristic style of argument is eloquent and forcible, but despite the judgment's legal formality and technical tone, it is not without its literary moments of virtuoso alliteration: "nothing … gave notice that the falling package had in it the potency of peril to persons thus removed" (2). Still, this decision is a model of what Richard Posner calls the pure style – it sees the law as logical, objective, and constrained. The writing is impersonal, refined, solemn, and professional. It is directed at a legal audience. The issue is carefully and narrowly defined – wrong is only in relation to the holder of the package; Palsgraf has no legally protected interest; an innocent and seemingly harmless act does not take on the quality of a tort just because something bad happens and somebody gets injured. Since "no hazard was apparent to the eye of ordinary vigilance" (3), the guards had no duty of care to Palsgraf.

On the surface, Cardozo's argument appears to epitomize the appeal to logic, but in the world of torts, it would seem, analogy proves to have a fatal attraction. After concluding that "the plaintiff sues in her own right for a wrong personal to her, and not as the vicarious beneficiary of a breach of duty to another" (3), Cardozo ponders alternative scenarios.

> A different conclusion will involve us, and swiftly too, in a maze of contradictions. A guard stumbles over a package which has been left upon a platform. It seems to be a bundle of newspapers. It turns out to be a can of dynamite. To the eye of ordinary vigilance, the bundle is abandoned waste, which may be kicked on or trod on with impunity. Is a passenger at the other end of the platform protected by the law against the unsuspected hazard concealed beneath the waste? If not, is the result to be any different, so far as the distant passenger is concerned, when the guard stumbles

over a valise which a truckman or porter has left upon the walk? The passenger far away, if a victim of a wrong at all, has a cause of action, not derivative, but original and primary. His claim to be protected against invasion of his bodily security is neither greater nor lesser because the act resulting in the invasion is a wrong to another far removed. In this case, the rights that are said to have been violated, the interests said to have been invaded, are not even of the same order. The man [the fireworks carrier] was not injured in his person nor even put in danger. The purpose of the act [of helping him board the train], as well as its effect, was to make his person safe. If there was a wrong to him at all, which may very well be doubted, it was a wrong to a property interest only, the safety of his package. Out of this wrong to property, which threatened injury to nothing else, there has passed, we are told, to the plaintiff [Mrs Palsgraf] by derivation or succession a right of action for the invasion of an interest of another order, the right to bodily security. (3)

This is a confusing passage for several reasons: first, it is mainly written in the hypothetical and conditional mode, making it hard to tell whether the questions posed are real or rhetorical; second, it takes us rapidly through a series of images and analogies – a maze of contradictions, a bundle of newspapers, the eye of ordinary vigilance, a can of dynamite, a valise; third, it shifts focus to the case at bar by using an ambiguous prepositional phrase, "in this case," a phrase that could be taken in a non-legal sense; and, fourth, it uses vague expressions such as "the man" and "the purpose of the act."

The first analogy posits a guard stumbling over a package that turns out to be a can of dynamite even though to the eye of ordinary vigilance, it seems to be a bundle of newspapers. Cardozo seems to suggest that a passenger at the other end of the platform is not protected by law under these circumstances. I say "seems" because the matter is cast in interrogative form, and the nature and extent of the passenger's injuries are not made clear. The "if not" that begins the next sentence does not make things clearer. Cardozo implies in the conditional rather than stating in the declarative that the distant passenger is not protected by law. We are then asked to contemplate whether things would be different for the passenger if "the guard stumbles over a valise which a truckman or porter has left upon a walk" (3). Though the contents of the valise remain a mystery, we are told that the distant passenger, if he is a victim of a wrong at all, has a cause of action that is "not derivative, but original and primary" (3). Why this is so is not explained. Instead,

Cardozo says that "his claim to be protected against invasion of his bodily security is neither greater nor lesser because the act resulting in the invasion is a wrong to another far removed" (3). Does the wrong to another far removed refer to the guard or to the passenger? The pronoun references are rather opaque. Moreover, the distant passenger would seem to be in a position analogous to Mrs Palsgraf's, but the invasion of rights Cardozo turns to is that of the man carrying the package. Someone has been seriously injured by way of an explosion, but Cardozo's focus is on the safety of the package containing the explosives. "The orbit of duty," he concludes, is "the orbit of danger as disclosed to the eye of ordinary vigilance" (3).

What Cardozo seems to be saying could probably be better said without any analogy at all: namely, that the passenger has no claim against either of the stumblers. He would only have a claim against someone whose negligence was directed at him. Applied to the case at bar, this construal of the issue means that the fireworks carrier is liable to anyone within the orbit of danger, while the guard who negligently causes him to fall, unaware of the fireworks in the package, is liable to the carrier but not to others within the foreseeable zone of danger. This may be the correct legal conclusion, but the analogical reasoning that leads to it is confusing. Nevertheless, instead of giving us the clarification we need, Cardozo gives us yet another analogy.

> One who jostles one's neighbor in a crowd does not invade the rights of others standing at the outer fringe when the unintended contact casts a bomb upon the ground. The wrongdoer as to them is the man who carries the bomb, not the one who explodes it without suspicion of the danger. Life will have to be made over, and human nature transformed, before prevision so extravagant can be accepted as the norm of conduct, the customary standard to which behavior must conform. (3)

But if the man carrying the bomb is the wrongdoer, why is not the man carrying the fireworks the wrongdoer in the case before us? Why is he recklessly running after a moving train with a package of dangerous explosives? Does he not owe a duty of care to his fellow travellers? Or is the point that because nothing bad happened to anyone within the orbit of danger, he is off the hook? With analogy, there is always the danger of lurking antithesis. Analogies have a tendency to keep on ramifying, which is why they need to be used with due care and attention. The zone of danger into which they lead a writer is not always foreseeable.

Dissenting against Cardozo's decision, Andrews construes the issue in terms of proximate cause and proximate consequences, not in terms of what a prudent person could reasonably perceive as a foreseeable zone of danger. Upon the facts of the case, he asks, where "the defendant's servant negligently knocked a package from [a passenger's] arms," may an intending passenger

> recover damages she has suffered in an action brought against the master? The result we reach depends on our theory as to the nature of negligence. Is it a relative concept – the breach of some duty owing to a particular person or to particular persons? Or where there is an act which unreasonably threatens the safety of others, is the doer liable for all its proximate consequences, even where they result in injury to one who would generally be thought to be outside the radius of danger? This is not a mere dispute as to words. We might not believe that to the average mind the dropping of a bundle would seem to involve the probability of harm to the plaintiff standing many feet away whatever might be the case as to the owner or to one so near as to be likely to be struck by its fall. If, however, we adopt the second hypothesis we have to inquire only as to the relation between cause and effect. We deal in terms of proximate cause, not of negligence. (5–6)

Note the difference between Andrews's opening and Cardozo's. Andrews loads the dice by inserting the word "negligently," a legally charged adverb. But even though he is writing in dissent, a mode in which an emotive rendering of the plaintiff's suffering is a standard ploy, he declines to delineate the concrete human story and adopts what Posner calls an impure style, a style that sees the law as less logical, objective, and constrained than its purer counterpart. With the exception of a few archaisms, Andrews deploys a plain style for the most part and writes in a conversational and accessible language, avoiding technical terms and seeking illuminating illustrations. The audience he imagines is comprised of average minds and reasonable people, people just like us, as is revealed by his recurrent use of the pronoun "we." Mrs Palsgraf, however, barely exists; she is an injured plaintiff and intending passenger only.

Andrews's is a much broader theory as to the nature of negligence, reinforcing the Aristotelian point that all conclusions are foregone conclusions once we have determined our enabling assumptions. In law, framing the question is everything. To see through the lens of cause and effect is to direct our attention towards empirical events rather than legal niceties. For Andrews, negligence is an act or omission that unreasonably affects the rights of others, or that unreasonably fails to protect them from the dangers resulting from such acts. "Should we drive down Broadway at a reckless speed," he writes, "we are negligent whether we strike an approaching car or miss it by an inch. The act itself is wrongful. It is a wrong not only to those who happen to be in the radius of danger but to all who might have been there – a wrong to the public at large. Such is the language of the street" (6).

According to Andrews, if the act is wrongful, the doer is liable for its proximate results. He imagines a legal world and human community where everyone owes a duty of care to his or her fellow citizens:

> The proposition is this. Everyone owes to the world at large the duty of refraining from those acts that may unreasonably threaten the safety of others. Such an act occurs. Not only is he wronged to whom the harm might reasonably be expected to result, but he also who is in fact injured, even if he be outside what would generally be thought the danger zone ... [A]ll those in fact injured may complain ... Unreasonable risk being taken its consequences are not confined to those who might probably be hurt. (7)

But Andrews, it would seem, is addicted to analogies, the proliferation of which ends up undermining the concept of proximate cause itself. Wantonly using analogy in a passage that openly says analogy is of little aid, Andrews seems to have stumbled upon chaos theory before it became part of the modern mindset. According to chaos theory, the flapping of a single butterfly's wings is capable of producing a tiny change in the atmosphere so that in a month's time a tornado that would otherwise have missed a small provincial town instead devastates it. Andrews has similar thoughts about the vagaries of proximate cause:

> These two words [proximate cause] have never been given an inclusive definition. What is a cause in a legal sense, still more what is a proximate cause, depend in each case on many considerations, as does the existence of negligence itself. Any philosophical doctrine of causation does not help us. A boy throws a stone in a pond. The ripples spread. The water level rises. The history of that pond is altered to all eternity. It will be altered by other causes also. Yet it will be forever the resultant of all causes combined. Each one will have an influence. How great only omniscience can say. You may speak of a chain, or if you please, a net. An analogy is of little aid. Each cause brings about future events. Without each the future

would not be the same. Each is proximate in the sense that it is essential. But that is not what we mean by the word. Nor on the other hand do we mean sole cause. (8)

This paragraph is a seemingly self-defeating exercise in negative definition whereby Andrews tries to define proximate cause in terms of what it is not. He starts with a boy throwing a stone in a pond and thereby altering the history of that pond to all eternity even if other subsequent causes will also have an equally permanent influence. One might assume that this analogy is meant to be illustrative, but Andrews goes on to say that "an analogy is of little aid," that to speak of chains or nets of causation sheds scant light. Whether large or small, each cause brings about future events and is thus "proximate in the sense that it is essential" (8). This is his first attempt to say what proximate cause is not. It is not every cause, nor is it the sole cause.

Having just conceded that analogy is of little aid, Andrews nevertheless invokes the analogy that he prefers: causation as a stream:

Should analogy be helpful, however, I prefer that of a stream. The spring, starting on its journey, is joined by tributary after tributary. The river, reaching the ocean, comes from a hundred sources. No man may say whence any drop of water is derived. Yet for a time distinction may be possible. Into the clear creek, brown swamp water flows from the left. Later, from the right comes water stained by its clay bed. The three may remain for a space, sharply divided. But at last, inevitably no trace of separation remains. They are so commingled that all distinction is lost. (8)

With the assistance of this putatively helpful analogy of causation as a stream, we are led by Andrews to follow that stream from the spring to the ocean, but by the time we get to the ocean so many tributaries have joined this stream that "no trace of separation remains. They are so commingled that all distinction is lost" (8). On the face, it is difficult to see how this analogy is "helpful," since the sceptical point made is that a given cause generates effects that merge with other causes and effects in their joint journey downstream, making it impossible to distinguish or determine all the effects of a given cause. As Andrews puts it,

[w]e cannot trace the effect of an act to the end, if end there be. Again, however, we may trace it part of the way. A murder at Sarajevo may be the necessary antecedent to an assassination in London twenty years hence.

An overturned lantern may burn all Chicago. We may follow the fire from the shed to the last building. We rightly say the fire started by the lantern caused its destruction.

A cause, but not the proximate cause. What we do mean by the word "proximate" is that because of convenience, of public policy, of a rough sense of justice, the law arbitrarily declines to trace a series of events beyond a certain point. This is not logic. It is practical politics. (8)

To multiply so many analogies to arrive at a pragmatic criterion that could have been invoked without advancing any analogy at all seems confusing at best, for all that Andrews discovers is what proximate cause is not. It would seem that when the foundational concept in question is as nebulous, elusive, and self-subverting as proximate cause, a judge runs the risk of drowning in an ocean of analogies. Despite this risk, Andrews soldiers on, offering yet another example.

He imagines a scenario in which a chauffeur negligently collides with another car filled with dynamite. A man on the sidewalk is killed (with the law as it is, Andrew says, damages definitely will be awarded), a man in an office near the sidewalk is cut by flying glass (here damages probably will be awarded), another man a block away is also cut by flying glass (here damages probably will not be awarded), and a nurse ten blocks away drops a baby (here damages definitely will not be awarded). Even though none of these injuries would have been sustained without the precipitating event of the collision,

[i]t is all a question of expediency. There are no fixed rules to govern our judgment. There are simply matters of which we may take account ... There is in truth little to guide us other than common sense. [Nevertheless,] there are some hints that may help us. The proximate cause, involved as it may be with many other causes, must be, at the least, something without which the event could not happen. (9)

In the end, all we can do is "draw an uncertain and wavering line, but draw it we must as best we can" (9). To function at all, the law must arbitrarily decline to trace a series of events beyond a certain point:

It may be said that this is unjust. Why? In fairness, [the chauffeur] should make good every injury flowing from his negligence. Not because of tenderness toward him we say he need not answer for all that follows his wrong. We look back to the catastrophe, the fire kindled by the spark, or the explosion. We trace the consequences – not indefinitely, but to a certain point. And to aid us in fixing that point we ask what might ordinarily be expected to follow the fire or explosion. (10)

After many analogical detours in a judgment of several thousand words, Andrews finally arrives at the case before him, a case to which he devotes only two paragraphs. In his view, even though the defendant knocked an apparently harmless package onto the platform, the act was negligent, and the railroad is liable for its proximate consequences. But for the explosion, Palsgraf would not have been injured. "Under these circumstances," he writes, again showing his propensity for the negative, "I cannot say as a matter of law that the plaintiff's injuries were not the proximate result of the negligence" (10). What could have been a powerful conclusion is rendered impotent by its backhanded phraseology.

Andrews's obsession with tracking down the implications of the analogies he adduces causes him to lose sight of his best point, a point he entertains in passing in the middle of his dissent but fails to return to in his conclusion: namely, that for a cause to be proximate there has to be temporal and spatial propinquity between act and result. But for the explosion, the plaintiff would have sustained no injury. There was a natural and continuous sequence between cause and effect, explosion and injury, so that the two events were virtually simultaneous. (Is this not why the family of the dead man on the sidewalk gets damages and the nurse who drops a baby ten blocks away does not?) In my view, this is the most cogent inference to be drawn from Andrews's analogical reasoning, an inference that helps establish why Mrs Palsgraf's injuries should be seen as proximate consequences of the falling package even if it cannot establish that the acts of the running man or the helping guards were negligent. (Common sense, however, would seem to suggest that a man who is running recklessly after a moving train with a package of incendiary rockets under his arm owes a duty of care to his fellow passengers. Whether he is worth suing is a different issue.)

With its plethora of examples, Andrews's decision is itself a river with many tributaries – a reckless driver on Broadway, a boy throwing a pebble in a pond, a stream of causation, a murder at Sarajevo, an overturned lantern that burns all Chicago, a negligent chauffeur – but the overall effect of these metastasizing analogies is to deconstruct the very concept of causation he relies on, making everything a question of expediency and common sense.

If Andrews fails to fashion a logical argument, he does succeed in fashioning an appealing judicial self. He projects the image of a fair and reasonable person grappling as best he can with a complex philosophical concept and trying through analogy after analogy to arrive at a pragmatic criterion. Yet the criterion arrived at does not seem to have much to do with the analogies proffered. And despite his appealing authorial image, Andrews creates a world that has no room for Mrs Palsgraf. Give a jurist like Lord Denning the same scenario to work with and imagine what his dissent might look like:[3]

It was summer time in New York City. Helen Palsgraf was the mother of two daughters. To augment the family income, she worked long hours as a housekeeper so that she and her girls might enjoy some of the comforts of life, on this day a trip to Rockaway Beach to escape the sweltering heat of the city. Awaiting the train that would take them to the seashore, the three of them stood on a Long Island Railroad platform. As they bided their time, another train pulled into the station. Moments later, after the train started to leave the platform, two men, one of whom was carrying a package, emerged into view and ran to catch the moving cars. In a few seconds, they were alongside a car. While they struggled to climb aboard, one railroad guard on the ground and another on the train tried to help them. The guards succeeded in hoisting them aboard, but as they did so, the package tumbled to the ground. A thunderous explosion rang out. A large scale toppled. A stampede erupted as panicking and injured passengers tried to escape. The scale fell on Mrs. Palsgraf, striking her on the arm, hip, and thigh. Her terrified daughters looked on. Ambulances sirens were shrieking in the distance. With great difficulty, Mrs. Palsgraf was able to get up and walk. But the injuries were so debilitating that she was unable to continue her job as a housekeeper. The trauma of the experience caused her to suffer from nervous shock. Her sleep was fitful, and she could not speak without stuttering.

Even though the explosion and the resultant injuries to Mrs. Palsgraf would not have occurred but for the negligent actions of the railroad's guards, the railroad says that it bears no liability for what happened: the employees did not know that the package contained incendiary rockets, nor could they foresee that Mrs. Palsgraf was in a zone of danger. The

---

3 I engage in the sincerest form of flattery to try to show that Andrews had stylistic options. A rhetorically if not legally compelling narrative was there to be told, a narrative, moreover, that better expresses his argument from propinquity.

railroad owes nothing to this permanently disabled woman – no duty of care, no compensation for damages. Even if the majority decision is able to twist the law of torts to arrive at this unconscionable conclusion, it is bad law and the wrong conclusion. For the real issue here is proximate cause, not foreseeability. But for the explosion, there would have been no injury to the plaintiff. There was a natural and continuous sequence between cause and effect, explosion and injury. The two events were virtually simultaneous. Whatever his intent, a defendant is liable for the proximate consequences of a negligent act even when the victims might generally be thought to be outside the foreseeable zone of danger.

These different stories and styles show that legal thinking and judicial writing are above all compositional activities. A judgment is an imaginative construction of the most probable story that emerges from the material facts found and the legal criteria invoked. In this case, as we have seen, it makes a big difference whether the issue is construed as foreseeability or proximate cause.

Cardozo's decision adopts one side's brief, the railroad's. Andrews's decision is a stream with many tributaries. In both decisions, analogies proliferate to the point of unintelligibility: jostlers in crowds, chains or nets or streams of causation, negligent chauffeurs, and so on. Both judges are attempting to be illustrative, but in the case of Andrews the effect of his illustrative analogies is to deconstruct the very concept of causation he relies on, making everything a question of expediency and common sense.

In *Palsgraf v. Long Island Railroad*, one would be foolhardy to say that a right conclusion exists *a priori* in precedents from the law of torts. This is why both judges resort to illustrative analogies and hypothetical scenarios. Yet despite their different views as to the legitimacy of Palsgraf's suit, neither judge is at all interested in relating Palsgraf's story. And, strangely enough, neither judge is at all interested in taking into account the laws of science. Could an explosion of rockets with a certain firepower cause a scale of a certain weight to topple? Or did a panicky passenger knock the scale down? These would seem to be essential questions of fact, questions that pertain to issues of both liability and proximate cause.

In the case of Andrews, the omission of scientific considerations follows from his desire to exclude anything that might compromise his assumption that explosion and injury were simultaneous and that the one was the proximate cause of the other. In the case of Cardozo, the omission follows from his framing the question so as to exclude proximate cause as an issue. But even if he came to the correct conclusion in not awarding damages to Mrs Palsgraf, he should have a made a sympathetic gesture towards her ongoing suffering, and he should have accurately described the circumstances of the accident. The legal world he imagines in this judgment is a world of rules and outcomes, not a world of people.

Also significant is the fact that neither judge attempts to see the case in a broader social perspective. In 1924, the year of Mrs Palsgraf's injury, trains were a perilous means of transportation. In "Cultures of Facts," Kim Lane Scheppele summarizes the historical research of Judge John T. Noonan:

> As Noonan reports, in 1924, the year of Mrs. Palsgraf's injury, trains were in general quite dangerous. Across the United States, 6,617 people were killed by trains that year and another 143,739 people were injured. On the Long Island Railroad alone in 1924 ... 108 passengers were killed and 3,229 were injured. (364)

On that year on the Long Island Railroad, then, there was nearly one death every three days, and there were nearly ten injuries every day. The Palsgraf case, Scheppele notes, was "part of a long history in which the railroad industry imposed substantial costs on the broader society, costs that were never added to the ledgers of the railroads" (364). Most train accidents were not even litigated. Had Cardozo taken into account "just how dangerous trains were and how much death and destruction they left in their path" (364), he might have been less inclined to think the railroad owed no duty of care to Mrs Palsgraf.

The case of *Palsgraf v. Long Island Railroad* illustrates that rhetoric is an indispensable part of judicial decision-making because many legal questions cannot be resolved by empirical evidence and legal reasoning alone. To say this is not to endorse a sceptical conclusion. Scepticism, as Binder and Weisberg point out, presumes that unshakeable conceptual "foundations must be established for judgments to be legitimate; pragmatism presumes that because such foundations cannot be established, they cannot be necessary" (461).[4] Indeed, it is the foundational concepts in law that are the most elusive, and the rhetorical flexibility that such

---

4 For a more detailed discussion of scepticism, pragmatism, and antifoundationalism, please see "Postscript: Rhetoric, Postmodernism, and Scepticism."

elusiveness permits is precisely what gives judges the ability to draw their uncertain and wavering lines, as best they can, especially in hard cases. And whether they would regard themselves as such or not, the best judges are pragmatists more often than not, nimble rhetoricians already dancing to a deconstructionist tune.

As the judgments of Cardozo and Andrews attest, unbridled figuration can sometimes be a dangerous thing, but something essentially human is lost if judicial writing seeks to purge itself of eloquence by enshrining fact and law above all else. Analogy and figure, *pathos* and *ethos*, story and style – these too have vital parts to play in the creation of legal worlds and the fashioning of judicial selves. Such rhetorical devices no doubt open up zones of danger not always foreseeable. But every time we venture to say or decide anything, the minefields are always there. All we can do is try to dance through them, as best we can.

4 Murder, They Wrote: The Rhetoric of Causation in the Language of the Law

In his dissent against Justice Cardozo's majority opinion in the famous 1927 tort case *Palsgraf v. Long Island Railroad*, as we have seen, Justice Andrews laments the inutility of "any philosophical doctrine of causation" and says of proximate cause that "these two words have never been given inclusive definition. What is cause in a legal sense, still more what is proximate cause depend in each case upon many considerations as does the existence of negligence itself" (8). "What we mean by the word 'proximate,'" he concludes,

> is that because of convenience, of public policy, of a rough sense of justice, the law arbitrarily declines to trace a series of events beyond a certain point. This is not logic. It is practical politics … It is all a question of expediency. There are no fixed rules to govern our judgment. There are simply matters of which we may take account … There is in truth little to guide us other than common sense. [Nevertheless,] there are some hints that may help us. The proximate cause, involved as it may be with many other causes, must be, at the least, something without which the event could not happen. (8–9)

Causation in law, then, like causation in philosophy, is a vexing and elusive concept. As David Hume points out in his well-known sceptical argument, when we investigate causal sequences, we only discover relations of contiguity and succession. Insofar as causation is supposed to be something more than contiguity and succession, it is something that can be neither empirically demonstrated nor logically defined. Building on Hume's insights, but moving towards a pragmatic rather than a sceptical conclusion, I portray causal distinctions in law as self-subverting concepts that perpetually run the risk of sinking into a quicksand of adjectival excess. Though no doubt sincerely applied by the appellate courts, causal criteria cannot deliver the precision they promise, and the rhetorical power of vivid factual narratives ends up carrying as much argumentative weight as the logical force of erudite causal distinctions.

That storytelling has persuasive value in law is hardly news. Every Canadian lawyer and judge is intimately acquainted with the legendary beginnings of Lord Denning's appellate decisions – "It was bluebell time in Kent," "Old Herbert Bundy was a farmer," "Mr. Plenty had a milk round." But that storytelling is integral to the fashioning and application of standards of causation in murder cases might seem less self-evident. In *R. v. Harbottle*, Justice Cory is well aware of the power of storytelling, in this case the sickening power of the direct discourse of the appellant. Cory first frames the issue and then lets the appellant hang himself:

> The appellant James Harbottle together with his friend Shawn Ross forcibly confined Elaine Bown. While she was still confined with her hands tied, Shawn Ross strangled her while Harbottle held her legs to prevent her from continuing to kick and struggle. What must be determined on this appeal is whether Harbottle's participation was such that he can be found guilty of first degree murder … In a statement to the police the appellant recounted in grim detail the sordid sequence of events which included the sexual assault, forcible confinement and ultimately the murder of the victim … The forcible confinement and murder of the victim are depicted in the statement of the appellant in these chilling words:

>> [Shawn Ross] cut [Elaine Bown], put an "X" on her chest and uh, with a razor, and then stabbed her with a knife in the arm. And uh, after that – well, he tied her up too and stuff and gagged her. And then after that he – me and him went into another room actually and uh, I said now what are you going to do? You cut her up and stuff and uh, he said why don't we kill her. And uh, I said well I don't know, maybe. And then he said well why not. And I said okay, fine. And I carried her downstairs and what not. And then I said why don't we kill her nicely, you know. I didn't want her to go through any pain or anything. So he said why don't we cut her wrists. And I said go for it. And she said she didn't want to die. He said well I'm going to have to do it. So he started slashing her wrists but she pulled away what

not, so he couldn't do that. So then he said why don't we strangle her. And I said go for it then. *And he cut off her bra, take her bra, wrapped it around her neck. I grabbed her leg cause she started kicking and [Ross] strangled her to death.* Then we put her under the couch and we left and went and panhandled for some glue and got a little high on glue. Then went back – back about 3 o'clock in the morning or something like that and torched the place. (5–6)

It is hard to imagine anything more revelatory of depraved indifference than Harbottle's own words. That Harbottle, in a deadpan and semi-literate style, can equate slashing the victim's wrists with killing her nicely and painlessly says more than any judge could ever say. His lack of affect towards killing and torching descends into the psychopathic abyss. Once Harbottle casually and callously relates what happened, his fate is sealed. That he will be convicted of first degree murder is an all but foregone conclusion. Though the Court rigorously analyses the concept of causation in law and finds that Harbottle was "an essential, substantial and integral" link in the uninterrupted causal chain of events that led to Ms Bown's death, the vivid imagery, grisly narrative, and explanatory examples are just as decisive in resolving the issue of whether he is guilty of first degree murder as is Justice Cory's cogent legal reasoning.

"At the Court of Appeal," Justice Cory notes, "it was conceded that Harbottle was a party to the murder of Elaine Bown while participating in her forcible confinement or sexual assault. The sole question for determination was whether or not his participation was such that he could be found guilty of first degree murder [under] s. 214(5) of the *Criminal Code*" (7).

The minority ruled that he could not be found guilty of first degree murder. They said that the words in s. 214(5) "caused the death" (7) mean that the Crown must prove that Harbottle physically caused Ms Bown's asphyxiation, that his acts were the pathological or diagnostic cause of her death. They concluded that he was a party to her death and legally responsible for its consequences, but that the act of strangulation was performed by Ross alone.

The majority refused to accept such a narrow interpretation of the words "caused the death." They found that because Ross was ten pounds lighter than Ms Bown, Harbottle's holding the victim's legs while Ross strangled her was necessary for her death to occur. "If Harbottle had not done this, she might have resisted any attempts to strangle her just as she had successfully resisted the attempts to cut her wrists" (8)

Cory believes "that there was ample evidence upon which the jury could have found that the murder of Elaine Bown was planned and premeditated." Nevertheless, he continues, "the trial judge told the jury that she had difficulty pointing to evidence of planning and deliberation. Therefore, the jury was charged as well on the basis that the murder could have occurred while the victim was being sexually assaulted or forcibly confined" (8). So it is impossible to know on which basis the jury reached its verdict. The interpretation of s. 214(5) thereby becomes crucial. If the judge's charge with regard to it was incorrect, there must be a new trial.

This section says that irrespective of whether a murder is planned or deliberate, it is first degree murder "when the death is caused by [a] person" who is also engaged in sexual assault, sexual assault with a weapon, aggravated sexual assault, or kidnapping and forcible confinement. What must be determined, then, is the meaning of the words "when death is caused by that person" (9).

Cory canvasses earlier cases in order to determine what causal effect is required by the phrase "death caused by that person." He concludes that a test based on physical, pathological, or diagnostic cause is too restrictive. His argumentation, not rehearsed here, is subtle and perspicuous, but his imagery is even more compelling. As he puts it:

> In the case at bar, it would be unreasonable to suggest that, in order to be liable under s. 214(5), Harbottle must have pathologically caused the death of the victim by pulling one end of the brassiere strap while his co-accused pulled the other. I find it impossible to distinguish between the blameworthiness of an accused who holds the victim's legs thus allowing his co-accused to strangle her and the accused who performs the act of strangulation. (14)

It is the imagery that lends cogency and concreteness to Cory's conclusions about blameworthiness and causation.

The test for causation under s. 214(5) is a strict one. The Crown must establish "that the accused has committed an act or series of acts which are of a such a nature that they must be regarded as a substantial and integral cause of the death ... The substantial causation test requires that the accused play a very active role – usually a physical role – in the killing. Under s. 214(5), the actions of the accused must form an essential, substantial, and integral part of the killing of the victim" (15–16). Already the adjectives are beginning to accumulate – physical, pathological, and diagnostic, on the one side, essential, substantial, and integral, on the other. It is the concrete examples, however, that do the real explaining.

Cory concedes that to get a conviction under s. 214(5), the accused, in most cases, must physically cause the death of the victim:

> However, while the intervening act of another will often mean that the accused is no longer the substantial cause of death ... there will be instances where an accused could well be the substantial cause of the death without physically causing it. For example, if one accused with the intent to kill locked the victim in a cupboard while the other set fire to that cupboard, then the accused who confined the victim might be found to have caused the death of the victim pursuant to the provisions of s. 214(5). Similarly an accused who fought off rescuers in order to allow his accomplice to complete the strangulation of the victim might also be found to have been a substantial cause of the death. (16)

Again it is the images, examples, and analogies that illustrate how an accused can be the substantial cause of the victim's death without physically causing it. Cory concludes by noting that

> [t]he facts of this case clearly established that Harbottle was a substantial and an integral cause of the death of Elaine Bown. It will be remembered that Ross, who actually strangled the victim, weighed only 130 lb. and was about 5' 7" in height. Elaine Bown, although three inches shorter, was 10 lb. heavier. There was no indication in her blood of any alcohol or drugs so that it can be inferred that she was not impaired. Rather the bruising on her neck indicates she struggled valiantly. Indeed, it is apparent that even when her hands were bound, she successfully resisted the attempts of both Ross and Harbottle to cut her wrists. There is every reason to believe that, had it not been for Harbottle's holding her legs, she would have been able to resist the attempts to strangle her. In those circumstances, it is difficult to believe that Ross could have strangled her in the absence of the assistance of Harbottle.
>
> The evidence adduced clearly established all the elements of the test. The appellant was guilty (1) of at least one enumerated offence of domination (forcible confinement); (2) he participated in and was found guilty of the murder; (3) his participation in the murder was such that he was a

substantial and integral cause of the death of the victim; (4) there was no intervening act of another which resulted in the accused's no longer being substantially connected to the death of the victim; and (5) the crimes of domination and murder were part of the same series of acts or transaction. (17)

I reproduce this lengthy excerpt to show how the facts and the law sustain each other. The first paragraph deals with the facts; the second, with the law. And the concrete images in the first, I would submit, give us a clearer picture of what substantial cause looks like than do the abstract elements of the test in the second. I would almost go so far as to say that substantial cause cannot be logically defined no matter how many adjectives one piles up; it can only be shown through imagery, narrative, analogy, and example. Deprived of its vivid imagery, grisly narrative, and explanatory examples, Cory's carefully wrought decision would be far less convincing and effective.

Towards the end of this decision, Cory mentions in passing that the substantial cause test for first degree murder is much more rigorous than the test described in *Smithers v. The Queen*, a decision that dealt with the offence of manslaughter. That decision held "that sufficient causation existed where the actions of the accused were 'a contributing cause of death, outside the *de minimis* range'" (16). Cory does not say whether the test for second degree murder is substantial cause or contributing cause. His silence on this matter sets the stage for *R. v. Nette*.

Upheld by the Supreme Court of Canada in 2001, *R. v. Nette* is a 1999 British Columbia Court of Appeal decision that builds on *Harbottle* in its attempt to distinguish between the standard of causation for first degree murder and the standard of causation for second degree murder. In *R. v. Nette*, Mrs Loski, a ninety-five-year-old woman, is left hogtied in her bed and dies two days later. Nette is charged with first degree murder, a charge, the court maintains, that demands a "substantial and integral cause of death," "a more direct and substantive cause" than the "contributory and not insignificant" cause necessary to find second degree murder (3). In practice, however, as the adjectives begin to multiply, this distinction proves to be difficult to apply, and the rhetorical performances of the two appellate courts dance around such recondite matters as whether there is a difference between a significant contributing cause and a contributing cause that is not insignificant.

In the end, *R. v. Nette* and *R. v. Harbottle* are not so much arguments for particular standards or kinds of causation as they are arguments for relatively more or less serious degrees of criminal responsibility. In such cases, the horrible facts scenario is unfailingly invoked in all its nauseating detail, engendering moral revulsion and justifying the severe stigma and intensified blameworthiness that attach to first degree murder. In *R. v. Nette,* a ninety-five-year-old woman is rendered immobile and left to die. And as we have seen in *R. v. Harbottle,* a young woman is forcibly confined, sexually assaulted, repeatedly tortured, and eventually killed. James Harbottle watches his companion rape the victim and mutilate her with a knife. After the companion fails to kill her by slashing her wrists, the two men discuss other ways of killing her, in Harbottle's word, "nicely." Harbottle holds her legs down while his companion strangles her with her own brassiere. In finding Harbottle guilty of first degree murder, is the court really distinguishing between a cause that is substantial and integral as opposed to one that is contributory and not insignificant? Or is it saying that Harbottle's involvement in the forcible confinement of the victim, along with his active role in such a morally revolting "planned and deliberate" strangulation, deserves the stigma of a first degree murder conviction? The causal criteria, though no doubt sincerely applied, sink in the quicksand of adjectival excess, and, as I have said, the rhetorical power of vivid factual narratives carries as much argumentative weight as the logical force of erudite causal distinctions.

These cases illustrate that rhetoric is an indispensable part of judicial decision-making because many legal questions cannot be resolved by empirical data or logical distinctions. These questions often unsettle concepts as foundational as liability and cause. Logic can only take us so far. The limits of logic are seen in *R. v. Nette,* a decision that tries to establish distinct standards of causation for first and second degree murder.

Nette's first appeal from a conviction of second degree murder was heard by the British Columbia Court of Appeal. As noted earlier, he and a friend bound and gagged a ninety-five-year-old woman. They robbed her and left her hogtied on the bed. She died of asphyxiation two days later. Nette wanted a new trial because the trial judge supposedly erred in his charge to the jury by saying that the standard of causation to be proved for second degree murder was the standard of contributing cause beyond the insignificant or trivial, and not the standard of substantial cause. That the jury returned a verdict of second degree murder instead of first might have meant they thought the accused's actions were not a substantial cause of the victim's death. If substantial cause, not contributing cause, is the correct standard of causation for second degree murder, then the accused deserves a new trial.

The appeal was dismissed. The appellate court found that two insignificant slips aside, the judge properly instructed the jury as to the correct standard for second degree murder – significant contributing cause or contributing cause that is not insignificant.

So the court ultimately finds, but counsel for the accused has room to manoeuvre because the two most important precedent cases do not explicitly address the standard of causation for second degree murder. *Smithers v. The Queen* finds that to convict for manslaughter the Crown must establish beyond a reasonable doubt that the act of the accused was a contributing and not insignificant cause of death ("greater than *de minimis*"), while *R. v. Harbottle* finds that to convict for first degree murder the Crown must establish beyond a reasonable doubt that the act of the accused was "an essential, substantial, and integral part of the killing of the victim." Counsel for the accused argues that the *Harbottle* standard (substantial cause), not the *Smithers* standard (contributing cause beyond the insignificant or trivial), should apply to second degree murder.

Having laid out the only issue to be resolved – the correct standard of causation for second degree murder – Justice Lambert proceeds "to state the facts as they must have been found by the jury in returning a verdict of second degree murder" (3). It is at this moment that what Lambert's language is saying on the denotative or referential level begins to clash with what his language is doing on the connotative or rhetorical level, for if Harbottle's holding down the legs of the victim while his companion strangles her is found to be a substantial cause of her death meriting conviction for first degree murder, then Nette's actions seem equally blameworthy, as the judge's rendition of the horrible facts confirms. Lambert's undoubtedly genuine attempt to present a literal description of the facts that logically led to the jury's verdict has entirely the opposite effect; his description mystifies the outcome and becomes, perhaps inadvertently, a textbook instance of *litotes*, the rhetorical trope that creates emphasis through understatement. According to Justice Lambert, the facts found by the jury must have been these:

> Nette knew that Mrs. Loski, a 95-year old widow, lived alone in her own house in Kelowna. He and a male companion entered the house, tied Mrs. Loski's hands together with wire, tied her feet together with wire, and tied her feet behind her back. They wrapped some clothing round her head.

Either the tying occurred when Mrs. Loski was on the bed, or the two men placed her on the bed after she was tied. They then stole all the money they could find in the house and left. As time passed, Mrs. Loski must have wriggled about. She fell off the bed onto the floor. Some 24 to 48 hours after Mrs. Loski was tied up, she died of asphyxiation. By that time her dentures had come loose in her mouth and the item of clothing originally placed around her head was fairly tightly wound around her neck. Of course, Mrs. Loski could not loosen the clothing around her neck or remove her dentures because her hands and feet remained cruelly bound until the end. (3)

Though the only overtly emotive word in this apparently neutral and referential description of the facts is the adverb "cruelly," the solidity of specification in Lambert's account generates repugnant images – wire tying Mrs Loski's already wire-bound feet to her already wire-bound hands, her clothing wrapped tightly round her head, her wriggling about on the bed, her falling to the floor, her inability to remove dentures that had come loose in her mouth. All of these images accentuate the prolonged ordeal that eventually led to her death by asphyxiation. Intentionally or not, Lambert makes a devastatingly effective appeal to *pathos*, his verbal scene-painting seeming to justify, if not demand, the severe stigma and intensified blameworthiness that attach to first degree murder. The audience cannot help but wonder how, on these facts, a jury could ever have returned a verdict of second degree murder.

The possibly flawed verdict, however, was not a product of flawed instructions, for Lambert demonstrates convincingly that the trial judge accurately informed the jury as to the difference between substantial cause and contributing cause and that this difference is what distinguishes first degree murder from second degree murder or manslaughter. Counsel for the accused, of course, accepts the difference between the two kinds of cause but argues that the standard for second degree murder is the same as that for first degree murder. He maintains that the verdict in R. v. Nette should have been manslaughter, the bright line drawn by causation being between manslaughter and murder, not between first and second degree murder. Counsel for the Crown adduces "another plausible reason why the jury could have brought in a verdict of second degree murder rather than first degree murder" (5). They could have "decided, rightly or wrongly, to find that it had not been proven beyond a reasonable doubt that the actions that constituted the offence of forcible confinement ... were sufficiently closely integrated with the actions which caused the death" (5).

To suggest that the jury might have decided "wrongly" in not bringing in a verdict of first degree murder reinforces the doubt already engendered by Lambert's disturbing narration of the facts, and the Crown's introduction of the offence of "forcible confinement" into the discussion complicates the agenda considerably. Though the Criminal Code states that "murder is first degree murder when it is planned and deliberate" (5), it also states that murder is first degree murder irrespective of whether it is planned and deliberate when the perpetrator is committing or attempting to commit an offence that falls under particular sections of the Criminal Code, one of which is forcible confinement, as we saw with respect to *Harbottle*. Thus, as *R. v. Farrant* maintains, "the distinction between first and second degree murder ... is not based upon intent; it is based upon ... the presence of planning and deliberation ... the identity of the victim ... or the nature of the offence being committed at the time of the murder" (6).

Harbottle unanimously endorses *Farrant*, saying that first degree is in essence a sentencing provision for "an aggravated form of murder and not a distinct substantive offence" (6). Once an accused is seen to be guilty of murder, "what the jury must then determine is whether such aggravating circumstances exist that they justify ineligibility for parole for a quarter of a century ... The gravity of the crime and the severity of the sentence both indicate that a substantial and high degree of blameworthiness, above and beyond that of murder, must be established in order to convict an accused of first degree murder" (6).

Once the act of the accused is classified as murder, the substantial cause test is applied to determine whether the murder is first or second degree, but, as the above quotation indicates, *Harbottle* introduces or makes manifest moral criteria. According to *Harbottle*, it is not simply a question of "requiring that the accused play a very active role – usually a physical role – in the killing"; it is also a question of determining the blameworthiness of the accused and the heinousness of the crime, its "aggravating circumstances" (7).

In the case of Nette, it would seem clear that his hogtying Mrs Loski and leaving her for dead indicate that first, he played an active and physical role in inaugurating the chain of causation that led to her asphyxiation; second, that he was "a substantial cause of the death of the victim"; third, "that there was no intervening act of another which resulted in the accused no longer being substantially connected to the death of the victim"; and, fourth, that the crime of domination (specifically, forcible confinement) was part of the series of events that led to her death (7). These would seem to be the implications that flow from *Harbottle,* and they all point towards a verdict of first degree murder in *Nette.*

Though Lambert declines to explicitly draw such an inference, he does make some salient points about the legal principles he derives from *Harbottle.* First, the decision "settles the standard of causation which must be met before a person may be convicted of first degree murder," and "that standard is called the substantial cause test" (7). Second, "the jury must first find that the murder has been committed by the accused before they embark on the substantial cause test to determine if there should be a conviction for first degree murder" (7). Third, this test is considerably more stringent than "the contributing cause test for manslaughter" (8). And finally, while there are these three important things that *Harbottle* does do, there is one important thing it does not do: it "does not address the standard of causation required in order to support a conviction of second degree murder" (8).

That said, Lambert still believes that "the *Harbottle* case indicates that the standard of causation for second degree murder is not the essential, substantial, and integral cause test and must either be the significant contributing cause test that is used for manslaughter or some intermediate causation test between the two" (8). He then cites two decisions of the Ontario Court of Appeal that reject any such intermediate test and declare that the *Smithers* test of contributing cause is the appropriate standard to support a conviction of second degree murder. He states that *R. v. Meiler* holds that "although *Harbottle* does not specifically say that the causation test for [second degree murder] is the same as that set out in *Smithers,* the reasoning in *Harbottle* leads toward that conclusion. The court held that the more restrictive test of substantial cause reflects a higher degree of blameworthiness for first degree murder than for murder, thereby implying that there is a less restrictive causation test for murder that is not first degree" (8–9).

The language of *Meiler,* however, is less than definitive, for leading towards a conclusion on the basis of implication is not the same thing as entailing a conclusion on the basis of logic. Nevertheless, performative utterances in judgments bring into being the causal distinctions they enunciate, at least for the case at bar, and once the Supreme Court says that substantial as opposed to contributory cause is the bright line between first and second degree murder, as it does in *R. v. Nette,* that distinction stands until a future Supreme Court decision says otherwise. As Justice Andrews points out in *Palsgraf v. Long Island Railroad,* "this is not logic. It is practical politics" (8). A line has to be drawn – that is what courts are in the business of doing – and to say that it is not drawn on the basis of inferential logic is not to say that it is illogical. Rhetoric works in the contingent realm of probability and plausibility – what Andrews calls convenience, public policy, a rough sense of justice, expediency, common sense – not in the apodictic realm of certainty and truth. Justice Lambert accepts the authority of the Ontario precedents because they are congruent with the reasonable distinction he wants to endorse, not because they establish what logically follows from *Harbottle* in relation to the standard of causation for second degree murder. Nothing determinate about this standard can ever logically follow from *Harbottle* because *Harbottle* remains forever silent about it. Nor will anything determinate ever follow from consulting "the terminology of causation" (9), but this is Lambert's next move.

First, Lambert notes, there is what Glanville Williams, Professor of Law, calls the "but for" test: the woman would not have died but for the actions of the accused. For Williams, this is the factual cause. However, the "but for" test is not enough in itself to create a sufficient causal connection to establish criminal liability. The action or willed inaction of the accused must also be "an operating cause in law" – "an 'imputable,' 'legal,' 'effective,' 'direct,' or 'proximate' cause, without embracing the precise accuracy of any of those descriptive adjectives" (9). For Williams, then, the factual cause must be distinguished from the legal cause.

In *Smithers,* Lambert notes, the relevant causal standard is described in the words "a contributing cause beyond *de minimis*" (9). Appropriate synonyms, he goes on to say, can be cast in either the positive, "a significant contributing cause," or in the negative, "a contributing cause that is not trivial or insignificant" (9). Analogous terminology, he maintains, is to be found in the leading English and Australian cases.

Without seeming to notice that "substantial" is one of the usual adjectives attached to cause in its first degree designation, Lambert regards the English phrase "an operating cause and a substantial cause," something that "contributed significantly" and was "more than negligible," as expressing "a standard identical to the standard of the *Smithers* test" (9). He does notice, however, that "a sufficiently substantial causal effect" (10) – a phrase used in a leading Australian case – is also identical to the *Smithers* standard, despite the strong (though adverbially qualified) adjective used. After reviewing these cases, he concludes that "the significant contributing cause test derived from *Smithers* is conceptually the same as the test for operating cause, no matter the precise terminology that is used for causation in relation to the offence of murder in England and Australia" (11).

To be fair to Lambert, one should point out that he affirms from the outset that "it is important to be guided by the concepts relevant to causality rather than by the terminology" (9). But it is not clear what insight into the *Smithers* standard emerges from equating imputable, legal, effective, direct, proximate, significant, contributing, not trivial, not insignificant, operating, substantial, more than negligible, and sufficiently substantial, especially when some of the adjectives are not readily distinguishable from those associated with the *Harbottle* standard. As far as clarification is concerned, this proliferation of supposedly synonymous adjectives is not entirely helpful, but to dwell on this adjectival excess is to obscure the point that actually does emerge: namely, that the adjectives are useless outside of the factual narratives in which they appear. The distinctions that make a difference derive from the persuasive power of narrative, not from logic or semantics.

In *R. v. Hallet*, a leading Australian case cited by Justice Lambert, "the accused had attacked his friend and left him wounded on the beach. The victim drowned either by rolling into the water, or by being covered by the rising tide. Hallet was convicted of murder" (10), and the Supreme Court of Australia upheld that conviction. Whatever terminology one chooses to use, it seems reasonable to conclude that Hallet's act of violence is so connected with the death of the victim that it must be regarded, in Canadian terms, as either manslaughter or second degree murder. The act does not seem "planned and deliberate" enough to constitute first degree murder, nor does it seem to have the same blameworthiness that one would attach to Harbottle's participation in a gruesome scenario of rape, mutilation, and torture, the culmination of which was his holding the victim down while his companion strangled her.

In the case of *Harbottle*, the real work of persuasion is accomplished by the horrible facts scenario. The narrative description concretely dramatizes what substantial cause looks like in a way no abstract analysis could approximate. The task of an author, as Joseph Conrad famously observes, "is, by the power of the written word, to make you hear, to make you feel, [and] before all, to make you see" (708). The grisly facts that judges relate are often there to make you "see," in all senses of the word. To be sure, judges also rely on the appropriate causal terminology, and such terminology is necessary and useful as far as it goes, but without the factual narrative to sustain it, the adjectives the terminology generates sink into conceptual quicksand. Concurring with Lambert's result while reaching it by a different route, Justice McEachern makes this point well. Although *Harbottle*, in his view, does not articulate a test applicable only to first degree murder, "the facts of this case, which are fully described by Mr. Justice Lambert, particularly with regard to the question of causation, are so aggravated that a conviction for second degree murder was inevitable regardless of which test for causation the jury might have been given" (14).

Lambert's decision was upheld by the Supreme Court of Canada. In the highest court's version of *R. v. Nette*, Justice Arbour agrees with Justice Lambert that the trial judge accurately stated the correct standard of causation, and she betrays a similar doubt about the jury's verdict. "Whatever the jury's reasons for acquitting the accused of first degree murder," she writes, "the jury's verdict of second degree murder is unimpeachable" (40–1). She too distinguishes between factual causation – medical, mechanical, physical – and legal causation – the accused's responsibility under the law. Legal causation, as per Professor Williams, is imputable causation that deals with the responsibility of the accused. Causation, for her, is a legal rule based on concepts of moral responsibility, not a mechanical or mathematical exercise. There is only one standard of causation for all homicide offences, the *Smithers* standard. For an accused to be convicted of first degree murder, other factors enter into play: the gravity of the crime, the high blameworthiness of the accused, the identity of the victim, and the nature of the offence. Like Justice Lambert, Justice Arbour has an array of adjectives to attach to the noun "cause," and she cannot resist juxtaposing, on the one side, efficient cause, effective cause, real cause, proximate cause, direct cause, decisive cause, immediate cause, with, on the other side, occasional cause, remote cause, contributory cause, inducing cause, condition. But the distinctions that are compelling are the ones she makes by juxtaposing the factual scenarios of *Smithers* and *Harbottle*, *Smithers* involving a fight in a parking lot after a junior hockey game where the accused kicked the victim while he was down, and the victim choked to death on his own vomit. The accused was convicted of manslaughter despite the victim's malfunctioning epiglottis. As in all thin skull cases, the wrongdoer must take his victim as he finds him. It is the contrast between the two factual narratives that clarifies the distinction between contributory and substantial cause, not the adjectives. (In a similar vein, one could carve out a distinction between manslaughter and second degree murder by juxtaposing *Smithers* with the Australian case wherein an unconscious victim of assault is left to drown, the degree of blameworthiness in the former being noticeably lower than that in the latter.)

Other Supreme Court Justices in their commentaries on *Nette* dispute Arbour's endorsement of Lambert's synonymizing significant contributing cause with a cause that is not trivial and not insignificant. They claim that the positive expression raises the threshold of causation for second degree murder and thereby alters the *Smithers* standard, a standard that has withstood the test of time. Whereas I would prefer to lose a not insignificant amount of money at the casino rather than a significant amount, I do not believe that this distinction, however meaningful in certain contexts, would make much of a difference in a judge's instructions to a jury. The differences that matter are made manifest in practice when material facts engage with legal concepts. In this context, storytelling is more than an instrument of persuasion; it is an integral part of decision-making.

5 Narrative Theory and the Art of Judgment: The Anatomy of a Supreme Court Decision

A Narratological Primer

Modern narrative theory is predicated on an enabling distinction between narrative content and narrative presentation, between what really or supposedly happened (*l'histoire*, the actual chronological and causal series of events) and how what really or supposedly happened is related to the reader (*le discours*, the textual sequence of events). The story of what really or supposedly happened can only be inferred and constructed by the listener or reader from the discourses he or she must absorb and synthesize. Story is crucial to legal decision-making because the primary task of the judge or jury is to make a plausible and coherent narrative out of the chaotic particulars of a case that is often awash in a sea of conflicting evidence, contradictory versions of events, incongruent precedents, unclear controlling laws, incompatible expert reports, ambiguous legal documents, and, in general, at least two opposed and competing discourses. As Paul Gewirtz notes:

> A trial consists of fragmented narratives and narrative multiplicity ... In addition, one side's narrative is constantly being met by the other side's counternarrative ... so that "reality" is always being disassembled with multiple, conflicting, and partly overlapping versions, each version being presented as true, each fighting to be declared "what really happened" – with very high stakes riding on that ultimate determination. (8)

To add to it, as James Boyd White points out, a judge necessarily proceeds "in an uncertain world in which he or she is comparing one case, defined in one way, with an array of other cases, defined another way, in which the definition of both items is always arguable; and in which, moreover, these definitions must determine the class of items on both sides that will be relevant" (*Heracle's Bow*, 130).

The compositional task of a judge, therefore, is not altogether unlike that of a novelist, for even though a judge finds facts rather than invents them, he or she is trying to construct a plausible and coherent narrative. To approach what really happened, he or she must mediate between the conflicting discourses to produce an authoritative discourse of his or her own, a discourse by definition authoritative unless and until over-turned by a higher court. In making this comparison between judges and novelists, however, I do not mean to imply that judgments are simply fictions. On the contrary, my intent is to affirm a middle ground be-tween, on the one hand, the traditional view that judicial reasoning, anchored in legal precedent and found facts, is simply a deductive mat-ter of applying universal laws to particular fact-situations, and, on the other, the postmodern view that precedents, facts, and controlling laws are entirely constructed by judges according to the various interpretive strategies they deploy and the various interpretive communities to which they belong. Following Robert Wess, I call this middle ground "rhetorical realism," "rhetorical" because similarities of fact and law are constructed by judges, "realism" because something really hap-pened even if that true story is never wholly accessible to the judicial opinion that seeks to encompass it.[1]

To encompass what really happened is a complex business because a judgment, like a novel, must relate events from a particular angle of vision and in a particular voice, and, to further complicate the issue, sometimes from more than one angle of vision and in more than one voice. In his seminal work *Narrative Discourse*, Gerard Genette makes the crucial distinction between focalizer, the agent who sees, and ver-balizer, the agent who says – between narrative perspective and narra-tive voice.

---

1 Because some readers may want to know how "rhetorical realism" relates to "the postmodern view," a postscript on rhetoric, postmodernism, and scepticism follows the final chapter. My likening the compositional task of the judge to that of the novel-ist concerns individual judgments only. In *Law's Empire*, Ronald Dworkin famously likens judges working in a legal tradition to novelists working on a chain novel (228ff). Stanley Fish provides an energetic critique of this simile in "Working on the Chain Gang: Interpretation in Law and Literature" (*Doing What Comes Naturally*, 87–102).

On its face, this distinction between focalization and verbalization might seem to belong to the arcana of literary criticism, but not much reflection is required to realize that the distinction has profound implications for judicial writing. How does a judge narrate a case? Does he or she focalize events from the perspective of the complainant or from that of the accused? Does he or she speak in an omniscient voice or allow the parties to speak in their own voices?

Most people see the traditional voice of the judge as that of the unlimited omniscient author: unlimited because the judge has access to the perspective of whomever or whatever he or she chooses to focus upon; omniscient, not because the judge really does know everything, but because whenever a judge finds something to be a fact or finds someone to be guilty, it is a fact and that person is guilty. Judicial utterances are performative; they bring into being the realities they pronounce.

An unlimited omniscient style allows a judge to exploit the resources of narrative telling and dramatic showing. When engaged in narrative telling, the judge tells the audience what happened in his or her own language. This way of telling gives the judge considerable freedom to enter the minds of agents and reveal their motives as well as to interpolate at will his or her own evaluation and analysis of agents and events. When engaged in dramatic showing, the judge lets agents have their say in a language that belongs to them. This way of showing allows characters to speak in their own voices through testimony, transcript, statement, dialogue, or social media. In a conventional judgment, narrative telling predominates over dramatic showing; the language of the judge overrides that of the agents or parties.

Though the unlimited omniscient point of view is posited as the norm, judgments at times can deploy the limited omniscient point of view wherein the judge knows everything but confines him/herself to the perspective of one of the characters. In this instance, there is an external narrator (the judge) plus a focal character (one of the parties). Though the perspective is limited to that of the party, the omniscient voice is that of the judge. That voice, however, is sometimes intermingled with the party's. The motives behind such a rhetorical strategy are various, but to see events from an affected party's angle of vision is usually to create sympathy for that party. Whether a judge is conscious of the type of focalization and verbalization incorporated into his or her judgments is of little import. Whatever a judge's intention, voice and perspective have a huge impact on the persuasiveness of a decision, a point not lost on Lord Denning:

To some this may appear to be a small matter, but to Mr. Harry Hook, it is very important. He is a street trader in the Barnsley Market. He has been trading there for some six years without any complaint being made against him; but, nevertheless, he has now been banned from trading in the market for life. All because of a trifling incident. On Wednesday, October 16, 1974, the market was closed at 5:30. So were all the lavatories ... They were locked up. Three quarters of an hour later, at 6:20, Harry Hook had an urgent call of nature. He wanted to relieve himself. He went into a side street near the market and there made water ... No one was about except one or two employees of the council, who were cleaning up. They rebuked him. He said: "I can do it here if I like." They reported him to a security officer who came up. The security officer reprimanded Harry Hook. We are not told the words used by the security officer. I expect they were in language which street traders understand. Harry Hook made an appropriate reply. Again, we are not told the actual words, but it is not difficult to guess. I expect it was an emphatic version of "You be off." At any rate, the security officer described them as words of abuse. Touchstone would say that the security officer gave the "reproof valiant" and Harry Hook gave the "counter-check quarrelsome." (*Regina v. Barnsley*, 1055)

Although the voice in these opening paragraphs is clearly Denning's – Harry Hook is not likely to be quoting Shakespeare's *As You Like It* – the perspective is clearly Harry Hook's. It is Denning who alludes to Touchstone's naming the degrees of the lie:

The first, the Retort Courteous; the second, the Quip Modest; the third, the Reply Churlish; the fourth, the Reproof Valiant; the fifth, the Countercheque Quarrelsome; the sixth, the Lie with Circumstance; the seventh, the Lie Direct. All these you may avoid but the Lie Direct; and you may avoid that too, with an If. I knew when seven justices could not take up a quarrel, but when the parties were met themselves, one of them thought but of an If, as, "If you said so, then I said so"; and they shook hands and swore brothers. Your If is the only peacemaker; much virtue in If. (V.iv.88–98)

The contrast between the courtly sophistication of Touchstone and the marketplace bluntness of Harry Hook and the security officer underscores the huge disparity between a lifetime ban and the piddling simplicity of the case at bar. And there is no doubt at all where this judgment is going. The focal agent in a judgment is more often than not the winning party. But focalization and agency work at deeper levels too, as Edward Berry has pointed out in *Writing Reasons*, using the 1975 Canadian Supreme Court decision *Harrison v. Carswell* as an illustration.[2]

Here the question before the court is whether the owner of a shopping mall has the right to eject a lawful picketer from the mall. Writing for the majority, Justice Dickson finds that the owner does have that right:

> Anglo-Saxon jurisprudence has traditionally recognized, as a fundamental freedom, the right of the individual to the enjoyment of property and the right not to be deprived thereof, or any interest therein, save by due process of law. The Legislature of Manitoba has declared in the *Petty Trespasses Act* that any person who trespasses upon land, the property of another, upon or through which he has been asked by the owner not to enter, is guilty of an offence. If there is to be any change in this statute law, if A is to be given the right to enter and remain on the land of B, it would seem to me that such a change must be made by the enacting institution, the Legislature, which is the representative of the people and designed to manifest the political will, and not by this Court. (para. 15)

Dickson's use of focalization and agency is persuasive because it looks at the case from the point of view of the law itself and gives agency to authority and its institutions (Anglo-Saxon jurisprudence, the Legislature of Manitoba, this Court). They, not people, are the actors. Moreover, his language is formal and impersonal, a style of writing that reinforces his argument that the role of the courts is sharply limited by tradition and statute. The choice of language, the angle of vision from which the issues are seen, and the imputation of agency to legal entities would seem to reflect a conservative judicial philosophy.

Justice Laskin, in dissent, takes a different tack:

> I come then to those issues, and they can only be understood if we look at the present case not only from the position asserted by the shopping centre owner, but as well from the position asserted by the lawful picketer. An ancient concept, trespass, is urged here in all its pristine force by a shopping

---

2 I am indebted to my colleague Edward Berry, Professor of English Emeritus, University of Victoria, for this example. As well as referring to it briefly in *Writing Reasons*, he used it in his presentation on style for the Judicial Writing Program sponsored by the Canadian Institute for the Administration of Justice.

centre owner in respect of the areas of the shopping centre which have been opened by him to public use, and necessarily so because of the commercial character of the enterprise based on tenancies by operators of a variety of businesses. To say in such circumstances that the shopping centre owner may, at his whim, order any member of the public out of the shopping centre on penalty or liability for trespass if he refuses to leave, does not make sense if there is no proper reason in that member's conduct or activity to justify the order to leave. (para. 30)

Laskin's use of focalization and agency is persuasive because it looks at the case from the point of view of the affected parties and gives agency to them (a shopping centre owner, a lawful picketer, operators of various businesses, members of the public). His language is informal and personal, a style of writing that reinforces his argument that ancient legal concepts must bend to new human situations. The tone, moreover, is somewhat ironic ("an ancient concept, trespass, is urged here in all its pristine force"). The everyday language, the human angle of vision from which the issues are seen, and the portrayal of people as actors would seem to reflect a more pragmatic judicial philosophy than Dickson's.

I adduce these examples to demonstrate that focalization, verbalization, and agency have an impact not only on the form of a judgment but also on its substance. Insofar as there is a telling, there must be a teller, a narrating voice – a spectrum going from narrators who are the least noticeable to those who are the most so, from the minimally narrated to the maximally narrated, Lord Denning's judgments being an obvious example of noticeable narration. Covert narration occupies the middle ground between the minimally narrated and the maximally narrated. Some interpreting person, say a judge or a lawyer, is converting the agent's thoughts into indirect expression, and we cannot tell whether a slant other than the agent's lurks behind the words. A covert narrator can impute motives, intentions, ideas, beliefs, values, and emotions to agents using a vocabulary that goes beyond what the agents themselves possess. Judges and lawyers routinely give expression to the positions of parties in a way the parties themselves would be incapable of doing. In a legal context, the indirect form in narratives implies a shade more intervention by the judge or lawyer, since we cannot be sure that the ideas and words in the decision or submission are precisely those thought and said by the agent to whom they are attributed.

In *Bumper v. North Carolina* (1968), Bumper was convicted of rape by the lower court.[3] A rifle was seized at his grandmother's house in an isolated rural area. Four white officers went to the house, and one said to the grandmother, a sixty-eight-year-old African American widow of limited education: "I have a search warrant to search your house." Mrs Leath responded: "Go ahead" (546–7). The warrant was never shown. During the trial, the prosecutor did not rely on the warrant but on her consent. The appellate court found the search to be unlawful. Of interest from a rhetorical perspective is what is buried in a footnote – a subtle narratological point about the deceptiveness of continuous first-person testimony. As Mr Justice Stewart shrewdly observes:

> The transcript of the suppression hearing comes to us … in the form of a narrative; i.e., the actual questions and answers have been rewritten in the form of continuous first person narrative. The effect is to put in the mouth of the witness some of the words of the attorneys. In the case of an obviously compliant witness like Mrs. Leath, the result is a narrative that has the tone of decisiveness but is shot through with contradictions. (547)

Compliant witnesses are amenable to coaching, and lawyerly questions are almost always leading questions. If the attorneys' questions are suppressed, we cannot determine the extent to which the questions contain concepts that are not part of the grandmother's repertoire, concepts that supply Mrs Leath with legal terminology concerning free will, coercion, duress, and so forth. Covert narration in judicial writing creates even more problems, for we cannot easily determine where party speech and judge speech begin and end. Focalized narration creates interesting ambiguities in literature but real problems in law.

Judgments as Heteroglot and Dialogical

Useful as the concepts of Genette's narrative theory undoubtedly are, they need to be supplemented by those of Mikhail Bakhtin so that we can get a more detailed picture of how language functions in judicial writing. For Bakhtin, language must be understood as social activity,

---

3 Peter Brooks discusses this case at some length in "Narrative Transactions."

as dialogue. Every linguistic act imagines, assumes, or implies an addressee. The word, as his colleague V. Volosinov notes, "is a two-sided act. It is determined equally by whose word it is and for whom it is meant. A word is a territory shared by both addresser and addressee, the speaker and his interlocutor" (86). Language, therefore, is essentially dialogical. Bakhtin writes that "the word in living conversation is directly, blatantly, oriented toward a future answer word. It provokes an answer, anticipates it, and structures itself in the answerer's direction" (*Dialogical Imagination*, 280). All language use is language use from a certain point of view, in a certain context, and for a certain audience. There is no such thing as language that is not ideological, contextual, and dialogic. The words we use come to us as already imprinted with the meanings, intentions, and accents of previous users, and any utterance we make is directed towards some real or hypothetical other. Moreover, each speaker "is himself a respondent" for he is "not, after all, the first speaker, the one that disturbs the eternal silence of the universe" (Bakhtin, *Speech Genres*, 69). Each speaker builds on previous utterances, polemicizes with them, or simply presumes that they are already known to the listener. Each utterance refutes, affirms, supplements, and relies on the others, presupposes them to be known, and somehow takes them into account. However monological an utterance may seem to be, however much it seems to focus on its own topic, it cannot help but be a response to what has already been said about the topic. For Bakhtin, then, "language is not a neutral medium that passes freely and easily into the private property of the speaker's intentions; it is populated – overpopulated – with the intentions of others. Expropriating, forcing it to submit to one's own intentions and accents, is a difficult and complicated process" (*Dialogical Imagination*, 294).

This is especially true of the language of the law, a language that is essentially heteroglot, polyglot, and dialogical, heteroglossia being Bakhtin's term for the multiple social languages that exist within a single national language – languages of social groups, professions, generations, and so on – and polyglossia being his term for different national languages. Judgments embrace both multiple social languages (those of experts, parties, lawyers, etc.) and different national languages (English, Latin, Norman French, etc.). The judge participates in the judgment (he or she is omnipresent in it) but not always with a direct language of his or her own. The language of the judgment is a system of languages that mutually and ideologically interinanimate one another. Therefore, it is misleading to describe and analyse judicial discourse as if it were a single unitary language emanating from an omniscient narrator. Any given judgment is part of the unending legal conversation that both precedes and outlives it. Judges are in dialogue with the precedent decisions of their forbears as well as with statute speech, charter speech, case law speech, appellate speech, Supreme Court speech, dissent speech, lawyer speech, witness speech, expert speech, party speech, police speech, and so forth.

In a judgment that gets the ultimate review, what often emerges is a complex dialogue between the court of first instance, the appellate court, and the Supreme Court, not to mention the sometimes dissenting voices within the last two. I shall trace the emergence of such dialogue in a controversial Canadian case, *R. v. Ewanchuk*, by examining the crucial yet largely unacknowledged role that verbalization and focalization play in the rhetoric of judgment and by comparing and contrasting how the case is narrativized differently by the participants in the trial, the trial judge, the appellate judges, and the Supreme Court judges.

A Bonnet and Crinolines

Steven Brian Ewanchuk, a woodworker in his thirties, brought a seventeen-year-old woman into his van for a job interview. After the interview Ewanchuk invited the woman into a trailer attached to the van to show her a portfolio and brochure displaying his craftwork. Once they were both inside, he began to make a series of increasingly sexual advances. Each time she said "no" to his advance he would stop, but, after the passing of some time, he would then renew his efforts. She testified at trial that during her time in the trailer she was too frightened to attempt to leave the trailer.

At trial, Ewanchuk's lawyer argued successfully that although the woman had initially said "no" to his sexual touching, she did not verbally object to or physically resist his subsequent advances, thereby giving "implied consent" to his conduct. The acquittal was upheld on appeal. In the decision of the Alberta Court of Appeal, Justice John McClung commented that "it must be pointed out that the complainant did not present herself to Ewanchuk or enter his trailer in a bonnet and crinolines" and that Ewanchuk's conduct was "far less criminal than hormonal." The issue before the Supreme Court was "whether the trial judge erred in his understanding of consent in sexual assault and whether his conclusion that the defence of 'implied consent' exists in Canadian law was correct." Justice Major, writing for the majority, held that there was no defence of "implied consent" to sexual assault and overturned the ruling of the Court of Appeal. "Implied consent" can only arise in the context of the defence of mistake of fact where the accused argues that the complainant gave her implied consent through her actions, conduct, or words. Madam Justice L'Heureux-Dubé held that such a defence of honest but mistaken belief cannot be used unless the accused took sufficient steps to ascertain consent. Here, the accused did not make any attempt to ensure that the complainant had consented when he moved from a massage to sexual touching. She also castigated Justice McClung's opinion severely, arguing that it reinforced myths and stereotypes about women and sexual assault.

In response to L'Heureux-Dubé's criticism, McClung wrote a letter to the *National Post* (27 February 1999) characterizing her ruling as a "graceless slide into personal invective." He also suggested that the judge's feminism was contributing to the high suicide rate among Quebec males, either knowing or not knowing that her husband had committed suicide. In a later interview with the same paper, he added fuel to the fire by saying that the complainant "was not lost on her way home from the nunnery."

The Trial Transcript of the Court of First Instance[4]
(Court of Queen's Bench of Alberta, Edmonton, 7 and 10 November 1995)

A transcript reproduces the direct discourse of those who led and gave evidence during the trial. It is as close as we can come to seeing what really happened in the courtroom, and it furnishes the raw data on which the trial judge relied in making his decision to acquit Ewanchuk. Missing, of course, are gestures and tonalities. Nevertheless, transcripts involve a minimal amount of narrativization even if the questions, answers, and arguments they contain are shaped to tell the different stories put forward by the complainant and the accused. In this case, the accused did not testify. (I have not reproduced the testimony of Constable Hilton since it is immaterial to the issue on which the case hinged.)

---

4 This transcript is a part of the court records. Since no one else is likely to have it before him or her, I have quoted at length from it, trying to capture its flavour by keeping indirect narration to a minimum. I have also quoted at length from the decisions in an attempt to display their dialogical qualities.

Testimony of the Complainant's Roommate

The first witness was an eighteen-year-old friend and roommate of the complainant. She was with the complainant the day before the alleged assault took place, and they had both talked to Ewanchuk at that time though only the complainant attended the interview the next day. In response to the Crown prosecutor, her roommate reported that Ewanchuk "said that if any of our boyfriends phoned him up, that we wouldn't get the job" (106). "He said that he liked clowning around with [his employees]" (109). Upon cross-examination, she revealed that she and the complainant shared an apartment with their boyfriends and that the complainant had a six-month-old child at the time of the incident. When counsel for the accused tried to suggest that the complainant was dressed provocatively in shorts and possibly not wearing any underwear, her roommate said that she could not remember what the complainant was wearing save for shorts and a top of some type. She also said that during her interview with Ewanchuk the day before the incident, he never touched her.

Testimony of the Complainant

The complainant testified that she felt creepy and uncomfortable when she and her roommate met Ewanchuk the day before the incident. "Any older man that pulls up to two girls and asks them if they're looking for work seems a little out of sorts" (129). When she met with him the next morning, she said she left the passenger door open because she was hesitant about talking to him. "He told me that he could tell that I was hesitant. He said, I see that you don't feel comfortable, and he just kept on saying, It's okay. I won't hurt you. You can trust me. You'll find that I'm a nice guy" (129). She thought it was funny he felt he had to say that. She told him that she was seventeen. The job paid eleven dollars an hour. At first, from her perspective, it seemed like a regular job interview.

   She told him about her boyfriend to make him feel "threatened" (130). He was much larger than she, and he was working so hard to make her feel relaxed. "Well, after we had talked some about personal ideas," she continued, "he told me that he was very friendly, a very affectionate person, but he told me that he again, he said, I won't hurt you. It's okay. You'll be fine. There's nothing to worry about. And then he asked me if I would like to see some of his work. And he said that he had some of his equipment and some of his work inside the trailer that was hitched to his van" (130). She entered the trailer and said she believed he locked the door. She felt she'd better do what she was told.

They had a ten to fifteen minute conversation about his portfolio and brochure. Then he asked questions about her personality, whether she was as friendly and affectionate as he was. He said that he liked clowning around with his employees, that he preferred a friend/friend relationship to a boss/employee one. He touched her hand. Then he touched her arm and shoulder with his hand. "I won't hurt you. You can be relaxed" (134). She mentioned her boyfriend to dissuade Ewanchuk from more touching. She said she didn't touch him back. He wanted a massage. She rubbed his shoulders. Even though she didn't want to give him a massage she "was afraid that if [she] put up more of a struggle that it would only egg him on more, and his touching would be more forced" (135). He then said that he wanted to "return the favour" (135) and began to massage her shoulders:

> I remained very stiff ... [H]e was saying, he kept on saying, you should be more relaxed, you know. I'm not going to hurt you. Don't be afraid. And he started to try to massage around my stomach, and he brought his hand up – or underneath my breasts, and he started to get quite close up there, so I used my elbows to push in between, and I said, "No" ... He did stop and he said – he put his hands on my shoulders, and he said, You see, I'm a nice guy, I stopped. Be relaxed. I'm not going to hurt you. But he did continue a little bit, but then I said, "no" ... He kept on like touching me a little bit more, but not in like private areas. He just kept on touching me a little more, and I just kind of moved and said "no," and he stopped, and then he said, See, I'm a nice guy. It's okay. (137)

Then he started to massage her feet. She complied, she testified, because "I was afraid. I was frozen. I just did what he told me to do" (136). Then matters began to escalate. She thought it was best to mask her fear and offer no resistance:

> He was massaging my feet, but he didn't stay there. He was moving up my leg more toward my inner thigh, my pelvic area, and then he'd move back again, and I just sat there, and I didn't – I didn't do anything. I knew something was going to happen, and I didn't want to fight, because I felt that I would just egg him on more. I've learned through learning about

sexual assault that often when you struggle and when you put up a fight, sometimes the person just feels a superior power over you, and that just will egg them on more. So I didn't – didn't fight and I didn't scream. I didn't say anything. And then he moved himself on top of me and laid very heavily a lot of his weight on me … I was laying on my back. I was bone straight. I didn't – didn't have my arms out. I was straight. My legs were probably not even shoulder distance apart. (137)

Next came the first mention of sexual activity, not something she wanted. "He was moving his pelvic area, and he was telling me that he could get me so horny so that I would want it so bad, and he wouldn't give it to me because he had self-control and because he wouldn't want to give it to me" (138). He asked her to touch his back. She declined to do so. Then he moved his pelvic area against hers. She asked him to stop, and he did. He said that he wouldn't hurt her, and she didn't struggle, fearing that if she did, he would force himself upon her.

She acknowledged to him that she was scared. He hugged her, laid himself on top of her again, and continued to do what he was doing. Then he rubbed his soft penis on her vaginal area, under her shorts but on top of her underwear. "He kept on telling me again and again not to worry, that he wouldn't hurt me, that he had self-control, and that even though I was so horny, he wasn't" (141). She didn't want him to know how scared she was, believing that it would get worse, that it would be more brutal; the tactic came from what she knew about sexual assault via television and the police – the Discovery Channel, the Learning Channel, a talk given at school.

When the episode was over, he gave her a hundred dollar bill for the massage and said that she shouldn't tell anyone about what happened, especially her boyfriend.

During his cross-examination, counsel for the accused made the point that if Ewanchuk had wanted to force intercourse on the complainant, he could have. He also established that she didn't check if the door was locked and that throughout the ordeal she tried to look comfortable and relaxed (145). She never asked to leave; she had subjective fear; she was genuinely scared, but there were no threats, no punches, and no forcible removal of her clothing (155). Moreover, Ewanchuk gave her his correct name, phone, and address; she wasn't showing her nervousness; she wanted to hide it (160). The complainant responded to his points, saying, "I was too scared to jump up, run, get tools thrown at my head, get the crap kicked out of me so I just froze, just did what he told me to do" (175). Counsel for the accused tried to get her to say that the hundred dollars was for the baby, but she refused to do so, and he concluded by reiterating that Ewanchuk stopped after each of the three "no's" (183).

Argument of the Crown

The Crown began by emphasizing that Ewanchuk had some sexual contact with the complainant, a fact not in dispute. The Crown must prove beyond a reasonable doubt that the complainant did not consent to this activity and that the accused was not under an honest but mistaken belief that she was consenting. The accused could not have reasonably believed that she was consenting. After the first "no," he didn't cease his sexual touching. He intensified it.

She opposed breast touching so how could she possibly want him to lie on top of her and grind his pelvis into hers? His constant refrain of "don't be afraid" meant that he knew there was no consent. Acquiescence is not consent. After "no" was pronounced, he stopped momentarily but then continued and escalated his sexual activity.

Section 273.1 of the Criminal Code excludes consent when the complainant expresses lack of agreement, through words or actions. Section 273.2 deals with the defence of honest but mistaken belief. For such a defence to be valid, there must be no recklessness or wilful blindness on the part of the accused. He must take reasonable steps to ensure the complainant is consenting.

The Crown argued that Ewanchuk was reckless and wilfully blind. Moreover, he failed to take reasonable steps to ensure consent. After the first "no," the ante was upped, but he continued nonetheless. She was entrapped, he was physically intimidating, he gave her hush money, and he later phoned to see if everything was okay.

Argument of the Defence

Counsel for the accused began his argument by noting that the Crown had not put forth the expected argument from abuse of power, trust, or authority. The failure to make this argument annoyed him because he had done his research. He submitted that the complainant was old enough to consent validly. The Crown must prove that she did not consent and that the accused knew that she did not consent. She wasn't consenting, he conceded, but she kept her true feelings secret. The issue wasn't bad taste or clumsiness on the part of the accused, but serious criminal misconduct. From the outset, she said the situation was creepy but she met him nonetheless and went into his trailer. Counsel for the accused's main point was that "You can't keep non-consent a secret" (203).

In response, the Crown referred explicitly to Parliament's 1992 changes to laws concerning sexual assault and directed the Court's attention to Section 273.2 (b) of the Criminal Code, a section which requires that the accused take reasonable steps to ascertain that the complainant is consenting. There is no longer such a thing as implied consent, nor can the accused assume consent unless and until there is resistance. The accused has some burden to determine whether or not the complainant is consenting. The defence claimed that fear cannot be entirely subjective, that there must be some objective behaviour to manifest it to the accused. The Crown argued that this was an incorrect focus and that the more immediate concern was the steps taken by the accused to ensure the consent of the complainant.

The Decision of the Trial Judge, Mr Justice Moore

The trial judge's narrativization of the case is chronological and sets out the events in much the same way as the complainant's testimony sets them out. The style of narration is third-person omniscient, the narrative voice is virtually unnoticeable, and the account is unbiased for the most part even if the judge does point out that "underneath [the complainant's] shorts and T-shirt [she] wore a brassiere and panties," a seemingly baseless and gratuitous observation. Would unwanted sexual touching be less criminal if she wasn't wearing undergarments? He also mentions that Ewanchuk showed her "*beautiful* pieces of woodwork" (219, emphasis added). Having set the scene, the trial judge gets to the heart of the matter.

> During this time period of two and one half hours A [Ewanchuk] did three things which B [the complainant] did not like. When A was giving B a body massage, his hands got close to B's breasts. B said "no," and A immediately stopped.
> When B and A were lying on the floor, A rubbed his pelvic bone area against B's pelvic area. B said "no," and A immediately stopped. Later on A took his soft penis out of his shorts and placed it on the outside of B's

clothes in her pelvic area. B said "no," and A immediately stopped. During all of the two and one half hours that A and B were together, she never told A that she wanted to leave. When B finally told A that she wanted to leave, she and A simply walked out of the trailer.

The charge is sexual assault and consent is the issue. (218)

Sexual assault involves the application of force or the threat or fear of the application of force. "B says that she had a fear that A would apply force. However, are there any reasonable grounds for B to fear that A would apply force? This question must be answered objectively, not answered on the basis of subjective speculation" (220). He concludes:

B is a credible witness, and I know that she was afraid. All of B's thoughts, emotions, and speculations were very real for her. However, she successfully kept all her thoughts, emotions, and speculations deep within herself. She did not communicate most of [them] ... She did clearly communicate with the one word "no" on three separate occasions, and on each occasion A stopped.

B says that she did not want to let A know that she was afraid. Like a good actor, she projected an outer image that did not reflect her inner self. B did not communicate to A by words, gestures, or facial expressions that she was "frozen" by a fear of force. B did not communicate that she was frozen to the spot, and that fear prevented her from getting up off the floor and walking out of the trailer.

The Crown must prove lack of consent (and A's knowledge of lack of consent) beyond a reasonable doubt. Consent may be implied or expressed, and clearly in this case we are dealing with implied consent. (220–1)

That the judge could acquit on the basis of a defence that no longer exists in Canadian law and that he could totally ignore Section 273.2 (b), especially after it was explicitly brought to his attention, is strange. Even stranger is his supposition that saying "no" three times does not signify lack of consent. His flawed reasoning notwithstanding, he treats the complainant decently, at times compassionately, and he tries to be fair according to his lights. Indeed, his copious quotation from the complainant's testimony, testimony that is credible and convincing, puts her case forward in a way that effectively undermines his decision. His narration, unlike McClung's, is sympathetic to the complainant. It is not focalized through the eyes of the accused.

The Alberta Court of Appeal: Justice McClung for the Majority

(This section on the majority decision repeats points made and passages cited in chapter 1. The repetition, I hope, helps maintain continuity and coherence.)

McClung commences by noting that he has read Chief Justice Fraser's dissent. For him, the issue is jurisdiction, and he believes that an appellate court has no jurisdiction "to upset trial findings of fact that have evidentiary support" (para. 1). He then quotes at length (four pages single-spaced) from the trial judge's decision. (The key parts of this quotation have already been cited above, and it is noteworthy that McClung avoids quoting those parts of the decision that contain the complainant's direct discourse.) He concludes:

> The facts revealed by the record establish that the accused had no proven intention of forcibly pursuing his way with the complainant during the two and one-half hours they were alone in his trailer. The Crown tried to prove that what occurred did so against her apparent consent, but did not succeed. Whether or not the sexual activity took place with or without consent is a question of fact and the absence of consent was a finding that was refused at this trial. (3)

That McClung was mistaken in his belief that the case hinges on a question of fact is not relevant here. What is relevant is that Justice McClung's endorsement of the trial judge's reasons has surface plausibility, and his seeing no error in law is a defensible though erroneous finding that a rational appellate judge might come to. But his finding is vitiated by his trivialization of the victim's complaint through his diction and imagery:

> The complainant's television-suggested plan (from the evidence drawn from the Family Channel) to rebuff Ewanchuk by a display of bravura confidence was her choice, and it was a choice for which she cannot be criticized. But it is not clear from the evidence that her inner concerns emanated from what the accused Ewanchuk said or did or were influenced by what she had learned on television. The Chief Justice draws condemnatory inferences against Ewanchuk because his age was estimated to be about thirty and that he substantially outweighed the complainant, who was seventeen. But the record does not reveal that size or age disparities

were in any way determinative of what took place here between two persons who were both over the age of consent. The Chief Justice's concerns aside, it must be pointed out that the complainant did not present herself to Ewanchuk or enter his trailer in a bonnet and crinolines. She told Ewanchuk that she was the mother of a six-month old baby and that, along with her boyfriend, she shared an apartment with another couple. (I point out these aspects of the trial record, but with no intention of denigrating her or lessening the legal protection to which she was entitled.) (4)

As we already know, the complainant never referred to the Family Channel. Her strategy derived from the Discovery Channel, the Learning Channel, and a talk given by a police officer. The phrase "bravura confidence" is subtly demeaning – this, after all, is a young woman who gets such confidence, along with her knowledge of sexual assault, from supposedly watching the Family Channel. Moreover, McClung's dialogue with the Chief Justice brings the latter's "condemnatory inferences against Ewanchuk" into the picture, and even if the narration in this paragraph is unfocalized, we can detect a movement towards Ewanchuk's camp. "Bonnet and crinolines" is openly demeaning, the complainant being characterized as an unwed teenage mother who lives with her boyfriend, possibly in an open relationship with another couple. In his letter to the *National Post*, as we have seen, McClung uses a different though equally demeaning figure of speech when he says that the complainant was not lost on her way home from the nunnery. The implication that the complainant is a person of loose morals who dresses provocatively is hardly mitigated by the paraliptic parenthesis saying that the judge intends neither to denigrate the complainant nor to lessen the legal protection to which she is entitled. The intention is accomplished by the very act of disavowing it. After referring to "three clumsy passes by Ewanchuk," as if the lovable oaf lacked skill in the art of prosecuting what the judge inaptly calls "his romantic intentions," McClung goes further. I cite the relevant passage again:

Three overtures were made by Ewanchuk. The first two were marginally identifiable, if at all, as sexual in nature. They involved mutual body massages which, while they neared her sexual organs, were not in contact with them. Nonetheless, the last was clearly a sexual activity; a deliberate exposure of his sexual anatomy as he rubbed himself against her clothed pelvic area. This performance, if viewed in isolation ... would hardly raise Ewanchuk's stature in the pantheon of chivalric behaviour, but it did take

place in private and following her protest – "No!" – led to nothing. The
record would indicate that the one clearly sexual activity in the case ended
swiftly with her injunctive "No!" (13)

It is right that we be constantly reminded that sexual assault can intractably erode the present and future integrity of its victims. Clearly this is so.
Yet we must also remain aware that nothing can destroy a life so utterly as
an extended term of imprisonment following a precipitately decided sexual assault conviction. In the search for proof of guilt, sloganeering such as
"No means No!," "Zero Tolerance!," and "Take back the night!" which,
while they marshall desired social ideals, are no safe substitute for the or-
derly and objective judicial application of Canada's criminal statutes. (14)

At this point, Ewanchuk has become the focal character. McClung
borrows the adjective "clumsy" from the trial transcript and depicts
Ewanchuk as a hapless lover whose less than "chivalric behaviour" is
oafish rather than criminal. That he made his unwanted advances in
private is somehow a mitigating factor. They "led to nothing" even
though a frightened young woman was confined for two and a half
hours and subjected to pelvic grinding and an exposed penis. The complainant, however, is not the focus; Ewanchuk is. "Nothing can destroy
a life so utterly as an extended term of imprisonment following a precipitately decided sexual assault conviction." Yet a carefully decided
sexual assault conviction can also destroy a life, and the Chief Justice's
dissent and the Supreme Court's reversal are dense with detailed analyses of the legal meaning of consent; they are anything but precipitate.
And the attack on "sloganeering such as 'No means No'" is entirely
gratuitous even if McClung disingenuously says that the slogans
"marshall desired social ideals."

Unsurprisingly, as we have seen, McClung finds in favour of the accused and declines to take the high road in his conclusion:

In my reading of the trial record, this Crown appeal must be dismissed.
Beyond the error of law issue, the sum of the evidence indicates that
Ewanchuk's advances to the complainant were far less criminal than hormonal. In a less litigious age going too far in the boyfriend's car was better
dealt with on site – a well-chosen expletive, a slap in the face, or, if necessary, a well-directed knee. What this accused tried to initiate hardly quali-
fies him for the lasting stigma of a conviction for sexual assault and Alberta's
current bullet-train removal to the penitentiary for prolonged shrift.

To advocate swearing, slapping, and kneeing as methods for countering unwanted hormonal advances is not to give appropriate counsel. Equally inappropriate is the language of stigma and shrift. A previously convicted sexual offender is not a likely candidate for the cross. And "going too far in the boyfriend's car" evokes the world of the late 1950s and early 1960s, a world romanticized in television shows like *Happy Days* and in films like *American Graffiti*, a world where teenage couples make out in parked cars, a world where "no" doesn't necessarily mean "no." As Chief Justice Fraser caustically observes in her dissent: "Women in Canada are not walking around the country in a state of constant consent to sexual activity unless and until they say 'No' or offer resistance to anyone who targets them for sexual activity" (67).

The Alberta Court of Appeal: Chief Justice Fraser in Dissent

For Chief Justice Fraser the case raises six issues:

1 what is meant by "consent";
2 what the Crown must prove to establish "lack of consent";
3 what is meant by "implied consent";
4 the standard which applies in evaluating whether fear vitiates consent;
5 the effect in law of stating "No" in the course of sexual activity; and
6 when the Crown must prove that an accused knew that a complainant was not consenting or was wilfully or recklessly blind to this fact.

The trial judge found no proof of lack of consent despite believing that the complainant feared for her safety and submitted to Ewanchuk's advances out of that fear, despite the fact that she said "no" three times, and despite the fact that no evidence was called by the defence (27). The trial judge erred in law as to what constitutes consent. "Simply because the trial judge, in applying the law, did so by reference to found facts does not make the errors any less errors of law" (28). If Ewanchuk, two to three times the size of the complainant, did not take reasonable steps to ascertain consent, then the defence of mistake of fact is not available to him.

Fraser quotes at length from the trial transcript to narrativize the events in the direct discourse of the complainant. She adds and emphasizes some suggestive details: "To put what transpired here in context, it is noteworthy at the time of the subject incident, the complainant was

17 years old; 5'1" tall and about *105 pounds* and had met the Respondent accused, Steven Brian Ewanchuk, for a *job interview*. Ewanchuk was about *30* years old, *over 6' tall* and about *2 to 3 times the size of the complainant"* (29). She notes Ewanchuk's refrain of "I won't hurt you. You can be relaxed." She notes that the first "no" is uttered when he tries to touch the complainant's breast. "You see, I'm a nice guy," he says. "I stopped. Be relaxed. I'm not going to hurt you." Fraser takes us through the complainant's supposed horniness, Ewanchuk's supposed self-control, his failure to discuss her receptiveness to sexual activity, his pelvic grinding, his acknowledgment that he had her worried, his starting sexual activity anew, his placement of his soft penis on her vaginal area, and her final "no."

Fraser notes that the trial judge found the complainant to be a credible witness and knew she was afraid. Unfortunately, she remained frozen and did not communicate her fear. This lack of communication he wrongly equates with implied consent. The judge, she goes on to say, does not understand the meaning of consent under Section 273.1 (1) of the Criminal Code, which was amended in 1992. For him, "consent may be implied or expressed, and clearly in this case we are dealing with implied consent." The term "implied consent" could be used in the context of the defence of mistake of fact where the accused argues that the complainant gave her implied consent through her actions, conduct, or words. McClung sees the case as a mistake of fact case where the defence has an air of reality that is sufficient to raise reasonable doubt on the issue of consent. The trial judge does not consider mistake of fact, wrongly believing that the defence of honest but mistaken belief can only emerge if it comes from the accused himself:

> The trial judge began his analysis with a misunderstanding of the legal test for valid "consent." He then proceeded, wrongly, to equate submission out of fear, where that fear has not been communicated to an accused, with the complainant's implied consent. Not only is this, by itself, an error in law, but the trial judge then compounded these errors by imposing a strictly objective test on the assessment of the fear sustained by the complainant. And then, he went even further by ignoring, as part of the totality of events which transpired here, the legal effect of the "No's" which, according to his own fact findings, the complainant uttered. (50)

What comes next is a lengthy essayistic foray into the context of the 1992 amendments to the Criminal Code (Bill C-49), amendments "designed to promote equality rights and to protect women from the inappropriate use of stereotypical assumptions about women and their sexuality in cases involving sexual assault" (52). These amendments "included new rape shield provisions designed to protect complainants from invasive cross-examination about irrelevant aspects of their past sexual conduct" (54).

After 1992, "the mistake of fact defence is not available to an accused unless he first took 'reasonable steps' to ascertain consent" (56). This qualification shifts the focus "away from the self-conscious wrong-doing of the accused. The new focus is on the culpability inherent in the accused's failure to take reasonable steps to determine if the act he is about to engage in is in fact mutual and consensual" (57). The responsibility to ascertain consent lies with the initiator of sexual activity. Consent is voluntary agreement, and the issue should be "whether the complainant *positively affirmed* her willingness to participate in the subject sexual activity as opposed to whether she *expressly rejected it*" (59). In the old days, the Crown had "to prove that the complainant had expressed her non-consent. In other words, did she say 'No' or give the accused a slap in the face or well-placed knee in the groin or some other incontrovertible overt 'No' signal?" (59). Women are seen to be sexually available all the time, and the default position is assumed to be consent. By 1992 consent means voluntary agreement.

"The real inquiry is whether [the complainant] said 'Yes' (or its equivalent), *either expressly in words or writing or impliedly by her conduct*" (61). "And in order to determine whether she gave either her expressed or implied consent, one must have regard to the *state of mind of the complainant only*" (62). Did she voluntarily agree to engage in the activity? Between actual consent and reasonable belief in consent, there is no other category such as implied consent. The only legitimate term is "*actual consent implied through conduct*" (66). "I would suggest," she writes, "that judges avoid the use of the term 'implied consent' in sexual assault cases so long as the lingering myths of victim resistance continue to find a welcome greeting in some courtrooms in this country" (66). Words or actions must evince or imply a voluntary agreement by the complainant. "Women in Canada are not walking around this country in a state of constant consent to sexual activity unless and until they say 'No' or offer resistance to anyone who targets them for sexual activity" (67).

"Parliament chose to change the approach to consent from a negative notion to a positive notion of sexual mutuality and agreement and its purpose in doing so ought not to be judicially undermined or ignored" (68). Silence or lack of resistance is not to be equated with consent. The trial judge erred in assuming that the complainant had to express her opposition to Ewanchuk's conduct. He based implied consent on what the complainant did not do, but fear inducing submission or lack of resistance need only be subjective, need only be what a reasonable person would have felt. Locked in a trailer with a physically intimidating man who is supposed to be conducting a job interview, this reasonable young woman need not fight back. Saying "no" and "stop" more than once, as she did, is more than enough to indicate lack of consent.

"A woman does not consent to sexual activity in a vacuum. Nor is she in a state of constant consent and subject to sexual contact unless and until she says 'No'" (87). Because the test is subjective – and the judge found that the complainant was afraid – her lack of resistance does not matter. She did not positively consent by words or action; she did not voluntarily agree to engage or to continue to engage in the activity; she said "no" three times; Ewanchuk did not stop doing what he was doing until the third "no" was uttered. "'No' to one level of sexual activity can hardly be taken to mean 'Yes' to an increased level of sexual activity" (93). "No" does not mean "try harder." Once "no" is said, that's it. The man must attain a clear and unequivocal "yes" before doing anything else. "Unless the defence of mistaken belief is a live issue, it is enough that the Crown proves beyond a reasonable doubt that the complainant did not consent to the objectionable sexual conduct" (100).

Sexual assault is touching, in a sexual manner, without consent. There are three possible mental states for the accused: he knows she is not consenting or is wilfully blind to the fact that she is not consenting; he is unsure about whether she is consenting and therefore reckless in pursuing his desires; he mistakenly believes that she is consenting. The first involves criminal intent and knowledge; the second involves recklessness; the third involves mistaken belief.

Only with the defence of mistaken belief does the Crown have to prove *mens rea*, the accused's state of mind. If there is intent, knowledge, wilful blindness, or recklessness in his mind, then he is guilty of the offence. If mistaken belief is guiding his actions, there must be an air of reality to this defence, and the question must emerge as to whether he took reasonable steps to ensure there was consent.

In this case, the trial judge did not consider wilful blindness and recklessness, two alternative states of mind that would prove criminal culpability. He only considered whether Ewanchuk knew the complainant was not consenting. Furthermore, he viewed non-communication of fear and lack of physical resistance as proof that Ewanchuk did not know she wasn't consenting. *Mens rea* for sexual assault includes sexual touching without having first received positive consent. The Crown can prove communication of non-consent, but it can also prove no communication of consent. "The emphasis is not on whether an accused got 'No' or its equivalent (a kick in the groin, a poke in the eye, etc.) but whether he got a 'Yes' or its equivalent" (110). The complainant said "No" on two occasions prior to the final "No," and the judge failed to give legal effect to her words. The message was delivered to Ewanchuk and received by him. Defence of mistake of fact is not available to Ewanchuk because "consenting to give and even receive a back massage is not consent to sexual touching" (114). He thus did not meet the reasonable steps threshold.

Dialogue, Polemic, and Heteroglossia: McClung v. Fraser

In the first line of his judgment McClung says it is has been "an advantage" for him "to have read, in draft, the judgment of Chief Justice Fraser" (1). She is one of the objects of his polemic, and her characterization of Ewanchuk's exoneration as a "perverse acquittal" rankles him.

Just as he was once under the sway of a powerful female, his formidable grandmother Nellie McClung, a leading Canadian feminist and member of the Famous Five, he is now under the sway of another powerful female, his formidable Chief Justice. Even though he says that "every right-minded Canadian, male or female, deplores violence against women" (7), his judgment is a scarcely veiled attack on feminism and political correctness, a series of provocative conclusory remarks rather than detailed legal analyses. Moreover, there is a personal element at play.

The Chief Justice has catalogued what she urges are errors of law in Moore J.'s reasons:

> I do not think it is necessary or prudent to either ally myself to her criticisms or defend the trial reasoning. This is because any suspected errors of law in the trial judgment are overridden by an acquittal which was based on Ewanchuk's lack of proven criminal intent – here an unproven determination on Ewanchuk's part to pursue sex at any cost, including disregard of the complainant's wishes. There is no room to suggest that Ewanchuk knew, yet disregarded, her underlying state of mind as he furthered his romantic intentions. He was not aware of her true state of mind.

Indeed, his ignorance about that was what she wanted. The facts, set forth by the trial judge, provide support for the overriding trial finding, couched in terms of consent by implication, that the accused had no proven preparedness to assault the complainant to get what he wanted. (8)

It would seem that there is indeed room to speculate about what might have been going on in Ewanchuk's mind. He never testified to anything. What he thought can only be inferred from the testimony of others. To conclude that "he was not aware of her true state of mind" is simply to make an assertion. The question, as McClung properly says later, is whether there was "proven preparedness to assault."

Conspicuous is the lack of analysis in McClung's reasons. He says in the next paragraph: "I agree with my colleague, the Chief Justice, that consent by conduct (implied consent) may be invoked as a defence in cases of sexual assault" (9). (She, in fact, as we saw above, argues that implied consent can only arise in the context of a mistake of fact, and she favours banishing the term and replacing it with "actual consent implied by conduct.") "Where we disagree," he continues, "is in her conclusion that implied consent in these cases has no legal footing other than that allowed by the 1992 amendments to the Criminal Code (Bill C-49) which sets the parameters of the defence of 'honest but mistaken belief in consent'" (9). Her conclusion, however, is backed up by rigorous argument. His is merely an assertion: implied consent and honest but mistaken belief in consent "are distinct defences" (9). So he says, but he offers no reasons why and fails entirely to engage with the complex, nuanced arguments of his colleague, arguments that actually confront the niceties of the law.

In sum, McClung is as much making a social statement as giving reasons for his decision. Ewanchuk is *l'homme moyen sensuel*. Driven by hormones, the clumsy oaf went a bit too far, but he did not batter or rape the complainant. His "performance ... led to nothing" (11). To make him the sacrificial victim of feminism, political correctness, and ideological sloganeering would be to stigmatize him forever as a sexual offender.

Fraser is aware of McClung, as we have seen above, and her references to his judgment are mostly ironic. Her parodies of McClung's own words mock and undermine his stylistic flourishes while at the same time demonstrating her intimate knowledge of the decision she is writing against. Before 1992, she writes, the Crown had "to prove that the complainant had expressed her non-consent. In other words, did she say 'No' or give the accused a slap in the face or well-placed knee in the groin or some other incontrovertible overt 'No' signal?" (59). "The emphasis is not on whether an accused got 'No' or its equivalent (a kick in the groin, a poke in the eye, etc.) but whether he got a 'Yes' or its equivalent" (110). For the most part, Fraser does not return rhetorical fire though at times there is a mordant bite to her writing. She simply cannot believe that the trial judge does not see that "No" means "No." Furthermore, his saying that Ewanchuk "stopped" after each "No" and his believing this point to be significant puts her over the edge. If Ewanchuk had stopped, she says, "the complainant would not have ended up with [an] exposed penis stuck between her legs" (97). Appearing in the final sentence of a section on lack of consent, this graphic image is meant to be unsettling. Even if it oversimplifies the legal questions she has so painstakingly addressed, it emphatically reminds us that this case is about sexual assault, not about bonnets and crinolines or making out in the backseat of a car.

The legal world Fraser imagines is very different from McClung's and much more heteroglot. It is a world of assault narrative, dense legal argument, academic discourse, sociological commentary, and public education. It would seem that Fraser believes that when a controversial issue is socially significant, the task of the judge is to educate as well as to adjudicate.

"To deconstruct the several errors in the trial judge's understanding of the law of consent," she writes, "it is necessary to step back and examine the context in which the 1992 amendments to the *Criminal Code*, including those dealing with 'consent,' were passed ... In analysing the effect of these amendments, it is appropriate that the reality of that context – historical, legal, societal, and experiential – be taken into account" (51). Bill C-49 was "designed to promote equality rights and to protect women from the inappropriate use of stereotypical assumptions about women and their sexuality in cases involving sexual assault" (52). What follows is in essence a lengthy academic essay (ca. 3,500 words), buttressed with not only quotations from previous sexual assault decisions but also with quotations from scholarly treatises and articles – among them, *Confronting Sexual Assault: A Decade of Legal and Social Change*, "Judging Sexual Assault Law Against a Standard of Equality," "Bill C-49 and the Politics of Constitutionalized Fault," "The Reform of Sexual Assault Laws," *Convention on the Elimination of All Forms of Discrimination Against Women*, and *Declaration on the Elimination of Violence Against Women*. Like McClung, Fraser is making a social statement, but hers is a statement based on research and scholarship,

not on animadversions against political correctness. I cannot do justice
to her edifying arguments here. Suffice it to say, however, that a judgment comprising ninety-four single-spaced lengthy paragraphs does
not equate with "a precipitately decided sexual assault conviction."

The Decision of the Supreme Court of Canada

Once this matter reaches the Supreme Court, most of the heavy lifting
has already been done by Chief Justice Fraser of the Alberta Court of
Appeal. The Court's decision borrows liberally from her dissent, in-
gesting, as it were, her discourse into its own. Even Justice L'Heureux-
Dubé's disquisition on myths and stereotypes is in some measure a
variation on Fraser's theme.

Writing for the majority, Justice Major bases his narrative on Fraser's
and duplicates her quotations from the trial transcript. I shall not
rehearse his arguments since they are virtually identical to hers.
L'Heureux-Dubé's reasons also echo Fraser's. "Violence against wom-
en," she notes, "is as much a matter of equality as it is an offence against
human dignity and a violation of human rights" (69). In this same paragraph she cites the same case – *R. v. Osolin* – that Fraser cites in paragraph 51 of her dissent. She also refers to the *Convention on the Elimination
of All Forms of Discrimination Against Women* and quotes Articles 1 and 2
of the Convention.

After briefly narrativizing the facts in much the same way as her pre-
decessors narrativized them, L'Heureux-Dubé gets to what she believes
is the heart of the matter. "This case is not about consent, since none
was given. It is about myths and stereotypes" (82). She then quotes
from Archard's *Sexual Consent*, not bothering to note that *R. v. Ewanchuk*
is about unwanted sexual touching, not about rape.

> Myths of rape include the view that women fantasize about being rape
> victims; that women mean "yes" even when they say "no"; that the sexu-
> ally experienced do not suffer harms when raped (or at least suffer lesser
> harms than the sexually "innocent"); that women often deserve to be raped
> on account of their conduct, dress, and demeanour; that rape by a stranger
> is worse than one by an acquaintance. Stereotypes of sexuality include the
> view of women as passive, disposed submissively to surrender to the sex-
> ual advances of active men, the view that sexual love consists in the "pos-
> session" by a man of a woman, and that heterosexual sexual activity is
> paradigmatically penetrative coitus. (82)

Like Fraser, L'Heureux-Dubé believes that one of the judge's roles is that of educator, and she refers to an impressive range of scholarly texts, among them "Rape Myths and Acquaintance Rape," "Possession: Erotic Love and the Law of Rape," *Acquaintance Rape: The Hidden Crime*, *Towards a Feminist Theory of the State*, and *Gender Equality in the Canadian Justice System*. Her real objects of attack, however, are the male judges who

> do not make the basic distinction that consent is a matter of the state of mind of the complainant and belief in consent is ... a matter of the state of mind of the accused. This error does not derive from the findings of fact but from mythical assumptions that when a woman says "no" she is really saying "yes," "try again," or "persuade me" ... It denies women's sexual autonomy and implies that women "are walking around this country in a state of constant consent to sexual activity." (87)

McClung compounds the error by demeaning the complainant ("she did not present herself to Ewanchuk or enter his trailer in a bonnet and crinolines"), by noting that she is an unwed teenage mother who shares an apartment with her boyfriend and another couple, and by insinuating that she is "a person of questionable moral character":

> These comments made by an appellate judge help reinforce the myth that under such circumstances, either the complainant is less worthy of belief, she invited the sexual assault, or her sexual experience signals probable consent to further sexual activity. "Inviting" sexual assault, according to these myths, lessens the guilt of the accused. (89)

She mentions the inappropriateness of applying the term "romantic intentions" to a scenario wherein two strangers are supposedly engaged in a job interview and one of them finds herself trapped in a trailer with a man almost twice her age and size. References to "clumsy passes" and "chivalric behaviour" are "plainly inappropriate in that context as they minimize the importance of the accuser's conduct and the reality of sexual aggression against women" (91). The same goes for McClung's characterization of Ewanchuk's advances as hormonal rather than criminal and his recommendation that a woman should use concerted physical force to repel an unwanted advance should expletives, slaps in the face, or knees in the groin fail. According to McClung, a woman is "not only to express an unequivocal 'no,' but also to fight her way out of such a situation" (93).

Citing various judgments, articles, and books to reinforce her main points, Justice L'Heureux-Dubé lives in a rich intertextual world. Like Fraser, she applauds Bill C-49 and sees the judiciary as a social institution with a duty to inform and edify the public:

> Complainants should be able to rely on a system free from myths and stereotypes, and on a judiciary whose impartiality is not compromised by these biased assumptions ... They should not be permitted to resurface through the stereotypes reflected in the reasons of the majority of the Court of Appeal. It is part of the role of this Court to denounce this kind of language, unfortunately still used today, which not only perpetuates archaic myths and stereotypes about the nature of sexual assault but also ignores the law. (95)

In her contribution to the decision, Justice McLachlin concurs with

> Justice L'Heureux-Dubé that stereotypical assumptions lie at the heart of what went wrong in this case. The specious defence of implied consent ... rests on the assumption that unless a woman protests or resists, she should be "deemed" to consent ... On appeal, the idea also surfaced that if a woman is not modestly dressed, she is deemed to consent. Such stereotypical assumptions find their roots in many cultures, including our own. They no longer, however, find a place in Canadian law. (103)

Conclusions

Judgments are not monologues. They are instances of what Bakhtin calls living heteroglossia, dialogues composed of many social languages. As a case that attracted the attention of the media, *R. v. Ewanchuk* spawned multifarious responses, and the many voices it subsumed and provoked contributed to a heightened awareness across Canada of the standards of consent that pertain to sexual touching. Ironically, perhaps, the main catalyst was McClung himself, the grandson of a famous suffragette.

McClung did not respond well to L'Heureux-Dubé's criticisms. Shortly after the Supreme Court decision was published, he wrote a letter to the *National Post*. As noted earlier, he condemned her "graceless slide into personal invective" and held her feminism responsible for the high suicide rate of Quebec males. Such inappropriate comments published in a national newspaper added a whole new layer to the commentary surrounding this case. McClung made national headlines not only for venting his disrespectful views publicly but also for knowing or not knowing that L'Heureux-Dubé's husband had committed suicide in 1978. Strangely enough, McClung's own father had committed suicide decades before, leaving his son an orphan at the age of thirteen.

What is interesting from a dialogical point of view is that having been accused of being biased, McClung defends himself by reversing the charge, a charge not altogether without merit. Justice L'Heureux-Dubé, however justified, is clearly out to get him, and many of her strongest points pertain to rape, not to unwanted sexual touching. Nevertheless, McClung's charge ought not to have been aired in the media. This case was already receiving considerable attention. On the decision's release, the story made the front page of the *Globe and Mail*, and the headline read "No Means No." McClung's letter and interview gave the case an even higher profile, drawing countless feminists, journalists, editorial writers, newspaper readers, and other concerned citizens into the dialogical fray. Because of the letter and interview, a new agent intervened, and McClung ended up being soundly rebuked by a panel of the Canadian Judicial Council though he was not asked to step down from the bench, the ultimate penalty the panel could have imposed. And so it goes. To do an online search of this case today is to be overwhelmed by a superabundance of voices.

Nevertheless, one voice remains salient, and that voice belongs to the complainant, a young woman whose direct discourse is credible, cogent, and, more importantly, fatal for the trial judge and Justice McClung. The facts were never really in dispute, and since Ewanchuk refused to testify, her version of them appears in every narrativization of the case.

This is not to say that direct discourse always works in favour of the speaker. In *R. v. Harbottle*, as we have seen, the appellant's own chilling words relating to the forcible confinement and murder of the victim are far more condemnatory than any judicial narration of the facts could be.

Like novelists, judges are always making narratological choices. Once Harbottle speaks, his fate is sealed. The more the complainant speaks, the more her terrifying ordeal in the trailer comes to life. Had the trial judge been a calculating and amoral rhetorician whose only purpose was to make his decision convincing, he would never have let her speak.

6 The Look in His Eyes: *Rusk v. State, State v. Rusk*

Edward S. Rusk v. State of Maryland is a sexual assault case from the late 1970s that features multiple and sometimes conflicting discourses.[1] As the headnote says:

> Defendant was convicted ... of rape in the second degree and of assault, and he appealed. The Court of Special Appeals, Thompson, J., held that the evidence was legally insufficient to warrant a conclusion that the defendant's words or actions created in the mind of the victim a reasonable fear that if she resisted, he would have harmed her, or that faced with such resistance, he would have used force to overcome it, notwithstanding the victim's testimony that she was afraid and submitted because of "the look in his eyes," and that after both were undressed and in bed and she pleaded that she wanted to leave, he started to lightly choke her. (624)

Writing for the majority, Judge Thompson reverses the rape conviction but affirms the assault conviction. Writing for the minority, Judge Wilner vehemently dissents:

> The majority have trampled upon the first principle of appellate restraints. Under the guise of judging the sufficiency of the evidence presented against appellant, they have tacitly ... substituted their own view of the evidence for that of the judge and jury. In doing so, they have not only

---

1 Peter Brooks discusses this case in "Narrative Transactions."

improperly invaded the province allotted to those tribunals, but, at the
same time, have perpetuated and given new life to myths about the crime
of rape that have no place in our law today. (629)

The case proceeded to the Court of Appeals of Maryland. Writing for
the majority, Chief Judge Murphy reversed Judge Thompson's decision
and held that the evidence was sufficient to permit the trier of fact to
find the defendant guilty of rape. Writing for the minority, Judge Cole
argues that the previous court was right: the evidence was insufficient
to convict Rusk of rape. In Cole's discourse exempla go viral. He cites
and summarizes almost two dozen cases. He also makes the edifying
comment that the assault victim "certainly had to realize that [she and
the appellant] were not going upstairs to play Scrabble" (734).

Rusk was sentenced by the trial court to concurrent terms of ten
years for rape and five years for assault. At the Court of Special Appeals, presided over by Judge Thompson, Rusk did not challenge the
sufficiency of the evidence supporting the assault conviction. Only
Judge Wilner notices this curiosity. "It would seem," he remarks in a
footnote, "that if there was not enough evidence of force, or lack of
consent, to permit the rape conviction, there was an equal insufficiency
to support the assault conviction" (636). Because Rusk put forward no
challenge to the assault conviction, "the majority is spared ... the need
to deal with that thorny dilemma" (636).

As we have seen in other instances, factual narratives have persuasive power. If one side's version of the facts and framing of the issues
prevail, that side is likely to win. All conclusions are foregone conclusions once we have selected our enabling premises. This is why the law
is so scrupulous about what stories get to be told in court. Stories that
may prejudice jurors are often excluded – stories, for example, that involve convictions for past crimes similar to the alleged crime currently
before the court. In Rusk Judges Thompson and Wilner are both working with essentially the same set of facts, the set of facts found by the
trial judge, but they put radically different spins on these facts, deploy
markedly different strategies of inclusion and exclusion, and create
strikingly different portraits of the victim, who, it would seem, is as
much on trial as the appellant. These contrasting narrativizations are
crucial; they compel the legal reasoning that follows in their wake. The
conclusion arrived at is already implicit in the story told, and even
though precedents are cited and reasons elaborated, much of the argumentative labour is being done by narrative.

Narrative Strategizing: Thompson v. Wilner

Writing in dissent, Wilner has the advantage of having the majority opinion before him. What he presents on one level is a rhetorical and narratological critique of its shortcomings. He is thus able to fashion his own version of the facts in the light of those perceived shortcomings. Neither Wilner nor Thompson, however, tells the whole story. Details are included or excluded in accordance with their own argumentative exigencies.

Thompson starts with his conclusion: the evidence supporting Rusk's conviction for rape is insufficient. However, as noted above, since Rusk did not challenge the conviction for assault, the court has no choice but to affirm the assault conviction. According to Thompson:

> The prosecutrix was a twenty-one year old mother of a two-year old son. She was separated from her husband but not yet divorced. Leaving her son with her mother, she attended a high school reunion after which she and a female friend, Terry, went bar hopping in the Fells Point area of Baltimore. They drove in separate cars. At the third bar the prosecutrix met the appellant. (625)

Thompson identifies the victim of the assault, Pat, as the prosecutrix. He never refers to her by name. He never refers to Rusk by name either. Rusk is always the appellant. This lack of familiarity is meant to convey neutrality. Thompson points out that Pat is separated but not divorced. Why is this fact relevant? Is he implying that separated women have looser moral standards than married women? He also describes her behaviour as "bar hopping," hardly a neutral term. Are she and Terry women on the prowl, out for a night on the town, out to drink to excess and maybe even to find a man? The inferences are not explicitly drawn, but at the very least, Pat is portrayed as a mother who leaves her two-year-old son at home to go bar hopping. Also inexplicit is the reason why she and Terry drove in separate cars. Are they assuming they will be leaving the bar in the company of somebody else?

Wilner notes that "Judge Thompson recounts most, but not all, of the victim's story" (631). For Wilner she is a victim, not a prosecutrix:

> The victim – I'll call her Pat – attended a high school reunion. She had arranged to meet her girlfriend Terry there. The reunion was over at 9:00, and Terry asked her to Fell's Point. [A footnote tells us this is an old section

of Baltimore extensively renovated as part of urban renewal in the 1970s, an upscale place by the harbour now a part of the city's night scene.] Pat had gone to Fell's Point with Terry on a few prior occasions, explaining in court: "I've never met anybody [there] I've gone out with. I met people in general, talking in conversation, most of the time people that Terry knew, not that I have gone down there, and met people at dates." She agreed to go, but first called her mother, who was babysitting Pat's two-year old son, to tell her that she was going with Terry to Fell's Point and that she would not be home late. It was just after 9:00 when Pat and Terry, in their separate cars, left for Fell's Point alone. [A footnote tells us that Pat and Terry lived at opposite ends of town and that Fell's Point was midway between their respective homes.] (631)

As noted, Wilner identifies Pat not only by name but also by her status as victim. He humanizes her and goes to some length to suggest that she is a responsible mother, not a woman out on the town drinking to excess and looking for male companionship. He lets her speak in her own voice to reinforce the point that her motives for going to the bar were not to hook up with an eligible male. He also notes that Terry initiated the rendezvous and that Pat attended to her parental responsibilities by calling her mother and saying she would not be home late. We are also told why Pat and Terry left the reunion in separate cars – they lived at opposite ends of town – a fact strategically omitted by Thompson. The additional facts supplied by Wilner can hardly be said to be central to the case, but they do dispel the impression engendered by Thompson's terse descriptions, descriptions that evoke carefree exuberance on the part of barhopping young women possibly out for erotic adventure.

Thompson relates how Terry and the victim ended up talking to Rusk at the bar. Pat had never met him before but Terry knew him, only casually, as is later revealed:

[The appellant and prosecutrix] had a five or ten minute conversation in the bar; at the end of which the prosecutrix said she was ready to leave. Appellant requested a ride home and she agreed. (625)

These two sentences omit significant details about the time frame and the number of drinks consumed. Thompson's narrative corresponds with the impression he has been trying to convey. After a few minutes of conversation, Pat has found what she is looking for – an eligible man to go off with.

Wilner describes things differently:

> [Pat and Terry] went to a place called Helen's and had one drink. They stayed an hour or so and then walked down to another place (where they had another drink), stayed about a half hour there, and went to a third place. Up to this point, Pat conversed only with Terry, and did not strike up any other acquaintanceships. Pat and Terry were standing against a wall when appellant came over and said hello to Terry, who was conversing with someone else at the time. Appellant then began to talk with Pat. They were both separated, they both had young children; and they spoke about those things. Pat said that she had been ready to leave when the appellant came on the scene, and that she only talked with him for five or ten minutes. It was then about midnight. Pat had to get up with her baby in the morning and did not want to stay out late.
>
> Terry wasn't ready to leave. As Pat was preparing to go, appellant asked if she would drop him off on her way home. She agreed because she thought he was a friend of Terry's. She told him however, as they walked to her car "I'm just giving a ride home, you know, as a friend, not anything to be, you know, thought of other than a ride." He agreed to that condition. (631)

Wilner's rhetorical strategy consists of adding narrative details that shut down inferences that might be drawn from Thompson's account. Pat and Terry have one drink at Helen's, a name that conjures up the face that launched a thousand ships rather than a sleazy pick-up joint. They then have a drink in two other places. Wilner stresses that Pat conversed only with Terry; she was not trying to interact with anyone else. Rusk meets Pat through Terry, whom he had met previously and knew by name. What Pat did not know at the time was that Terry knew little more about Rusk than his name.

That Pat and Rusk talk about the trials of separation and young children is significant. From Pat's point of view, Rusk is a fellow parent, not a predatory male on the make. Pat wants to leave because she is concerned about getting up with her "baby" in the morning, the noun "baby" having more sentimental resonance than "son" or "boy," a point not lost on Wilner in his choice of diction. She agrees to give Rusk a ride home and makes it clear that romance is not on the table.

After the two arrive at Rusk's place, according to Thompson:

> The prosecutrix parked at the curb on the side of the street opposite his rooming house but did not turn off the ignition. She put the car in park and appellant asked her to come up to his apartment. She refused. He continued to ask her to come up, and she testified that she then became afraid. While trying to convince him that she didn't want to go to his apartment she mentioned that she was separated and if she did, it might cause her marital problems particularly if she were being followed by a detective. (625)

That Pat might be under the surveillance of a detective is not a detail that appears in Wilner's narrative. He too is not without his sins of omission. In Thompson's account, the fact of surveillance seems to suggest that being caught in an adulterous situation is of more concern to Pat than committing an adulterous act. That she has no interest other than giving the supposed friend of a friend a ride home and getting back to her baby is overshadowed by the possibility of a furtive detective lurking in the background, camera in hand, waiting for the commission of a sexual act.

Wilner's narrative stresses that Pat was in a strange place, surely an important fact:

> Pat was completely unfamiliar with the appellant's neighbourhood. She had no idea where she was. When she pulled up to where the appellant said he lived, she put the car in park, but left the engine running. She said to appellant, "Well, here, you know, you are home." Appellant then asked Pat to come up with him and she refused. He persisted in his request, as she did in her refusal. (631)

None of the four opinions specifies what sort of neighbourhood Rusk lived in. However, Thompson describes Rusk's place first as a "rooming house" (625) and later as "a rowhouse" (625). In addition to the subsequent revelation that the room was not Rusk's principal residence but a room he shared with a friend as a "pit stop" (723), the descriptors "rooming house" and "rowhouse" suggest that this was not an affluent middle-class neighbourhood. Not for nothing was the television series *Homicide: Life on the Streets* set in Baltimore. That series was based on David Simons's book *Homicide: A Year on the Killing Streets*, a book that was also the basis for Simons's own series, *The Wire*. In the 1970s

Baltimore was notorious for its poverty and crime. A young woman in a strange and unfamiliar area of the city would have good cause to be apprehensive, especially when trying to deal with a persistent young man refusing to accept that "no" means "no."

Thompson continues:

> The appellant then took the keys out of the car and walked over to her side of the car, opened the door and said, "Now will you come up?" The prosecutrix then told him she would. (625)

Thompson then cites the direct discourse of the victim.

> At that point, because I was scared, because he had my car keys, I didn't know what to do. I was some place I didn't even know where I was. It was in the city. I didn't know whether to run. I really didn't think at that point, what to do. Now, I know I should have blown the horn. I should have run. There were a million things I could have done. I was scared, at that point, and I didn't do any of them. (625)

No doubt Thompson believes that this testimony is inculpatory – Pat now knows that she should have done something proactive – but as we saw with the complainant in *Ewanchuk*, it is sometimes dangerous for a judge to use the direct discourse of a victim. To my mind, Pat's testimony is credible. Her terse sentences appear to be unrehearsed. Her jerky style evokes the genuine fear of a young woman in an unknown place in a dangerous city, a woman whose best means of escape, her car, is now unavailable to her. Blowing the horn in a possibly sketchy urban neighbourhood or trying to run away from a possibly violent predator might have subjected her to more harm than would acquiescing to Rusk's demand to follow him up to the room.

Thompson continues:

> The prosecutrix followed appellant into the rowhouse, up the stairs, and into the apartment. When they got into appellant's room, he said that he had to go to the bathroom and left the room for a few minutes. The prosecutrix made no attempt to leave. When appellant came back, he sat on the bed while she sat on the chair next to the bed. He started to pull her onto the bed and also began to remove her blouse. She stated she took off her slacks and removed his clothing because "he asked [her] to do it." After they both undressed, prosecutrix stated:

"I was still begging him to please let, you know, let me leave. I said, 'you can get a lot of other girls down there, for what you want,' and he just kept saying, 'no,' and then I was really scared, because I can't describe, you know, what was said. It was more the look in his eyes; and I said, at that point – I didn't know what to say; and I said, 'If I do what you want, will you let me go without killing me?' Because I didn't know, at that point, what he was going to do; and I started to cry; and when I did, he put his hands on my throat, and started lightly to choke me; and I said, 'If I do what you want, will you let me go?' And he said, yes, and at that time, I proceeded to do what he wanted me to."

She stated that she performed oral sex and they then had sexual inter-course. (625–6)

Again, the use of direct discourse is a questionable move on Thompson's part, given the interpretation he wishes to impose on the facts. When someone says "If I do what you want, will you let me go without killing me?," the words are not suggestive of a consensual situation; indeed, they emphatically suggest the contrary. So does Rusk's starting "lightly to choke [her]." Nevertheless, Thompson concludes "that in all of the *victim's* testimony we have been unable to see any resistance on her part to the sex acts and certainly we can see no fear as would overcome her attempt to resist or escape" (626, my emphasis). His inadvertent use of "victim" instead of "prosecutrix" perhaps subconsciously betrays his own uneasiness about his portrayal of the case.

Like Justice McClung, Judge Thompson has an affection for paralipsis, the trope of feigned omission, the trope through which one says what one has to say under the guise of not saying it. As an intermediate appellate judge in the State of Maryland, Thompson is required by law to view the evidence in the light most favourable to the prosecution. Nevertheless, he cannot resist saying that Rusk and two of his friends testified. "Their testimony painted the episode in a manner more favourable to the accused, but there is no need for us to recite that testimony because ... we are obligated to view the evidence in the light most favorable to the prosecution" (626). In truth, it is not a question of not needing to recite the testimony, but of not being permitted to recite it. Thompson is debarred from discussing exculpatory evidence issuing from the appellant, but he makes sure the reader knows it exists.

Wilner concedes that Pat followed Rusk into the rowhouse:

Finally, [Rusk] reached over, turned off the ignition, took her keys, got out of the car, came round to her side, and said to her, "Now, will you come up?"

   It was at this point that Pat followed appellant to his apartment, and it is at this point that the majority of the Court begins to substitute its judgment for that of the jury. (631)

Wilner's next move is a narratological *tour de force*. He steps outside of the continuous narrative he has been unfolding and foregrounds the constructedness and artificiality of all narratives, especially assault narratives that are second-hand reconstructions of what was said in the court of first instance:

We know nothing about Pat and appellant. We don't know how big they are, what they look like, what their life experiences have been. We don't know if appellant is larger or smaller than she, stronger or weaker. We don't know what the inflection was in his voice as he dangled her car keys in front of her. We can't tell whether this was in a jocular vein or a truly threatening one. We have no idea what his mannerisms were. The trial judge and the jury could discern some of these things, of course, because they could observe the two people in court and could listen to what they said and how they said it. But all we know is that, between midnight and 1:00 a.m., in a neighborhood that was strange to Pat, appellant took her car keys, demanded that she accompany him, and most assuredly implied that unless she did so, at the very least, she might be stranded. (631–2)

What Wilner calls "interrupt[ing] the tale for a moment and consider[ing] the situation" is a brilliant rhetorical tactic (632). It calls attention to the selective nature of the facts presented by any appellate judge, including himself, a judge who has no access to the demeanour of the witnesses – their tonalities, gestures, mannerisms, and body language. Wilner goes on to quote the same piece of Pat's testimony that Thompson does, but quotes more, not cutting her off after the seemingly inculpatory admission that there were a million things she could have done:

"There were a million things I could have done. I was scared, at that point, and I didn't do any of them." What, counsel asked, was she afraid of?

"Him," she replied. What was she scared that he was going to do? "Rape me, but I didn't say that. It was the way he looked at me, and said, 'Come on up, come on up'; and when he took the keys, I knew that was wrong. I just didn't say, are you going to rape me?" (632)

One can see why Thompson left out this testimony. It puts the events in a light unfavourable to Rusk. Uttered under oath to a jury, the words of a young woman expressing her fear she is about to be raped by a man who has taken the keys to her car would have a powerful impact. By omitting much of Pat's direct discourse and quoting "it was the way he looked at me" out of context, Thompson makes her fear seem subjective and unreasonable.

Wilner continues:

So Pat accompanied appellant to his apartment. As Judge Thompson points out, appellant left her in his apartment for a few minutes. Although there was evidence of a telephone in the room, Pat said that, at the time, she didn't notice one. When appellant returned, he turned off the light and sat on the bed. Pat was in a chair. She testified: "I asked him if I could leave, that I wanted to go home, and I didn't want to come up. I said, 'Now, I came up. Can I go?'" Appellant, who, of course, still had her keys, said that he wanted her to stay. He told her to get on the bed with him, and, in fact, took her arms and pulled her on to the bed. He then started to undress her; he removed her blouse and bra and unzipped her pants. *At his direction*, she removed his clothes. She then said:

"I was still begging him to please let, you know, let me leave. I said, 'you can get a lot of other girls down there, for what you want,' and he just kept saying, 'no,' and then I was really scared, because I can't describe, you know, what was said. It was more the look in his eyes; and I said, at that point – I didn't know what to say; and I said, 'If I do what you want, will you let me go without killing me?' Because I didn't know, at that point, what he was going to do; and I started to cry; and when I did, he put his hands on my throat, and started lightly to choke me; and I said, 'If I do what you want, will you let me go?' And he said, yes, and at that time, I proceeded to do what he wanted me to." He "made me perform oral sex, and then sexual intercourse." (632)

For obvious reasons Wilner stresses the fact that Pat removes Rusk's clothing at his direction. She is not a willing participant in this encounter.

Convincing the reader of her lack of consent is at the core of Wilner's argument. Thus he reminds us yet again that Rusk "still had her keys." Thompson's account of how the two became disrobed and had sex reads: "She stated she took off her slacks and removed his clothing because 'he asked [her] to do it' ... She stated she performed oral sex and then they *had* sexual intercourse" (626, my emphasis). Thompson's indirect discourse has a very different impact than Pat's direct discourse: she says that he "*made* me perform oral sex, and then sexual intercourse" (my emphasis). Normal people *have* sex; rapists *make* people submit to sex without their consent and against their will.

Thompson's narrative stops after Pat leaves, refuses to give Rusk her telephone number, and says she might see him at Fell's Point some time. Wilner's narrative takes the story further. With a constructed narrative, where one chooses to begin and end is as significant as the details one chooses to include or exclude.

After Rusk returned her car keys and escorted her to her car, she drove off. Wilner lets her tell the story in her own words and then critiques the majority's construction of the events:

> "I stopped at a gas station, that I believe was Amoco or Exon (sic), and went to the ladies' room. From there I drove home. I don't know – I don't know if I rode around for a while or not; but I know I went home, pretty much straight home and pulled up and parked the car.
> "I was just going to go home, and not say anything.
> "Q Why?
> "A *Because I didn't want to go through what I'm going through now.*
> "Q What, in fact did you do then?
> "A I sat in the car, thinking about it a while, and I thought I wondered what would happen if I hadn't of done what he wanted me to do. So I thought the right thing to do was to go report it, and I went from there to Hillendale to find a police car." (633, emphasis supplied by Wilner)

Pat's direct discourse is revealing. Her decision to report the rape was neither precipitously made nor emotionally driven. She reported it some two hours after the incident. She also seems well aware that testifying in court will be an ordeal, an ordeal that puts her on trial. Moreover, her motives appear to be altruistic. The violence that Rusk might inflict on future victims is what convinces her to do "the right thing." The ungrammaticality of "I thought I wondered what would happen if I hadn't of done what he wanted me to do" shows Pat to be a forthright person. She seems neither designing nor calculating, and Wilner recognizes the persuasive value of giving her a voice. He also recognizes the persuasive value of his own authoritative voice:

> How does the majority Opinion view these events? It starts by noting that Pat was a 21-year old mother who was separated from her husband but not yet divorced, as though that had some significance. To me, it has none, except perhaps (when coupled with the further characterization that Pat and Terry had gone "bar hopping") to indicate an underlying suspicion, for which there is absolutely no support in the record, that Pat was somehow "on the make." Even more alarming, and unwarranted, however, is the majority's analysis of Pat's initial reflections on whether to report what had happened. Ignoring completely her statement that she "didn't want to go through what I'm going through now," the majority, in footnote 1, cavalierly and without any foundation whatever, says:
>
> "If, in quiet contemplation after the act, she had to wonder what would have happened, her submission on the side of prudence seems hardly justified. Indeed, if *she* had to wonder afterward, how can a fact finder reasonably conclude that she was justifiably in fear sufficient to overcome her will to resist, at the time." (Emphasis in the original.)
>
> It is this type of reasoning – if indeed "reasoning" is the right word for it – that is particularly distressing. The concern expressed by Pat, made even more real by the majority Opinion of this Court, is one that is common among rape victims, and largely accounts for the fact that most incidents of forcible rape go unreported by the victim. (633)

Unlike Thompson, Wilner looks at the broader social picture of rape and its victims.

Logical Strategizing: Thompson v. Wilner

Both judges agree that the Court of Appeals of Maryland last spoke on the amount of force required to support a rape conviction in *Hazel v. State* (1960). According to the only part of *Hazel* that Thompson quotes:

> Force is an essential element of the crime and to justify a conviction, the evidence must warrant a conclusion either that the victim resisted and her resistance was overcome by force or that she was prevented from resisting by threats to her safety. (626)

Thompson's conclusion is unequivocal.

> In all of the victim's testimony we have been unable to see any resistance on her part to the sex acts and certainly can we see no fear as would overcome her attempt to resist or escape as required by *Hazel*. Possession of the keys by the accused may have deterred her vehicular escape but hardly a departure seeking help in the rooming house or in the street. We must say that "the way he looked" fails utterly to support the fear required by *Hazel*. (626)

A later decision, *Winegan v. State* (1970), says that in cases where there is no visible evidence of wounds, bruises, disordered clothing, or the like, "the lack of consent could be shown by fear based on reasonable apprehension" (627). For Thompson, "the evidence that the accused 'started lightly to choke me' as well as the circumstances of being in a somewhat strange part of town late at night were [not] sufficient to overcome the will of a normal twenty-one year old married woman" (627). He is "not impressed with the argument [from lack of consent and reasonable fear] ... Whatever appeal this argument might have in other cases, it has none here where there is nothing whatsoever to indicate that the victim was anything but a normal, intelligent, twenty-one year old, *vigorous* female" (627, my emphasis). Paraliptically speaking, the chauvinism implicit in portraying the victim as a libidinally energetic person capable of fending for herself need not be mentioned.

Thompson cites *Farrer v. the United States* (1959), a case that precedes *Hazel* and thus is not binding. In *Farrer* the judge addresses the issues of what constitutes reasonable fear and non-consent when force is absent.

> As I understand the law of rape, if no force is used and the girl in fact acquiesces, the acquiescence may nevertheless be deemed to be non-consent if it is induced by fear; but the fear, to be sufficient for this purpose, must be based upon something of substance; and furthermore the fear must be of death or severe bodily harm. A girl cannot simply say, "I was scared," and thus transform an apparent consent into a legal non-consent which makes the man's act a capital offence. She must have a reasonable apprehension, as I understand the law, of something real; her fear must be not fanciful but substantial. (627–8)

After exploring others cases that recognize the reasonable apprehension rule, Thompson comes to the incredible conclusion that "lightly choking" could signify a "heavy caress":

> Applying this reasoning to the record before us, we find the evidence le-
> gally insufficient to warrant a conclusion that appellant's words or actions
> created in the mind of the victim a reasonable fear that if she resisted, he
> would have harmed her, or that faced with such resistance, he would have
> used force to overcome it. The prosecutrix stated that she was afraid, and
> submitted because of "the look in his eyes." After both were undressed
> and in the bed, and she pleaded to him that she wanted to leave, he started
> to lightly choke her. At oral argument it was brought out that the "lightly
> choking" could have been a heavy caress. We do not believe that "lightly
> choking" along with all the facts and circumstances in the case, were suf-
> ficient to cause a reasonable fear which overcame her ability to resist. In
> the absence of any other evidence showing force used by appellant, we
> find that the evidence was insufficient to convict appellant of rape. (628)

Again he is inconsistent and lets the term "victim" slip into a discourse
that preponderantly uses the term "prosecutrix." "Caress" is a word with
connotations of intimacy, affection, and gentleness. That light choking
can be seen as a heavy caress strains credibility, even as an oxymoron.
Caresses, by definition, are light, not heavy. A caress is "a gentle touch
or gesture of fondness, tenderness, or love." To caress is

1 To touch or stroke in an affectionate or loving manner.
2 To touch or move as if with a caress …
3 To treat fondly, kindly, or favourably; cherish. (thefreedictionary
   .com/caress)

More important, however, is what Thompson does not do: namely,
analyse *Hazel* itself. It is strange that an appellate judge should ignore
the binding precedent.

After noting that "the majority have trampled upon the first principle of appellate restraint … [by] substituting their own view of the evidence … for that of the judge and jury" (629), Wilner, unlike Thompson,
engages in legal analysis. He points out that the principles of law that
govern this case are whether there was enough evidence for the find-
er of fact to conclude that the appellant was guilty beyond a reasonable doubt and whether that evidence meets the legal requirements for
the crime of second degree rape. "A person is guilty of rape in the second degree if he (1) engages in vaginal intercourse with another person, (2) by force or threat of force, (3) against the will, and (4) without
the consent of the other person" (629). The evidence, Wilner notes, was

sufficient to show that the appellant had vaginal intercourse with the victim and that the sexual encounter took place against her will and without her consent. At issue is whether the intercourse was accomplished by force or threat of force. As Wilner emphatically puts it, *"consent is not the issue here, only whether there was sufficient evidence of force or the threat of force.* Unfortunately, courts ... often tend to confuse these two elements – force and lack of consent – and to think of them as one. They are not. They mean and require different things" (629).

He goes on to say that what seems to cause the confusion "is the notion that the victim must actively resist the attack upon her ... The focus is almost entirely on the extent of resistance – *the victim's acts, rather than those of the assailant"* (629). However illogical this focus might be, "it seems to be the current state of the Maryland law" (629), and Wilner accepts it as binding:

> But what is required of a woman being attacked or in danger of attack? How much resistance must she offer? Where is that line to be drawn between requiring that she either risk serious physical harm, perhaps death, on the one hand, or be termed a willing partner on the other? (629–30)

Turning to *Hazel* and citing it at some length, Wilner directs our attention to subtleties bypassed in Thompson's quotation of but a single sentence from the opinion: "Force is an essential element of the crime and to justify a conviction, the evidence must warrant a conclusion either that the victim resisted and her resistance was overcome by force or that she was prevented from resisting by threats to her safety" (630). What Thompson does not tell us is that *Hazel* goes on to say that "no particular amount of force, actual or constructive, is required to constitute rape" (630). The court must look to the particular circumstances of the case. In the rape scenario discussed in *Hazel,* the court came to the conclusion that force existed without violence. As *Hazel* notes:

> *If the acts and threats of the defendant were reasonably calculated to create in the mind of the victim – having regard to the circumstances in which she was placed – a real apprehension, due to fear, of imminent bodily harm, serious enough to impair or overcome her will to resist, then such acts and threats are the equivalent of force ...*
>
> With respect to the presence or absence of the element of consent, it is true, of course, that however reluctantly given, consent to the act at any time prior to penetration deprives the subsequent intercourse of its

criminal character. *There is, however, a wide difference between consent and a submission to the act. Consent may involve submission, but submission does not necessarily imply consent. Furthermore, submission to a compelling force, or as a result of being put in fear, is not consent ...*

The authorities are by no means in accord as to what degree of resistance is necessary to establish the absence of consent. However, the generally accepted doctrine seems to be that a female – who was conscious and possessed of her natural, mental and physical powers when the attack took place – must have resisted to the extent of her ability at the time, unless it appears that she was overcome by numbers or was so terrified by threats as to overpower her will to resist ... Since resistance is necessarily relative, the presence or absence of it must depend on the facts and circumstances in each case ... *But the real test, which must be recognized in all cases, is whether the assault was committed without the consent and against the will of the prosecuting witness.*

The kind of fear which would render resistance by a woman unnecessary to support a conviction of rape includes, but is not necessarily limited to, a fear of death or serious bodily harm, or a fear so extreme as to preclude resistance, or a fear which would well nigh render her mind incapable of continuing to resist, or a fear that so overpowers her that she does not dare resist. (cited by Wilner at 630, his emphasis)

In the case at bar, Wilner maintains, Rusk's acts and words were reasonably calculated to create in the mind of the victim a real apprehension of imminent bodily harm and were thus the equivalent of force. Her fear was reasonable, and her submission was not the equivalent of consent. Sex was imposed upon her without her consent and against her will:

The concern expressed by Pat, [that reporting the rape would subject her to more suffering at trial], made even more real by the majority Opinion of this Court, is one that is common among rape victims, and largely accounts for the fact that most incidents of forcible rape go unreported by the victim. *See F.B.I. Uniform Crime Reports* (1978), p. 14; *Report of Task Force on Rape Control*, Baltimore County (1975); *The Treatment of Rape Victims In The Metropolitan Washington Area*, Metropolitan Washington Council of Governments (1976), p. 4. *See also Rape And Its Victims: A Report for Citizens, Health Facilities, and Criminal Justice Agencies*, LEAA (1975). If appellant had desired, and Pat had given, her wallet instead of her body, there would be no question about appellant's guilt of robbery. Taking the car keys under those circumstances would certainly have supplied the requisite threat of force or violence and negated the element of consent. No one would seriously contend that because she failed to raise a hue and cry she had consented to the theft of her money. Why then is such life-threatening action necessary when it is her personal dignity that is being stolen? (633)

That theft is taken more seriously than sexual assault appalls Wilner. Like Justices Fraser and L'Heureux-Dubé, Judge Wilner goes beyond the law and delves into sociology and criminology, seeing his role as an officer of the court to be educative as well as adjudicative. Like his Canadian counterparts, he believes that the taboos and myths surrounding rape must be demystified:

Rape has always been considered a most serious crime, one that traditionally carried the heaviest penalty. But until recently, it remained shrouded in the taboos and myths of a Victorian age, and little real attention was given to how rapes occur, how they may be prevented, and how a victim can best protect herself from injury when an attack appears inevitable. The courts are as responsible for this ignorance and the misunderstandings emanating from it as any other institution in society, and it is high time that they recognize reality. (633)

He points out that the *F.B.I Uniform Crime Reports* show that rape is on the increase, that physical force is absent in over half of the reported cases, and that in one-third of the cases no weapon is involved. Noting that verbal resistance is resistance, Wilner states that FBI statistics show that rape victims who physically resisted are more likely to be injured than ones who did not. In fact, "the United States Department of Justice … has published a pamphlet that warns, among other things:

"If you are confronted by a rapist, stay calm and maximize your chances for escape. *Think* through what you will do. You should not *immediately* try to fight back. Chances are, your attacker has the advantage. Try to stay calm and take stock of the situation."

Where does this leave us but where we started? A judge and a jury, observing the witnesses and hearing their testimony, concluded without dissent that there was sufficient evidence to find beyond a reasonable doubt that appellant had sexual intercourse with Pat by force or threat of force against her will and without her consent; in other words, that the extent of her resistance and the reasons for her failure to resist further were reasonable. No claim is made here that the jury was misinstructed on the law of rape. Yet a majority of this Court, without the ability to see and hear the witnesses, has simply concluded that, in *their* judgment, Pat's fear was not a reasonable one, or that there was no fear at all (a point that appellant conceded at oral argument before the Court *en banc*). In so doing, they have ignored the fact of a young woman alone in a strange neighborhood at 1:00 in the morning with a man who had taken her keys and was standing at her open car door demanding that she come with him; they have ignored that she offered the very type of verbal resistance that is prudent, common, and recommended by law enforcement agencies; they have ignored that the reasonableness of Pat's apprehension is inherently a question of fact for the jury to determine. (635)

Chief Judge Murphy v. Judge Cole

Judge Murphy's account of the facts is more akin to Wilner's than to Thompson's. He says Pat and Terry went to Fell's Point "to have a few drinks" (721) and cites virtually the same portions of Pat's direct discourse that Wilner cites. New details, however, do emerge. We are told that Terry corroborated Pat's testimony and said Pat "was drinking screwdrivers that night but normally did not finish a drink" (721). Terry also "testified about her acquaintanceship with Rusk: 'I knew his face, and his first name, but I honestly couldn't tell you ... how I know him. I don't know him very well at all'" (722). We also learn that Officer Hammett received the rape complaint at 3:15 a.m. and accompanied Pat to Rusk's apartment. The officer entered the multi-dwelling apartment house and arrested Rusk in a room on the second floor. Hammett testified that Pat was sober and that an examination at the hospital "disclosed that seminal fluid and spermatozoa were detected in Pat's vagina, on her underpants, and on the bed sheets recovered from Rusk's room" (723). The trial court judge denied Rusk's motion for a judgment of acquittal. His decision foregrounded the forcible taking of the car keys, the look in Rusk's eyes that put Pat in fear, Rusk's starting "to strangle her softly" after she begged him to let her leave, and her plea to him not to kill her if she submitted. The trial court judge concludes that even though "there was no weapon, no physical threatening testified to" (723), Rusk's actions were the equivalent of force; he had sex with Pat without her consent and against her will.

At this higher level of appeal, evidence favourable to the defendant, Rusk, is permissible, and Judge Murphy notes that Rusk and two of his friends, Michael Trimp and David Carroll, testified on the defendant's behalf. The friends said that the three of them went to the bar to dance, drink, and try "to pick up some ladies" (723). Trimp and Carroll left to get something to eat, and when they returned Rusk was walking down the street arm-in-arm with a woman and told them that she was giving him a ride home. When Trimp returned around two to the "pit stop" (723) he and Rusk rented as a place in which to crash after partying downtown, Rusk was alone in the room.

Rusk testified that earlier in the evening he and Pat talked about their marital situations and their children. He said that Pat asked him if he was going to rape or beat her because she had been raped before and her husband used to beat her. He claimed that she turned off the ignition and removed the keys. He describes a scene of seduction – petting leading to kissing leading to intercourse. After Pat willingly came to his room, he sat on the bed across from her and reached out

> and started to put my arms around her, and started kissing her and we fell back into the bed, and she – we were petting, kissing, and she stuck her hand down in my pants and started playing with me; and I undid her blouse, and took off her bra; and then I sat up and I said "Let's take our clothes off"; and she said, "Okay"; and I took my clothes off, and she took her clothes off; and then we proceeded to have intercourse. (724)

Pat "got uptight" after the intercourse and "started to cry" (724). She then walked out with Rusk to her car and left. Rusk denied using force or threats of force to get Pat to have intercourse with him.

Chief Judge Murphy rehearses what went on in the lower courts. For him, the applicable standard is "whether, after viewing the evidence in the light most favorable to the prosecution, *any* rational trier of fact could have found the essential elements of the crime beyond a reasonable doubt" (725). Once it is established that vaginal intercourse took place, the remaining elements of rape in the second degree are force – actual or constructive – and lack of consent.

In *Hazel* common law rape is defined as "the act of a man having unlawful carnal knowledge of a female over the age of ten years by force without the consent and against the will of the victim" (725). It is interesting, indeed frightening, to note that at the time of the judgment the age of consent in Maryland was ten. In *Hazel v. State*, Hazel followed the victim into her home,

> put his arm around her neck, said he had a gun, and threatened to shoot her baby if she moved. Although she never saw the gun, Hazel kept one hand in his pocket, and repeatedly stated that he had a gun. He robbed the prosecutrix, tied her hands, and took her into the cellar. (725)

He ordered her to lie on the floor and then had intercourse with her while her hands were tied. "The victim testified that she did not struggle because she was afraid for her life" (725). The question was whether her failure to struggle and resist amounted to consent in law. The Court noted that the judges who heard the evidence, and who sat as the trier of fact in this non-jury case, concluded that "in light of the defendant's acts of violence and threats of serious harm, there existed a genuine and continuing fear of such harm on the victim's part, so that the ensuing act of sexual intercourse under this fear 'amounted to a felonious and forcible act of the defendant against the will and consent of the prosecuting witness'" (726). The issue "was one of credibility, properly to be resolved by the trial court" (726). Murphy applies this reasoning to *Rusk* and echoes Judge Wilner's sentiments that the majority decision of the Special Court of Appeals "trampled upon the first principle of appellate restraint" – deference to the trial court on questions of fact. "The reasonableness of Pat's apprehension of fear was plainly a question of fact for the jury to determine" (727). "It was for the jury to observe the witnesses and their demeanour, and to judge their credibility, and weigh their testimony. Quite obviously, the jury disbelieved Rusk and believed Pat's testimony" (727). "Just where persuasion ends and force begins in cases like the present is essentially a factual issue, to be resolved in light of the controlling legal precepts" (728). With those observations, Chief Judge Murphy reverses the judgment of the Special Court of Appeals.

As I suggested in an earlier chapter, argument from analogy is a perilous business even if it is frequently the only game in town. Precedents are grounded in analogical thinking, and no two fact-situations are ever precisely the same. The fact-situation in *Hazel* featured overt violence: the defendant tied up the victim's hands and gagged her. In *Rusk* the victim's fear was generated by stolen keys, a strange neighbourhood, and a look in the defendant's eyes. Even if the gun in *Hazel* was imaginary, the threat of having one's baby shot is terrifying. I do not make these observations to suggest that either verdict was wrong. Quite the contrary. I make them to reinforce the point that the realm of law is a realm of rhetoric, a realm where contingency, plausibility, and probability reign supreme. Even if it has powerful persuasive value, analogical reasoning cannot lead to mathematical certainty or apodictic truth.

In his dissenting opinion, Judge Cole is big on analogy but skimpy on the reasoning that makes it persuasive. For the victim's fear to be reasonable, he says, "the conduct of the defendant ... must clearly indicate force or the threat of force such as to overpower the prosecutrix's ability to resist or will to resist" (729). For Cole, "there is no evidence to support the majority's conclusion that the prosecutrix was forced to submit to sexual intercourse, certainly not fellatio" (729). Why a person cannot be forced to commit fellatio is not clear.

Judge Cole, it seems, was on the panel for *Hazel*. In that decision, he notes, "by way of illustration we cited certain cases." Cole devotes some two thousand words to describing the particulars of these cases and comes to the conclusion that

[i]n each of those twelve cases there was either physical violence or specific threatening words or conduct which were calculated to create a very real and specific fear of *immediate* physical injury to the victim if she did not comply, coupled with the apparent power to execute those threats in the event of non-submission.

While courts no longer require a female to resist to the utmost or to resist where resistance would be foolhardy, they do require her acquiescence in the act of intercourse to stem from fear generated by something of substance. She may not simply say, "I was really scared," and thereby transform consent or mere unwillingness into submission by force. These words do not transform a seducer into a rapist. She must follow the natural instinct of every proud female to resist, by more than mere words, the violation of her person by a stranger or an unwelcomed friend. She must make it plain that she regards such sexual acts as abhorrent and repugnant to her natural sense of pride. She must resist unless the defendant has objectively manifested his intent to use physical force to accomplish his purpose. The law regards rape as a crime of violence. The majority today attenuates this proposition. It declares the innocence of an at best distraught young woman. It does not demonstrate the defendant's guilt of the crime of rape. (733)

To say that this account epitomizes a sexist mindset is almost unnecessary. The condescension is palpable. Rusk is a seducer transformed into a rapist because Pat did not follow the natural instinct of every proud woman to resist unwanted sexual advances. At best, she is a distraught young woman. "Here we have a full grown married woman who meets the defendant in a bar under friendly circumstances" (733). When he asks her to come up to his room, she refuses, and he takes her keys. Cole points out that "there is no evidence of the tone of his voice when he asks her come up" (733), let alone a weapon or a threat to inflict physical injury:

> She also testified that she was afraid of "the way he looked," and afraid of his statement, "come on up, come on up." But what can the majority conclude from this statement coupled with a "look" that remained undescribed? There is no evidence whatsoever to suggest that this was anything other than a pattern of conduct consistent with the ordinary seduction of a female acquaintance who at first suggests her disinclination. (733)

Cole also notes that during the so-called choking Pat "was able to talk" (734) and to extract from the defendant a promise that he would let her go if she submitted to his will. Cole just cannot believe that fellatio can be performed unwillingly:

> I find it incredible for the majority to conclude that on these facts, without more, a woman was forced to commit oral sex upon the defendant and then to engage in vaginal intercourse. In the absence of any verbal threat to do her grievous bodily harm or the display of any weapon and threat to use it, I find it difficult to understand how a victim could participate in these sexual activities and not be willing.
>
> What was the nature and extent of her fear anyhow? She herself testified she was "fearful that maybe I had someone following me." She was afraid because she didn't know him and she was afraid he was going to "rape" her. But there are no acts or conduct on the part of the defendant to suggest that these fears were created by the defendant or that he made any objective, identifiable threats to her which would give rise to this woman's failure to flee, summon help, scream, or make physical resistance. (734)

Like McClung, Cole declines to take the high road in his conclusion. He goes further and points out that, as the defendant well knew, Pat "was not a child." She "was a married woman with children, a woman familiar with the social setting in which these actors met." "She certainly had to realize that they were not going upstairs to play *Scrabble*" (734). When he left the room for a few minutes, she did not even try the door to see if it was locked. He did not rip her clothes off. "As a matter of fact, there is no suggestion by her that he bruised or hurt her … or that the 'choking' was intended to be disabling" (734). Although she would not release her phone number, she said they might meet again at Fell's Point.

The twelve cases he cites and summarizes in the body of his opinion, however, are not enough for Judge Cole. In an appendix of another two thousand words or so, he cites and summarizes a half a dozen more cases in which "rape convictions were overturned because the requirement of force necessary to demonstrate lack of consent was not strictly complied with, or the facts were so sketchy or inherently improbable that this element could not be established, as a matter of law, beyond a reasonable doubt" (735). Only one of the opinions is published after *Hazel*. The final three cases he cites sustain the rape convictions on basis of the jury's finding of non-consent.

It would be tedious to go through the cases he cites, most of which involve fact-situations radically different from the one in *Rusk*. Moreover, the first twelve cases are cited in a decision that says force need not be actual; it can also be constructive. Since resistance is necessarily relative, *Hazel* concludes that the presence or absence of it must depend on the facts and circumstances in each case. The real test is whether the assault was committed without the consent and against the will of the prosecuting witness. The six cases that overturn rape convictions are so different from *Rusk* as to be largely unhelpful.

In *Zamora v. State* (1969), "it was held that the evidence was insufficient to sustain a conviction of rape by force and threats where the sixteen-year-old prosecutrix, who had been engaging in sexual relations with the defendant stepfather for about six years, went to his bedroom to take him coffee, did not try to leave, took off part of her clothes at his request, made no outcry, and did not resist in any way, even though she knew what was going to happen when she sat on the bed" (735). Leaving aside the moral horror of a stepfather having sex with his stepdaughter from when she was ten and Cole's description of this violation of a child's innocence as "engaging in sexual relations," one wonders how this case has any bearing on the one at bar. In this case, the Court ruled that the defendant's threats to put the girl in a juvenile home and to whip her younger siblings were made after the alleged act. The threats were "not made to cause the prosecutrix to yield but to prevent her from informing her mother" (735). Unlike Pat, the step-daughter had no reasonable fear of being injured or killed.

Some of the other cases are equally off the mark. In 1946, a man is convicted of kidnapping but acquitted of rape. (Rusk was convicted of both assault and rape.) The man's telling the victim that he would find out what kind of woman she was, in the absence of any resistance on her part, was not deemed to be a threat that would induce fear in a rea-sonable person. In another case where there was no threat of force or violence except for a knife that the frightened victim falsely believed the man had in his hand while "he was doing all the things she said he did over this two or three hour period" (736), the judge ruled that even though the victim testified that she felt something sharp and knife-like, she would have seen the knife if it had actually existed. Cole's inten-tions notwithstanding, what these pre-*Hazel* cases really show is that earlier courts were even more egregiously stereotypic and sexist in their attitudes towards sexual assault than later courts.

The various fact scenarios include a twenty-one-year-old married woman with two children who, fearing for their safety, struggled with her assailant until the child asleep in her bed woke up. After the child was awake, she eventually gave in to the assailant's demands. The court notes that "it is the natural impulse of every honest and virtuous female to flee from threatened outrage. Her explanation that she did not want to leave the children alone with the defendant is a rather weak one, to say the least" (737). It is a hard to see how refusing to leave one's young children with a rapist constitutes a weak reason for remaining at the scene of the crime. The court's pseudo-chivalric rhetoric of honesty and virtue is offensive to say the least. In another case "an eighteen-year-old high school student accepted a ride home from an acquaintance, which eventually led to her *seduction*. At no time did the defendant threaten her with any weapon" (737, my emphasis). That she had sex against her will and without her consent is immaterial. Such is the stuff as seduc-tions are made on.

As we have seen in this discursive exploration of a single assault case, it is amazing how one crime can generate so many stories, stories that are sometimes congruent with one another, sometimes incongru-ent. If one further considers the number of fact-situations and scenarios canvassed in the dozens of precedent cases cited by the four judgments under scrutiny, it is hard to escape the conclusion that storytelling is at the core of legal decision-making, which, despite its deductive logic of justification, is heavily reliant on analogical reasoning. Fact-situations, however, are at best similar; they are never identical. And analogies, however persuasive, cannot prove anything if proof is to be understood in apodictic terms. The next chapter deals with the problematic relationship between rhetoric, philosophy, and law. Aristotle sees the relationship in terms of the contingent and the absolute, whereas Plato sees it in terms of the apparent and the real. I shall argue that Aristotle gets it right.

7 Rhetoric, Philosophy, and Law

Mention the word "rhetoric" and people automatically conjure up images of immaculately attired and impeccably coiffed politicians spouting lies in the name of truth. Or their minds turn to the slaughter bench of history, and they conjure up images of genocidal demagogues whose charismatic powers of eloquence spurred heinous crimes and unspeakable atrocities. To most people, the very word "rhetoric" is disreputable if not evil. According to them, rhetoric deals with questionable if not downright false propositions and bedecks these propositions in glittery and seductive verbal ornamentation for the purpose of manipulating rather than enlightening an audience. Or, in an even worse scenario, rhetoric displaces reason with emotion for the purpose of appealing to an audience's primal instincts of prejudice, hatred, vengeance, or murder lust. This is rhetoric that invites the adjectives "mere" and "empty" in the first scenario, "base" and "incendiary" in the second. What our opponents say is rhetoric, ingratiating verbosity or coercive passion. What we say is unvarnished truth – logical, rational, and compelling. How easily we distinguish our reasons from their rationalizations, our ideas from their ideology. Theirs is the realm of deception, dishonesty, and mystification. Ours is the realm of clarity, logic, and truth. They have policies whereas we have principles. What they say is sheer rhetoric, propaganda at best, and this pejorative characterization of the term is its common meaning. The derogation of rhetoric is an old story. For a historical villain, one naturally turns to Plato and his legendary demolition of the sophists, the first teachers of rhetoric.

Plato's critique of rhetoric relies on his theory of forms. Reality, Plato maintains, is to be found only in the intelligible world of eternal and unchanging forms, of which the shifting phenomena of the sensible world are imperfect copies. There is the heavenly world of pristine archetypes and the material world of distorted images. The intelligible realm comprises real objects of knowledge – the true, the good, and the beautiful. The sensible realm comprises degenerate manifestations of the ideal. The intelligible is the realm of truth and philosophy – *episteme*. The sensible is the realm of opinion and rhetoric – *doxa*.

If, as Alfred North Whitehead famously suggests, the European philosophical tradition consists of a series of footnotes to Plato, then the foundational binary distinction between *episteme* and *doxa* is at the core of this tradition. For Plato, dialectic deals with the realm of true ideas, and rhetoric deals with the realm of illusory appearances. Rhetoric, for Plato, has nothing to do with truth. The people Plato hates most, next to tyrants, are sophists. Of the nine degrees of soul elaborated in the *Phaedrus*, the first comprises philosophers, artists, and musicians; the eighth comprises sophists, demagogues, and rhetoricians. Only tyranny, it would seem, is viler than rhetoric.

The sophists preached the good rather than the true. Truth won, and the good lost. The syllogistic reasoning of logic trumped the analogical reasoning of rhetoric. Unlike Plato, the sophists were not cosmologists. They were humanists. They sought to teach the beliefs of people, not the principles of the universe. Their aim was improvement. For the sophists, all principles, all truths, are relative. Humanity, Protagoras says, is the measure of all things. The dialecticians think truth is absolute, a matter of logical demonstration; the sophists think truth is relative, a matter of political consensus. Though not the source of all things, human beings are the measure of all things. The sophists use the language of ethical self-fashioning: *arête*, excellence, duty towards self and other. *Arête* implies a respect for the wholeness or oneness of life; like rhetoric, it reveres prowess in all domains and abhors specialization.

Notwithstanding his protestations to the contrary, Plato was a consummate rhetorician, and one not at all averse to using emotionally persuasive language for the ulterior purpose of making the weaker argument, the case for dialectic rather than rhetoric, appear the stronger. As the saying goes, we always condemn in others what we most fear in ourselves. And rhetoric, once equated with learning itself, becomes reduced to the teaching of techniques, strategies, mannerisms, and styles. Unlike philosophy, rhetoric, for Plato, is not a search for truth. It is merely an unscientific knack for stroking and stoking the prejudices of

its audience. Lawyers and judges get the truth in their academic cours-
es on law and pick up a little rhetoric along the way so that they can
argue persuasively and further their careers.

Plato attacks rhetoric from the start. In the *Gorgias* he characterizes it
as gratification and deception – greasy fast food that panders to popular taste, not genuine, curative medicine that heals the wounded soul.
Though rhetoricians themselves see their art as a practical means of
deliberation and judgment – an art that "invents terms, constructs arguments, criticizes faulty interpretations, and judges matters not susceptible to algorithmic rules" (*A Companion to Rhetoric*, xv) – for every
Cicero there is a Hitler, for every civic-minded statesman there is a dangerous and unscrupulous demagogue, an enemy of reason and com-
passion. Gorgias, however, is no innocent. "Speech," he admits, "is a
powerful lord, which by means of the finest and most invisible body
effects the divinest works: it can stop fear and banish grief and create
joy and nurture pity" (cited by Kastely, 222). According to Gorgias,
rhetoric has the power of unbridled emotion, a sovereign power that
arises not from reason or *logos*, but from passion or *pathos*, an amoral
power that exalts efficacy over virtue. For Gorgias, rhetoric operates
more in terms of psychic compulsion than rational persuasion. No
wonder Plato reviles it.

Even though there are few self-identified Platonists in the public fo-
rum today, Plato's view of rhetoric is commonplace. In this study, I
have insisted on using the term "rhetoric" in a neutral way. The means
of rhetoric, I have said, are neither virtuous nor vicious. They merely
exist. They can be put to noble or ignoble purposes. Eloquence is beyond good and evil. It is not necessarily anything – positive or negative.
To invoke the overused tautology of our day, it is what it is. But tau-
tologies, even if overused, are at least true. They are not, however, very
compelling or informative.

Aristotle's view of rhetoric embraces praxis. His strategic innovation
is to replace the appearance/reality binary with the contingency/ne-
cessity binary. As Dilip Parmeshwar Gaonkar notes, for Aristotle the
contingent is the scene of rhetoric. Gaonkar cites three reasons for
Plato's rejection of rhetoric as a defective and incomplete art:

> First, rhetoric is rooted in a false ontology. It is content to deal with what
> appears to be true and good rather than inquire into what it is in reality.
> Second, rhetoric is epistemically deficient because it seeks to impart a

mastery of common opinion rather than knowledge. Third, as an instrument of practical politics it exploits the resources of language to make the "weaker cause appear stronger" and to promote the acquisition of power as an end in itself without consideration for the well-being of the soul. Each of the three reasons for rejecting rhetoric – its reliance on appearance, its entanglement with opinion, and its linguistic opportunism – are marked, in Plato's imagination, by instability and danger. (5)

Because rhetoric traffics with appearance and exploits opinion, it cannot furnish any ultimate philosophical foundation for its persuasive enterprises. For Plato, as we have seen, it is an unscientific knack, a process of trial and error, not an art based on knowledge. For Aristotle, too, the realm of rhetoric is the realm of appearance and opinion, but to admit such for him is not to be put into a defensive and debilitating position. His radical solution is to change the binary opposition that will go on to inform nothing less than the whole trajectory of Western philosophy. Aristotle, as Gaonkar points out, replaces Plato's binary opposition between the real and the apparent with his own binary opposition between the necessary and the contingent. Once rhetoric is placed in the realm of the contingent, it can be viewed not as a distorted representation of reality deficient in epistemic substance and ontological truth but as a kind of workaday knowledge grounded in common sense and prudential wisdom. Such knowledge and wisdom constitute what Aristotle calls *phronesis*, practical thought.

As Gaonkar notes, Aristotle's conception of the contingent has two fundamental characteristics. "First, the contingent is posited simultaneously as the opposite of the necessary (or necessarily true) and in conjunction with the 'probable' or that about which one can generate probable proof" (7). "The contingent is a mark of human actions because in any given situation human beings can conceivably act in ways other than they do" (7). "According to Aristotle: 'Most of the things about which we make decisions, and into which we therefore inquire, present us with alternative possibilities. For it is about our actions we deliberate and inquire, and all our actions have a contingent character; hardly any of them are determined by necessity'" (cited by Gaonkar, 7–8).

Only in the face of contingent alternatives does it make sense for human agents to deliberate and choose, let alone try to influence the deliberations and choices of their fellow citizens. Such probable reasoning is based on enthymeme and example, enthymeme being a truncated form of deductive reasoning that leaves out premises an audience takes for granted, example being a loose form of inductive reasoning that builds on analogy. A probability is something that usually happens, and a contingent event has three characteristics: first, it may or may not occur; second, it is neither necessary nor impossible, for necessary or impossible things are not things on which we expend energy in debating; and third, it is within someone's power to make or prevent it from happening; it is within the sphere of voluntary human agency.

As we saw with legal concepts of causation, there are many things in human affairs that do not admit of logical demonstration or empirical verification. Propositions that are credible, consistent, and probable are all that a rhetorician can lay claim to, indeed, all that a judge or lawyer can lay claim to. In dialectic, the apodictic truth of logic is aloof and unsituated:

> In rhetoric, on the other hand, opinion is binding, audience is sovereign, time is of the essence, and judgment is inescapable. This renders rhetoric's grasp of the contingent tenuous and fragile. There are too many variables thrown together that generate further contingencies. Rhetoric can never catch up with the unfolding chain of contingencies. The latter maintain an irreparable lead. (Gaonkar, 14)

The same is true of law. It too lacks absolute foundations and can never succeed in corralling contingency. Antifoundationalism, alas, goes with living in a rhetorical world. As recent deconstructive and postmodernist theory has shown, this position can be metaphysically inflated into an all-encompassing linguistic, epistemological, and ethical nihilism, for rhetoric is the realm of the uncertain and the indeterminate as well as the usual and the common, nihilists stressing rhetoric's instability and undecidability, pragmatists stressing its givenness and availability. But when all is said and done, a nihilist is just a pragmatist with an attitude problem. As Stanley Fish points out, human beings are situated in interpretive communities:

> Anti-foundationalism teaches that questions of fact, truth, correctness, validity, and clarity can neither be posed nor answered in reference to some extracontextual, ahistorical, nonsituated reality, or rule, or law, or value; rather, anti-foundationalism asserts, all these matters are intelligible and debatable only within the precincts of the contexts or situations or paradigms or communities that give them their local and changeable shape. (344)

It follows from this that "all practice is situated practice. Regardless of what we are doing – whether interpreting a literary text, making a legal argument, rendering a moral judgment, or opting for a political strategy – we cannot escape our situatedness" (Gaonkar, 18).

Pragmatically understood, antifoundationalism does not generate anarchy. While it is true in an absolute sense that all interpretations are epistemically ungrounded, ours is not a view from nowhere. A situated agent is "a function of the conventional possibilities built into this or that context" (Fish, 346). Within the constraints of the interpretive strategies of the interpretive communities to which we always and already belong, we have no choice but to impute intentions to discourses we believe have been constructed for a purpose. True, there is no literal meaning or original intent we can pretend to construe; meaning and intention can only be established through construction and persuasion. But interpretation of intention is what everyone is in the business of doing, regardless of their philosophies. All that we can propound are propositions, propositions that emerge from the contingencies of subject, occasion, purpose, genre, and audience, propositions, we hope, that are credible, consistent, and probable, propositions that are above all convincing and persuasive. The assumption here is an old one. *Ought* cannot be derived from *is*. Positivistic science and dialectical logic cannot tell us how we ought to act or what we ought to say. Rhetoric, by contrast, offers prudential wisdom, equipment for living in the tumults and the chances of this wavering world. And in a wavering world where exactitude is unattainable, analogy is indispensable.

Especially relevant to Aristotle's conception of prudential wisdom is his

> view of the scope and limits of the kind of knowledge that can appropriately be expected in practical matters. Near the beginning of the *Nicomachean Ethics* Aristotle explains that it would be mistaken to hope for an equal degree of certainty in all fields of inquiry. The kind of certainty that one has a right to expect in matters of cognition is not apt to be forthcoming where human action is concerned. The two thus call for very different modes of discourse, and this serves as one of the grounds on which the divisions within philosophy can be made: "Our discussion," he says at the beginning of the *Nicomachean Ethics* "will be adequate if it has as much clearness as the subject matter admits of, for precision is not to be sought for alike in all discussions, any more than in all the products of the crafts." (Cascardi, 299)

Surety and comprehensiveness vary with the subject matter of one's inquiry. One no more expects probable reasoning from a mathematician than one expects demonstrative proofs from a rhetorician. As the counterpart of dialectic, rhetoric offers probable and analogical reasoning in contexts where apodictic certainty is unavailable, where what we need to know is how to act or what to say. An opinion, by definition, is any belief or proposition that could be otherwise.

"In classical rhetoric," Cascardi notes, "the example – narrative or otherwise – furnishes a viable mode of 'proof,' one that Aristotle regards as a counterpart of logical induction. Narrative examples have the rhetorical force of proof in the same way that an account by a witness may help to prove a case in legal contexts" (302). As we have seen with the citation of precedents, just how many examples are required cannot be precisely determined. Every rhetor must develop an acute and intuitive sense of what will suffice. When used to build a case, examples resemble induction. They are a form of analogical reasoning, and, for Aristotle, analogy is at the core of practical argumentation. Analogy provides new insight by establishing a relation between the known and the unknown, the familiar and the unfamiliar.

What Cicero calls *ingenium*, a heightened capacity to see similarity and difference, is the key to making apt analogies and gripping stories. Both depend on concrete particulars, vivid sensory images. Enthymemes, by contrast, resemble deduction. They appeal to generally accepted propositions, often leaving out the major premises. What Aristotle calls the persuasiveness of the given is a sort of pre-knowledge or common sense, a vast body of assumed information and shared values that every rhetorician relies on if context permits. Such pre-knowledge, of course, is anathema to Plato. He regards it as prejudice and preconception. Rather than being a common ground on which debate is based, what-goes-without-saying is for him precisely that which must be dialectically interrogated. For the rhetorician, however, everything depends on subject, occasion, purpose, genre, and audience. In some cases, received opinion must be submitted to deconstruction and demolishment, though, as we have seen, the cost of persuasion rises to the degree that one must move people away from what they already believe. Most people tenaciously believe that killers should be severely punished, and it is going to be inordinately difficult for a judge to convince them that the constitutional rights of the accused compel the inadmissibility of a murder weapon unveiled by an illegal search and seizure.

Black letter law, the law on the books, can only take us so far. As Robert P. Burns suggests,

> To understand law as a system of rules is to commit Whitehead's fallacy of misplaced concreteness, mistaking an abstract aspect of reality for its full actuality. The law in action succeeds when its linguistic practices form an absorbing and meaningful context of argument and feeling that elevates deliberation and enhances judgment. (442)

At trial, he points out, "the jury is asked to make a practical judgment that reconciles *in action and in context* incommensurable values – moral, legal, and political ... If the trial is the heart of the law, then the law is rhetorical, for rhetoric rules where action under uncertainty is necessary" (443–4). Though less dominant than it once was, the received view of conventional jurisprudence sees "the law as a system of rules that can be known 'scientifically.' Individual cases are decided ultimately by cognitive acts of (1) accurate, value-free fact-finding followed by (2) acts of fair categorization, judgments ultimately about the meaning of legal terms" (444).

What the received view represses are narrative, analogy, and enthymeme. At trial, as Burns points out,

> the opening statements present God's-eye narratives of what the evidence will show. Done artfully, this will be more than a recitation of expected evidence. It will rather be a "continuous dream" (Gardner 1983: 31) that weaves all of the evidence into a coherent narrative that illustrates, *shows*, the meaning of the events that have brought the case to trial. The opening statement answers in narrative fashion the rhetorical question that lawyers often put to themselves in opening statement, "What is this case about?" or, in the language of hermeneutics, "What should this case be seen *as*?" The opening is woven around what trial lawyers call a "theme," an implicit moral argument much like the plot of a novel, based on the values implicit in the life-world of the jury, the rhetorical resources implicit in the tacit practices, habits, cultural values, personal and social commitments, and so on that comprise our hermeneutical and rhetorical horizon of understanding: what Ludwig Wittgenstein calls *Lebensformen*, and Cavell our "mutual attunements." (445)

Opposing rhetors, of course, seek to counter each other's characterizations of a given case. For Justice Cardozo, as we have seen, *Palsgraf v. Long Island Railroad* is a case that should be seen as a question of liability and protected interests, an entirely legal issue. For Justice Andrews, *Palsgraf* should be seen as a question of proximate cause and proximate consequences, an empirical as well a legal issue. Cardozo sees the case as hinging on whether the guards had a duty of care to Mrs Palsgraf, whereas Andrews sees it as hinging on whether the conduct of the guards was the proximate cause of Mrs Palsgraf's permanent disability. In theory, both judges seem to understand that "the greatest weapon in the arsenal of persuasion is the analogy, the story, the simple comparison with a familiar object," since nothing can move people "more convincingly than an apt comparison to something they know from their experience is true" (Spangenburg, cited by Burns at 449). In practice, however, when it comes to concocting analogies, both judges are somewhat deficient in simplicity, familiarity, and aptness. Their analogies, as I have argued, spiral out of control. All analogies, of course, break down at some point. Similarity is not identity. As Kenneth Burke reflects,

> put similarity and dissimilarity ambiguously together, so that you cannot know for certain where one ends and the other begins, and you have the characteristic invitation to rhetoric ... The wavering line between the two cannot be "scientifically" identified; rival rhetoricians can draw it at different places, and their persuasiveness varies with the resources each has at hand. (*A Rhetoric of Motives*, 25)

Such incurable ambiguity is also the characteristic invitation to legal disputation. The scandal of composition is that the discovery of arguments in all fields has little to do with logic or reason and everything to do with analogy and metaphor. Indeed, the term "metaphor" is itself a metaphor derived from its literal meaning – to transfer or carry over. Metaphor transfers or carries over an image or idea from one semantic field to another, revealing similarity in dissimilar things, seeing A in terms of B, and B in terms of A. Although it might be desirable that similar cases be decided on similar grounds, fact-situations, as we have seen, are never identical, and controlling laws are not always self-evident. However much similarities may seem to be anchored in empirical fact or legal precedent, they are nonetheless discovered and constructed by judges. A fact is not a fact until found to be so by a judge. A law is not controlling until he or she makes it so. Judgments are performative utterances; they bring into being the reality they describe, even if that reality may be later redescribed by a higher court.

In *Heracles' Bow,* James Boyd White uses *Katz v. US* as an example of performative analogy. In *Katz* the police, without a warrant, place an electronic bug on top of a phone booth and later seek to use the overheard conversation in evidence. "The Supreme Court holds that the evidence should be excluded as the fruit of an unreasonable 'search' – even though there was no trespass on property or invasion of premises as the word 'search' was once thought to imply" (113). After that decision, the idea of search includes interference with a reasonable expectation of privacy. In a modest way, the reality of a new technological world has entered American jurisprudence. Electronic eavesdropping, the Supreme Court says, is analogous to trespassory invasion, a suggestive analogy that proves to have tremendous transformative power. The legal meaning of search has been extended.

Such analogical extension is central to how language works. Every writer relies on analogy for the discovery of arguments, a kind of thinking that works not by argument from general premises to conclusion, but by a process of comparison and contrast, perceived similarities and differences. Is the fact-situation in this case similar to the fact-situation in a precedent case? Does the same controlling law apply? The analogical origin of a decision, however, is often concealed in a judgment's final form, a form that features a logic of justification based on the deductive model of particular issue, relevant fact, controlling law, and entailed conclusion. That is to say, the structure of exposition wherein a court justifies its reasons for decision is different from the reasoning by analogy that led to the decision. Like all arguments, judgments are composed and constructed on the basis of analogy as well as logic.

Insofar as we focus on logic rather than analogy, we are focusing on the legal story and creating an abstract world defined by laws, statutes, charters, rights, precedents, and the like. As we move towards *pathos,* we are focusing on the human story and creating a concrete world of acts, agents, agencies, scenes, motives, images, passions, and dramas. With *ethos,* we are focusing on the messages judges perform, on a normative world in which ethical excellence is viewed not as a matter of result but as a matter of composition, of judicial self-fashioning, of how judges define themselves as judges and imagine legal worlds in which others must live, worlds that reinterpret the past, delimit the present, and shape the future.

This study has focused on legal world-making and judicial self-fashioning, on how judges create normative universes for us to live in and fashion ethical images of themselves as judges. *Ethos* is character as

it emerges in language, something judges construct, implicitly or explicitly, to accommodate themselves decorously to a particular subject,
occasion, purpose, and audience. *Ethos* is in some sense a hidden persuader, a product of all the rhetorical choices a writer makes. Consciously trying to establish *ethos* is like consciously trying to be sincere. More
often than not, the enterprise is doomed. Storytelling, however, is a
more open persuader, and the underlying assumptions of this study
have been that judicial writing is a form of narrative, that storytelling in
law is narrative within a culture of argument, and that narrative is an
integral element of legal argument. As James Boyd White notes,

> the lawyer is repeatedly saying, or imagining himself or herself saying:
> "Here is what happened"; here is "what it means"; and here is "why it
> means what I claim." The process is at heart a narrative one because there
> cannot be a legal case without a real story about real people actually lo-
> cated in space and time and culture. Some actual person must go to a
> lawyer with an account of the experience upon which he or she wants the
> law to act, and that account will always be narrative. (*Heracles' Bow*, 36)

Each legal case, of course, involves more than one account of an experience. Justice Paul Perell rightly sees the courtroom as a competition
among the narrative accounts of various storytellers:

> Each of the competing storytellers wishes to tell a story that will work. It
> is a complex competition to tell a story that will work because the parties
> or their lawyers do not have an artist's greater freedom to construct the
> story and the facts, for the story must be introduced through the filters of
> the frailties of human witnesses, the law of evidence, and the adversary
> system, and, because, under the gravity of the doctrine of *stare decisis* [the
> legal principle by which judges are obliged to respect the precedent estab-
> lished by prior decisions], the stories of the parties must not only compete
> in their ability to compel the favourable interest and attention of the judge
> but for a party to succeed in this effort, his or her story must connect with
> another judicial story, the story of the precedent case or the story that de-
> scribes the background to the creation of a legal document. (206)

Throughout this study I have argued that narrative is crucial to legal
decision-making because the primary task of the judge or jury is to
make a plausible and coherent story (*une histoire*) out of the chaotic

particulars of a case, a case that is often awash in a sea of conflicting evidence, contradictory versions of events, incongruent precedents, unclear controlling laws, incompatible expert reports, ambiguous legal documents, and, in general, at least two opposed and competing discourses. While it is true that logic as well as narrative enters into the deciding process, legal reasoning utterly depends upon the selection of factual and legal premises, premises, it would seem, that are almost always shrouded in factual and legal uncertainty. Reported by witnesses who are more or less informed, competent, and credible, facts are usually incomplete, inconsistent, and insufficient until they are winnowed down and shaped into a necessarily selective narrative. As for legal premises, first principles are posited rather than proven. They cannot be proved because they are points of departure, and points of departure cannot be the object of the logical analysis they enable.[1]

In the face of uncertainties and complications, formal logic founders. Justice Perell makes this point incisively:

> What is remarkable about all of these complications in the adjudication of disputes and in legal reasoning is that the complications cannot be resolved as a matter of deductive reasoning or formal logic. They cannot be resolved as a matter of strict logic because formal logic does not govern the selection of premises, and, ultimately, legal reasoning is about the selection of factual and legal premises and not about the ultimate formal structure of the argument that yields the conclusion. In the application of the seemingly deductive principle of formal justice that like cases be treated alike, the criterion of likeness is not specified, and the exercise of finding similarities and differences is itself a matter of choice or argument … Formal logic cannot guide us when we are concerned with the content and not with the form of the reasoning. The content, which comes from interpreting factual circumstances, from interpreting the legal document, from interpreting social policy, or from interpreting the influence of the precedent case, is essentially a matter of rhetorical or practical reasoning. (103–4)

---

1 How formal and informal logic function in legal writing is beyond the scope of this study, a study centred on how story and style function in a culture of argument. The works of Ronald Dworkin, Chaim Perelman, Stephen Toulmin, and many others offer insights into logic, rhetoric, argumentation theory, and law.

Persuasion, the cornerstone of rhetoric, is more important to legal reasoning than demonstration, the cornerstone of logic. Story persuades in a way that syllogism cannot. What we can perceptually see has more impact on us than what we can conceptually know. The perceptually seeable has what Chaim Perelman calls presence. He uses a Chinese tale to make his point. "A king sees an ox on its way to sacrifice. He is moved to pity for it and orders that a sheep be used in its place. He confesses he did so because he could see the ox but not the sheep" (cited by Perell, 33). The ox had presence. The sheep did not. Arguments with presence tend to prevail over those without it, though presence, like any rhetorical device, is not always a good thing. The bonnet and crinolines memorably evoked by Justice McClung had nothing if not presence.

Postscript: Rhetoric, Postmodernism, and Scepticism

In "Dancing Through the Minefield," Annette Kolodny says that

> our purpose is not and should not be the formulation of any single reading method or potentially Procrustean set of critical procedures nor, even less, the generation of prescriptive categories ... Instead as I see it, our task is to initiate nothing less than a playful pluralism, responsive to the possibilities of multiple critical schools and methods, but captive of none, recognizing that the many tools needed for our analysis will necessarily be largely inherited and only partly of our own making. Only by employing a plurality of methods will we protect ourselves from the temptation of so oversimplifying any text ... that we render ourselves unresponsive to ... its various systems of meaning and their interaction. (2064)

Such pluralism is at the core of rhetorical criticism. In embracing pluralism, Kolodny goes on to say that "we do not give up the search for patterns of opposition and connection – probably the basis of thinking itself. What we give up is the arrogance of claiming that our work is either exhaustive or definitive" (2064). Analogical reasoning, the capacity for similarity seeing and difference seeing, underwrites all discourse.

Chapter 5 of this study draws an analogy between writing judgments and writing fiction. In it I say that

> the compositional task of a judge ... is not altogether unlike that of a novelist, for even though a judge finds facts rather than invents them, he or she is trying to construct a plausible and coherent narrative. In making this comparison between judges and novelists, however, I do not mean to imply that judgments are simply fictions. On the contrary, my intent is to

affirm a middle ground between, on the one hand, the traditional view that judicial reasoning, anchored in legal precedent and found facts, is simply a deductive matter of applying universal laws to particular fact-situations and, on the other, the postmodern view that precedents, facts, and controlling laws are entirely constructed by judges according to the various interpretive strategies they deploy and the various interpretive communities to which they belong. Following Robert Wess, I call this middle ground "rhetorical realism," "rhetorical" because similarities of fact and law are constructed by judges, "realism" because something really happened even if that true story is never wholly accessible to the judicial opinion that seeks to encompass it.

What exactly is this middle ground, and how does it differentiate itself from postmodernist and sceptical takes on the relationship between rhetoric and reality? In its classical sense, rhetoric is the art of persuasion, the ability of speakers or writers to use the most efficient means of persuasion to achieve a desired effect or purpose. All discourse falls within the province of rhetoric because all language is laden with values and value judgments. All language reveals, betrays, or conceals the motives of its user. These motives do not have to be conscious or explicit. They can be unconscious or implicit.

Unconscious and implicit motives inform our habitual modes of perception and cognition. These modes of perception and cognition are the what-goes-without-saying, the given. They are a lens through which we view the world. What we cannot see is the lens itself. The facts do not speak for themselves, even in science. There is no such thing as a neutral observation-language. Every version of the world presupposes a model or paradigm, an interpretive or rhetorical strategy, a metaphor to live by, whether it be the cultural mosaic, the melting pot, the invisible hand, the withering away of the state, or whatever.

All vocabularies are formative vocabularies. They create things as well as reflect them. And rhetoric is about vocabularies of motive. A way of saying is a way of not saying just as a way of seeing is a way of not seeing. There is always an element of self-fulfilling prophecy in the terms we use. As Wittgenstein suggests, all seeing is *seeing as*. We can only see what our vocabularies allow us to look for. As Kenneth Burke puts it in *Language as Symbolic Action*, "even if any given terminology is a *reflection* of reality, by its very nature as a terminology it must be a *selection* of reality; and to this extent it must function also as a *deflection* of reality" (45). How accurately a vocabulary reflects reality is the stuff of argument. Only in cases of extreme psychosis or schizophrenia is there an utter disconnect between language and reality. But if you believe something and survive, even if what you believe – say, Scientology or Christian Science – is outside the mainstream, the fact of your survival demonstrates the adequacy of your belief.

Nevertheless, every terminology is necessarily selective. What Burke calls "terministic screens" direct the attention (45). Terministic is just his peculiar synonym for terminological. It combines terminology and determinism, the idea being that our terms in some measure determine our observations. As he puts it, "Not only does the nature of our terms affect the nature of our observations, in the sense that the terms direct the attention to one field rather than another. Also, many of the *'observations' are but implications of the particular terminology in terms of which the observations are made."* We see in terms of terms. "In brief, much that we take as observations about 'reality' may be but the spinning out of possibilities implicit in our particular choice of terms" (46).

All strategies of reading are learned strategies. You can read a judgment as a legal realist or an original-intent scholar. You can see it as reactionary or activist. What you cannot do is read it or see it innocently or naturally. As Burke points out, "'reality' could not exist for us, were it not for our profound and inveterate involvement in symbol systems" (48). We live in a world of symbolicity and virtuality – cyberspace, Facebook, Twitter, social media, the Internet. Where are nature and reality? What is natural and real in our world? "Even something so 'objectively there' as behaviour [or material objects] must be observed through one or another kind of terministic screen, that directs the attention in keeping with its nature" (49).

For Burke, there is no escape from terminology. "We must use terministic screens, since we can't say anything without the use of terms; whatever terms we use, they necessarily constitute a corresponding kind of screen; and any such screen necessarily directs the attention to one field rather than another" (50). We posit a rhetorical screen and affirm its superiority. "But are we not here 'necessarily' caught in our own net? Must we concede that a screen built on [a rhetorical basis] is just one more screen; and that it can at best be permitted to take its place along with all the others?" (52–3). What is the advantage of a rhetorical perspective? Is it just a perspective among others?

In one sense, yes, it is just a perspective among others. The terministic screen of rhetoric is at once reflective, selective, and deflective. A way of saying is a way of seeing, and every way of seeing is a way of not seeing. As Burke reflects, "every insight contains its own special sort of blindness" (*Attitudes*, 41). This perplexity Thorstein Veblen calls trained incapacity. A vocabulary of motives both capacitates us and incapacitates us. It gives us a skill set at the expense of other skill sets. This is why the rhetorical world view endorses pluralism. The more vocabularies we possess, the more capacities we possess.

If, as Nietzsche maintains, there are no facts, just interpretations, then interpretive strategies come in many sizes, shapes, and forms. So-called facts have to be interpreted, selected, and organized. And different strategies make for different realities. The religious fundamentalist in some sense lives in a different world than the secular rhetorician. Try advocating the right to choose in the midst of those who believe in the right to life. Where there are no shared premises, argument is futile. When do human rights emerge, at conception, at three months in the womb, at birth? There is no moral issue here. No one believes in murdering human beings who have inalienable rights to life. In dispute is what constitutes a human being and how such a being is to be defined – religiously, biologically, culturally, or in some other way.

As we have seen, the realm of rhetoric is a realm of contingency and probability, not a realm of necessity or certainty. Call such a view pragmatism or call it nihilism, but, whatever you call it, the honest rhetorician, if such a person exists, has to concede that there is no ultimate foundation for knowledge. Nor is there any ultimate metalanguage, any view from nowhere that looks down on other object languages and evaluates them objectively. There is no stable or unchanging code. Nature and reality do not ask to be described in any particular way. And rhetoric does not give us a metalinguistic platform from which to survey and judge the object-languages of other discourses. It gives us a perspective within the fray, not a platform above the fray.

Because the observer is part of the observation, the rhetorician has little choice but to embrace a soft version of what we might call the four dogmas of postmodernity: antifoundationalism, constructionism, coherentism, and relativism. Antifoundationalism is the belief that there are no unshakeable empirical facts or rationalist ideas upon which knowledge is grounded. There are no facts, just interpretations. Constructionism is the belief that everything is linguistically and socially constructed. There is no neutral observation-language, no realm of extra-linguistic facts or essences to appeal to. Coherentism is the belief that propositions do not correspond to any external frame of reference, that the only criterion for their validity is internal consistency. Language does not simply hold up the mirror to nature and society. Finally, relativism is the belief that everything is relative to the vocabulary and perspective of the observer, whose own situatedness makes objectivity impossible. The observer is inside the scene.

These beliefs, however, are neither life-threatening nor earthshattering. What should prevail, I have suggested, is rhetorical realism, rhetorical because our world is largely constructed by symbol systems, realism because there is something out there that we are trying to represent. As Robert Wess observes, "there are always multiple motivational discourses" (22). "Rhetorical realism concedes that we can't get outside the constructions of discourse but it insists that neither can we construct our way outside the materiality of living" (24). Whether you are a Platonist or a legal realist, if you ingest cyanide, you are going to die.

Just because there are no ultimate foundations for knowledge does not mean there are no foundations. That those foundations shift a bit is just the way things are. And just because there is no ultimate metalanguage does not mean that our codes do not overlap. As long as the margin of overlap is significant, we can more or less communicate. When people cannot talk to one another for whatever reasons, their codes are deficient in overlap.

That is why I have taken an instrumental approach to rhetoric, looking at it from a functional and pragmatic standpoint. Presumably, by carefully studying rhetoric, we can disentangle the motives of its practitioners, but this is a difficult, complex, and indeterminate process. As with everything else involved in the study of language, there is no single method that guarantees the correctness of an analysis. The best we can hope for is an approximation of the truth. And I believe that the best way to approach the truth is through a plurality of methods and vocabularies. As Richard McKeon says, "there is a sense in which truth, though one, has no single expression" (203–4).

I do not believe postmodernist rhetors would disagree with most of what has been said above. They would, however, disagree with the soft constructionism that undergirds it. In fact, the interpretive assumptions that enable Stanley Fish's postmodernist rhetorical project are none other than antifoundationalism (there is no text in this class, no autonomous and objective verbal structure), constructionism (the text is created and constructed by the reader's interpretive strategy), coherentism (criticism is a matter of rhetorical persuasion rather than logical demonstration), and relativism (everything is relative to the vocabulary and standpoint of the reader, whose own situatedness makes objectivity impossible). Fish's resolutely dualist scheme – persuasion versus demonstration, rhetoric versus logic – synonymizes and homogenizes opposing interpretive assumptions so that all beliefs in the mind-independent reality of the text become one and the same in their supposed endorsement of rationalism, objectivism, and realism. The fatal flaw of such dualism is to construe reason as something independent of rhetoric in the first place. With its oddly Platonic overtones, the rhetoric/reason dichotomy might seem an unusual starting point for a postmodern rhetor, but Fish is no stranger to all-or-nothing tactics.

Fish maintains that the interpretive strategy of the reader creates the text – legal or other – there being no text except that which a reader or an interpretive community of readers creates. Though common sense would concede that the text has some structure of determination, Fish challenges absolutely "the brute-fact status of the text" (75). Even at the most rudimentary level, he goes on to say, the very grammar, syntax, and semantics of a text are created by the reader. Textual features, he writes, "appear (or do not appear) as a consequence of particular interpretive strategies ... there is no distinction between what the text gives and the reader supplies; he supplies *everything*" (77), everything from the grammar of a text to its metaphysics.

In my view, a defensible claim that no priority can be ascribed to either the linguistic structure of the text or the interpretive strategy of the reader gets confused with a claim that is as unverifiable as it is irrefutable: namely, that the interpretive strategy of the reader entirely determines the intentionality of a text and its formal realization, that different strategies make different texts. That interpretation has no absolute foundation in linguistic factuality, that some principle of selection is unavoidable, one might readily admit. But this pragmatic admission need not be inflated into a metaphysical difficulty. For practical purposes one does treat words as linguistic facts, and in most contexts one does take grammar, syntax, and semantics at face value. To maintain, as Fish does, that interpretive terminologies shape and affect perception but that the verbal structure of the text does not is to be at once sensitive to the formative nature of terminologies and insensitive to the dialogical nature of the transaction between reader and text. The rhetorical realist assumes that reader and text intersect even if we cannot say precisely where.

In the end, however, Fish's position is not as radical as it seems. He combines audacious relativism – the interpretive strategy of the reader creates the text – with conservative professionalism – readers belong to interpretive communities, a fact that explains why modes of interpretation become normalized and why communication between interpreters is possible. Nevertheless, Fish's position is as irrefutable as it is indefensible. If all facts are interpretations, then rhetorical persuasion takes the place of logical demonstration, the latter being a species of argumentation that ultimately depends on a correspondence theory of truth whereby propositions match or do not match the facts of experience – facts that, for Fish, do not exist apart from their conventional acceptance by some interpretive community.

If interpretation is the only game in town, and if criteria of coherence supplant those of correspondence, then Fish's position can only be defended on the grounds that it is more persuasive than that of the rhetorical realist. In such a game, of course, the only permissible move is to rejoin that Fish's position is not as persuasive as the rhetorical realist's and that any position that denies the existence of grammatical and syntactical facts invites *reductio ad absurdum,* a rhetorical move that cannot refute a position but can only appeal to common sense by showing the improbable and implausible consequences that flow from holding such a position. Surely the text imposes some constraints; the reader cannot promiscuously make it mean whatever he or she likes without being subject to the derision of his or her peers. At the very least, the text has a skeleton of determinate meanings even if it is the reader who fleshes out these meanings and the implications they generate. This, however, is but a wishful assertion. The absolutist position that calls itself relativism cannot be so easily dismissed.

As M.H. Abrams observes in "How to Do Things with Texts," the postmodern rhetor is an "absolutist without absolutes" (438). According to such a rhetor, language, "to be determinately understandable," "requires an absolute foundation, and … since there is no such ground, there is no stop to the play of undecidable meanings" (438). "The absence of the transcendental signified," Derrida writes, "extends the domain and the play of signification infinitely" (213). He thus "puts out of play, before the game even begins, every source of norms, controls, or indicators which, in the ordinary use and experience of language, set a limit to what we can mean and what can be understood to mean": the speaking or writing subject, his or her intention to mean something, along with the rules of grammar, syntax, semantics, and usage (Abrams, "The Deconstructive Angel," 245).

As a counterstatement to such radical scepticism, rhetorical realism aligns itself with ordinary language philosophy. According to Wittgenstein, philosophy can in the end only describe the actual use of language. It cannot give it any foundation. Wittgenstein's conception of language is use-oriented and context-dependent.

In *Philosophical Investigations* Wittgenstein embraces the idea of language-games. He contends that "to imagine a language-game means to imagine a form of life" (8) and goes on to say that "the term 'language-*game*' is meant to bring into prominence the fact that the *speaking* of language is part of an activity, or a form of life" (11). Words, he insists, must be understood in terms of a context of situation, for linguistic and non-linguistic human behaviour intertwine. Language is communal in its nature. Words and the context of situation together define the language-game. The meaning of a word, then, is not the referent to which it points, the object for which it stands; "the meaning of a word is its use in language" (20).

For Wittgenstein, as for Stanley Cavell, the task of philosophy is to "bring words back from their metaphysical to their everyday use" (48). As Cavell reflects,

> philosophers before Wittgenstein had found that our lives are distorted or waylaid by illusion. But what other philosopher has found the antidote to illusion in the particular and repeated humility of remembering and tracking the uses of humble words, looking philosophically as it were beneath our feet rather than over our heads? (34)

Like Wittgenstein, Cavell confronts the temptation of scepticism and finds whatever victory there is to be found in "never claiming a final philosophical victory over (the temptation to) skepticism" (38). For such a victory could only mean "a victory over the human" (38).

Our very sense of the arbitrariness and conventionality of language, Cavell suggests, is itself a manifestation of scepticism as to the existence of the world, the self, and others. Appealing to shared criteria is not very helpful, for such criteria do not refute scepticism; they merely beg the question. But why, Cavell asks, do we expect otherwise? "Why are we disappointed in criteria, how do we become disappointed as it were with language as such?" (43). After all, as Wittgenstein observes, "explanations come to an end somewhere" (3), and to repudiate shared criteria is to speak outside language-games and to renounce the forms of talking life into which we symbol-using, symbol-misusing, and symbol-used animals are thrown. Nevertheless, this "straining of language against itself, against the commonality of criteria which are its conditions" (58), is perfectly natural. Our reflective encounters with language are often encounters with scepticism, and to bring us home to the ordinary, to nurture in us a distrust of the need for the profound, can neither prevent nor eliminate these bouts of scepticism. For the griefs to which language repeatedly comes are part of our inheritance and condition.

Cavell's ordinary language philosophy might initially seem to offer an antidote to the literary and linguistic scepticism that pervades postmodernist theory and criticism. It does not. The adequacy of shared criteria is precisely what postmodernism and deconstruction put in question. To appeal to such criteria is to refute Berkeley by kicking a stone or to refute Derrida by telling him there's egg on his tie and watching him look. All Cavell can offer is an alternative to what Michael Fischer aptly calls literary theory's "flight from the ordinary" (125). And, as Fischer's *Stanley Cavell and Literary Skepticism* affirms, it requires an extraordinary amount of effort to recover the ordinary and to lead words home.

Characterized by radical epistemological questioning, scepticism raises doubts as to whether we can know with certainty the existence of material objects or other minds. It is born of the need to give knowledge and language some unshakeable ontological foundation, some ultimate referent or transcendental signified. In the end, as I have said, scepticism is as indefensible as it is irrefutable. The absence of shared criteria makes argument futile, as volumes of writing for and against postmodernism and deconstruction would seem to attest.

"Deconstruction," Jay Cantor writes, "is a classical skeptical argument, recast using linguistic metaphors" (cited by Fischer, 7). "It is a version of skepticism which attacks the claim of consciousness that it has at its disposal a language that is representative of the world or even of consciousness itself. Deconstructive critics argue that signifiers cannot be adequately or reliably aligned with signifieds" (7). Hence the postmodern rhetor questioning the textual object – is there a text in this class? – resembles the traditional epistemologist questioning the existence of objects in the external world – how do you know there's a goldfinch in the garden? When Fish asks, "How do you know that Faulkner's 'A Rose for Emily' does not describe an Eskimo in the concluding tableau of Emily and her father in the doorway?," he is trying to suggest that doubt can unsettle seemingly irrefragable assumptions – that Faulkner al argument.

Such scepticism may be implausible but it is neither impossible nor inhuman. In fact, "nothing could be more human," Fischer writes, "than the skeptic's dissatisfaction with our ordinary ways of knowing" (31). Cavell goes further, making the interesting point that the violence of the sceptic's dissatisfaction with these ways of knowing may be typically male. It is as if the stubborn and recalcitrant autonomy of the world or text poses a threat and causes a separation that knowing would either overcome or destroy. "It is against the (fantasized) possibility of overcoming this hyperbolic separateness," Cavell suggests, "that the skeptic's (disappointed, intellectualized, impossible, imperative, hyperbolic) demand makes sense" (cited by Fischer, 31), for the imperious demand to master, possess, or penetrate the world or text is a demand whose absolutism guarantees its non-fulfilment.

According to Cavell, the sceptic's longing for knowledge goes too far and refuses to accept the contingency of the everyday. It is the unnaturalness of end-of-the-line deconstructionist thinking, thinking which raises the ante out of sight, that cries out for explanation. Why, Cavell insists, is the sceptic drawn "to just *this* form of self-defeat?" "Skepticism's 'doubt,'" he suggests, "is motivated not … by a (misguided) intellectual scrupulousness but by a (displaced) denial, by a self-consuming disappointment that seeks world-consuming revenge" (cited by Fischer, 31). What needs explaining, Cavell and Fischer conclude, is an obsessive and compulsive need to explain that manifests itself as a quest for a kind of certainty that cannot be attained in the contingent world of the everyday.

What should really amaze us is not the inescapable duplicity and mendacity of language but the extraordinary depth of the mutual attunement we ordinarily have with one another, the intimacy and pervasiveness of understanding and agreement, the sharing of feelings, values, judgments, concepts, and so on. These are unspectacular everyday achievements – the sharing of a joke or grievance – and in themselves they can hardly heal the cleavage between sign and meaning, the existence of which any mature user of language recognizes. But they do reveal the unnaturalness of dwelling on duplicity, of inflating it into a metaphysical difficulty, into an all-encompassing linguistic nihilism, and they perhaps underscore the unusual amount of denial, escape, and disappointment the sceptic necessarily embraces.

As Fischer notes, "the sense of a gap between us and others origi-
nates in our wishing to give up responsibility for maintaining those
shared forms of life linking us to others" (64). Unable to tolerate distance or separation, and eager to silence the claims that others have
upon us, the sceptic perpetuates isolation by absolutizing it. The sceptic
thereby steps outside ordinary language-games – the forms of life we
share with others – and this distancing exacerbates the sceptic's sense
that these games and forms are merely arbitrary and conventional.

As Fischer reflects:

> By linking skepticism to denial of the practical difficulty imposed by inti-
> macy, escape from the language games that ensure our communication
> with one another, and disappointment with the apparent lack of necessity
> or absoluteness that tarnishes our criteria, stigmatizing them as merely
> ours, Cavell is trying to characterize skepticism, not to refute it. There is no
> refuting skepticism any more than there is human life without disappoint-
> ment and desire. (66)

This is in many ways a compelling characterization, and it implies an
attractive alternative attitude. But it does seem to ignore the possibility
that insofar as deconstructionists belong to an interpretive community,
they are not, strictly speaking, stepping outside language-games. They
are simply playing a new language-game, one that allows its practitioners to be intimate with one another, to communicate with one another,
and to take pleasure in the apparent lack of necessity and absoluteness
that tarnishes our everyday criteria and stigmatizes them as merely
ours. True, there is something strange about the notion of a community
of sceptics – we traditionally picture the sceptic as alone in a study con-
templating the unreality of material objects and other minds – but no
one can deny that deconstruction is a powerful language-game with
many players.

In making this point, I am not at all gainsaying Fischer's astute observation that "what [Paul] de Man sees as the unruliness of language
Cavell sees as its practical resourcefulness" (129) and that "what
Derrida stigmatizes as arbitrary (because not transcendentally or absolutely grounded) Cavell accepts as natural – improvised and otherwise
dependent on human effort but not for that reason merely arbitrary or
conventional" (134). Cavell's appeal to how words are ordinarily or
actually used, however, neither does nor is meant to stop the free play
of signification. The ordinary and actual use of language is creative,

playful, diverse, and flexible. As Fischer points out, Cavell wants to secure words not by metaphysically delimiting their meaning but by tying them to everyday life. To tie words to everyday life, however, is not to endorse an uncritical acceptance of how people use language. As Emerson complains, "every word they say chagrins us and we know not where to set them right" (22–3). To be chagrined is to be realistic, but to ignore the poverty and richness of ordinary language is to deprive ourselves of insights into how we do things with words.

Other-minds scepticism, like external-world scepticism, cannot be refuted. We can only avoid or acknowledge our connections with others, express or repress our capacity for empathic projection. "We determine the humanity of others," Fischer writes, "on the basis of empathic projection – nothing more, but nothing less" (73). As Cavell reflects, we are creatures for whom language is our form of life, and language is everywhere we find ourselves. We should thus have a great deal of respect for the users and abusers of ordinary language, who can resist everything, it would seem, except the temptation of scepticism.

In the end, rhetorical realism is more of an attitude than a philosophy. Nevertheless, the fact remains that however you strategize, stylize, or narrativize a situation, if your verbal characterization "is too far out of accord with the nature of the situation, the 'unanswerable opponent,' the objective recalcitrance of the situation itself, will put forth its irrefutable rejoinder" (Burke, *Philosophy*, 131). Reality cannot be entirely captured by language, but if you do not believe in vaccinations, antibiotics, or blood transfusions, chances are reality will have the final say, sooner rather than later.

Works Cited

Brown v. Board of Education of Topeka, 347 U.S. 483 (1954).

Buck v. Bell, Superintendent, 274 U.S. 200 (1927).

Bumper v. North Carolina, 391 U.S. 543 (1967).

Cummings v. Granger (1977) Q.B. 397.

Harrison v. Carswell (1976) 2 S.C.R. 200.

Hinz v. Berry (1970) 2 Q.B. 40 (Court of Appeal).

Lloyd's Bank v. Bundy (1975) Q.B. 326 (Court of Appeal).

Miller v. Jackson (1977) Q.B. 966 (Court of Appeal).

Ontario (Ministry of Labour) v. Enbridge Gas Distribution Inc. (2011) Ontario Court of Appeal 24.

Osterlind v. Hill (1929). In *Poethics* 22–4.

Palsgraf v. Long Island Railroad, 162 N.E. 99 (N.Y. 1928). www.nycourts.gov/history/cases/palsgraf_lirr.htm, 1–11.

R. v. Ewanchuk (1998) Alberta Court of Appeal 52.

R. v. Harbottle (1993) Supreme Court of Canada 306.

R. v. Nette (1999) British Columbia Court of Appeal 2836.

R. v. Nette (2001) Supreme Court of Canada 78.

R. v. Simon (2010) Ontario Court of Appeal 4723.

Regina v. Barnsley Metropolitan Borough Council, ex parte Hook. *The Weekly Law Reports*. 5 November 1976. 1055–8.

Rusk v. State, 406 A.2d 624 (Md. Ct. Spec. App. 1979). *Atlantic Reporter, 2d Series*. 625–36.

State v. Rusk, 424 A.2d 720 (Md.1981). *Atlantic Reporter, 2d Series*. 720–38.

Abrams, M.H. "How to Do Things with Texts." In Adams and Searle, *Critical Theory Since 1965*. 436–49.

– "The Deconstructive Angel." In Lodge and Wood, *Modern Criticism and Theory*. 242–53.

Adams, Hazard, and Leroy Searle. *Critical Theory Since 1965*. Toronto: Scholarly Book Services, 2002.

Aristotle. *The Rhetoric and Poetics of Aristotle*. Trans. W. Rhys Roberts. New York: Modern Library, 1954.

Bakhtin, Mikhail. *Speech Genres and Other Late Essays*. Trans. Vern W. McGee. Ed. Caryl Emerson and Michael Holquist. Austin: University of Texas Press, 1986.

– *The Dialogic Imagination*. Trans. Caryl Emerson and Michael Holquist. Ed. Michael Holquist. Austin: University of Texas Press, 1981.

Berry, Edward. *Writing Reasons: A Handbook for Judges*. Peterborough: E-M Press, 2007.

Binder, Guyora, and Robert Weisberg. *Literary Criticisms of Law*. Princeton: Princeton University Press, 2000.

Booth, Wayne. *The Company We Keep: An Ethics of Fiction*. Berkeley: University of California Press, 1988.

Brooks, Peter. "Narrative Transactions – Does the Law Need a Narratology?" *Yale Journal of the Law and Humanities* 18, no. 1 (2006): 1–38.

– "The Law as Narrative and Rhetoric." In Brooks and Gewirtz, *Law's Stories*. 14–22.

Brooks, Peter, and Paul Gewirtz, eds. *Law's Stories: Narrative and Rhetoric in the Law*. New Haven: Yale University Press, 1996.

Burke, Kenneth. *Attitudes Toward History*, 3rd ed. Berkeley: University of California Press, 1984.

– *Language as Symbolic Action: Essays on Life, Literature, and Method*. Berkeley: University of California Press, 1966.

– *The Philosophy of Literary Form: Studies in Symbolic Action*, 3rd ed. Berkeley: University of California Press, 1973.

– *A Rhetoric of Motives*. Berkeley: University of California Press, 1969.

Burns, Robert P. "Rhetoric in the Law." In Jost and Olmsted, *A Companion*. 442–56.

Cardozo, Benjamin N. *Law and Literature and Other Essays and Addresses*. New York: Harcourt, Brace, and Company, 1931.

Cascardi, Anthony J. "Arts of Persuasion and Judgment: Rhetoric and Aesthetics." In Jost and Olmsted, *A Companion*. 294–308.

Cavell, Stanley. *This New Yet Unapproachable America: Lectures after Emerson after Wittgenstein*. Albuquerque: Living Batch Press, 1989.

Conrad, Joseph. *Heart of Darkness*. New York: Penguin Books, 1999.

– "The Condition of Art." In *The Portable Conrad*. New York: Penguin Classics, 2007.

Cover, Robert. "Violence and the Word." In *Narrative, Violence, and the Law: The Essays of Robert Cover*. Ann Arbor: University of Michigan Press, 1993. 203–38.

Derrida, Jacques. "Structure, Sign, and Play in the Discourse of the Human Sciences." In Lodge and Wood, *Modern Criticism and Theory*. 89–103.

Dershowitz, Alan. "Life Is Not a Dramatic Narrative." In Brooks and Gewirtz, *Law's Stories*. 99–105.

Dworkin, Ronald. *Law's Empire*. Cambridge, MA: Harvard University Press, 1986.

Emerson, Ralph Waldo. *Self-Reliance: An Excerpt from Collected Essays, First Series*. Rockville: Arc Manor, 2007.

Fischer, Michael. *Stanley Cavell and Literary Skepticism*. Chicago: University of Chicago Press, 1989.

Fish, Stanley. *Doing What Comes Naturally: Change, Rhetoric, and the Practice of Theory in Literary and Legal Studies*. Durham: Duke University Press, 1989.

Gaonkar, Dilip Parmeshwar. "Contingency and Probability." In Jost and Olmsted, *A Companion*. 5–21.

Gardner, John. *The Art of Fiction*. New York: Vintage Books, 1983.

Genette, Gerard. *Narrative Discourse: An Essay in Method*. Trans. Jane Lewis. Ithaca: Cornell University Press, 1980.

Gewirtz, Paul. "Narrative and Rhetoric in the Law." In Brooks and Gewirtz, *Law's Stories*. 99–105.

Goldfarb, Ronald, and James Raymond. *Clear Understandings: A Guide to Legal Writing*. New York: Random House, 1983.

Jakobson, Roman. "Linguistics and Poetics." In Lodge and Woods, *Modern Criticism and Theory*. 30–55.

Jost, Walter, and Wendy Olmsted, eds. *A Companion to Rhetoric and Rhetorical Criticism*. Oxford: Wiley-Blackwell, 2006.

Kastely, James L. "Rhetoric and Emotion." In Jost and Olmsted, *A Companion*. 221–37.

Kolodny, Annette. "Dancing through the Minefield: Some Observations on the Theory, Practice, and Politics of a Feminist Literary Criticism." In *The Norton Anthology of Theory and Criticism*, 2nd ed. Ed. Vincent B. Leitch. New York: W.W. Norton, 2010. 2048–66.

Levinson, Sanford. "The Rhetoric of Judicial Opinion." In Brooks and Gewirtz, *Law's Stories*. 187–205.

Lodge, David, and Nigel Wood, eds. *Modern Criticism and Theory: A Reader*, 2nd ed. New York: Pearson, 2000.

Makin, Kirk. "The Judge Who Writes Like a Paperback Novelist." *Globe and Mail*. 10 March 2011.

McKeon, Richard. *Rhetoric: Essays in Invention and Discovery*. Ed. Mark Backman. Woodbridge: Ox Bow Press, 1987.

Nussbaum, Martha. *Poetic Justice: The Literary Imagination and Public Life*. Boston: Beacon Press, 1995.

Perell, Paul M. *The Case for Rhetoric*. Doctor of Jurisprudence thesis, Graduate Program in Law, York University, Osgoode Hall Law School. Toronto, April 1998.

Posner, Richard. "Judges' Writing Styles (And Do They Matter?)." 62 *The University of Chicago Law Review*, 1995. 1421–49.

– *Law and Literature*. Cambridge, MA: Harvard University Press, 2002.

Rodell, Fred. "Goodbye to Law Reviews." 23 *Virginia Law Review*, November 1936. 38–45.

Scheppele, Kim Lane. "Cultures of Facts." *Perspectives on Politics* 1, no. 2 (2003): 363–9.

Volosinov, V. *Marxism and the Philosophy of Language*. Trans. Ladislav Matejka and I.R. Titunik. Cambridge, MA: Harvard University Press, 1986.

Walters, Jesse. In Goldfarb and Raymond, *Clear Understandings*, 71.

Weisberg, Richard. *Poethics and Other Strategies of Law and Literature*. New York: Columbia University Press, 1992.

Wess, Robert. *Kenneth Burke: Rhetoric, Subjectivity, Postmodernism*. Cambridge: Cambridge University Press, 1996.

White, James Boyd. *Heracles' Bow: Essays on the Rhetoric and Poetics of the Law*. Madison: University of Wisconsin Press, 1985.

– *Justice as Translation: An Essay in Cultural and Legal Criticism*. Chicago: University of Chicago Press, 1990.

Wittgenstein, Ludwig. *Philosophical Investigations*. Trans. G.E.M. Anscombe. Oxford: Basil, Blackwell, and Mott, 1958.

Index

Abrams, M.H., 163
agency, 93, 94
Alberta Court of Appeal, 97, 105–8
analogy: of causation as a stream,
   67–8; characteristic of, 64; as core
   of practical argumentation, 150;
   example of performative, 153; in
   judgments, use of, 36, 62–3, 64;
   logic and, 36; in writing and
   fiction, 157–8
Andrews, William Shankland,
   Justice: characteristic of narrative
   of, 70n3; on conclusions on the
   basis of politics, 85; on duty of
   care, 66; interpretation of *Palsgraf*
   case, 10, 60–1, 65, 69, 71, 152; on
   negligence, 66; on philosophical
   doctrine of causation, 74; on
   proximate cause, 66–7, 68, 69;
   style of, 65; use of analogy by, 11,
   66–7, 68, 69, 70, 71
antifoundationalism, 148, 149, 160
Antony, Marc, 19
Arbour, Louise, Justice, 87
arête, notion of, 145
Aristotle: conception of contingent,
   147; Plato and, 15, 143, 150; on

practical thought, 15; on pre-
   knowledge, 150; on prudential
   wisdom, 149; on relationship, 143;
   on rhetoric, 36, 147

Bakhtin, Mikhail, 12, 13, 95–6
Berry, Edward, 44, 93, 93n2
Bill C-49: An Act to amend the
   Criminal Code, 109–10, 113, 114
Binder, Guyora, 4, 18n5, 31
Booth, Wayne, 29, 33n12
Bown, Elaine, 75, 76, 77, 78
Braley, Henry K., Justice, 59
British Columbia Court of Appeal,
   79, 80
Brooks, Peter, 5, 99
Brown, Linda, 8, 31
Brown v. Board of Education of Topeka,
   8, 31
Brutus, Marcus Junius, 19
Buck, Carrie, 34, 35
Buck v. Bell, Superintendent, 9, 33, 36
Bumper v. North Carolina, 95
Bundy, Herbert, 40, 41–2, 43
Burke, Kenneth: *Language as
   Symbolic Action*, 158; on percep-
   tion of reality, 160; on rhetoric,

152; *A Rhetoric of Motives*, 27n10; on temporizing of essence, 26, 27n10; on terministic screens, 159; on terminology and reality, 158–9
Burns, Robert P., 151

Caesar, Julius, 19, 20
Cantor, Jay, 165
Cardozo, Benjamin, Justice: on form and substance, 38; on impact of judgment, 25; interpretation of *Palsgraf* case, 10, 60, 61, 71, 151–2; legal thinking of, 72; on proof of negligence, 62; on substance, 32, 38; use of analogy by, 62–3, 64; use of figures of speech by, 11; use of vague expressions by, 63; writing style of, 61–2
Cascardi, Anthony J., 150
causation: concept of, 74; definition in Criminal Code, 77–8; distinctions of, 12; doctrine of, 74; legal *vs.* factual, 87
cause: in relation to effect, 65–6; substantial *vs.* contributing, 82
Cavell, Stanley, 164, 165, 166, 167–8
chaos theory, 66
Chekhov, Anton, 28
Cicero, 150
coherentism, 160
Cole, Harry A., Judge: judgment of *Rusk* case, 120; on overturned rape convictions, 141; on performance of sexual activities, 140; rape cases cited by, 141–2; sexist mindset of, 139–40; on victim's behaviour, 139, 141
Conrad, Joseph, 33, 86
consent: characteristics of, 110; concept of, 22; Criminal Code on,

102, 110; debate on legal meaning of, 107, 108; *vs.* lack of resistance, 110–11; standards of, 14; stereotypical assumptions about, 117; *vs.* submission to the act, 134; use of force and lack of, 131, 133
constructionism, 160, 161
contingent, characteristics of, 147, 148
Cory, Peter deCarteret, Justice, 75, 76, 77, 78, 79
Court of Appeals of Maryland, 14, 120, 130
Cover, Robert, 3, 6
Cribb, Everton, 50, 51
cricket, 53–4
Criminal Code: 1992 amendments to, 109–10, 114; on first degree murder, 76, 77–8, 83; on forcible confinement, 83; on meaning of consent, 102, 103, 109; section 214(5), 76, 77–8; section 273.1, 102, 109; section 273.2 (b), 103
Cummings v. Granger, 55–7

deconstruction, 165
Denning, Alfred Thompson (Tom): on cause and effect, 71; characteristics of judgments of, 39, 41; on *Cummings v. Granger*, 55–7; depiction of Herbert Bundy by, 42; distinctive style of, 9, 40–1, 42–5, 49; legal reasoning of, 45; length of sentences, 41, 44; logic of exposition of, 45; on *Miller v. Jackson*, 53–4; noticeable introductions of, 39–40; opinion on Harry Hook case, 92; on *Palsgraf v. Long Island Railroad*, 70–1; on public *vs.* private interests, 53–4; racist remarks

of, 55; reliance on imagery and
narrative, 20–1; on signing bank
guarantee, 43; storytelling in appellate decisions, 8, 75; views of,
9, 55, 57; *What Next in the Law*, 54;
writing language of, 7, 20, 42
Derrida, Jacques, 163, 165, 167
Dershowitz, Alan, 8, 27, 28, 29
Dickson, Brian, Justice, 93
doxa (realm of opinion and rhetoric),
145
drama, Chekhov's conception of, 28
Dworkin, Ronald, 90

Edward S. Rusk v. State of Maryland.
See *Rusk v. State*
eloquence: consequences of, 18n5;
justice and, 32, 33, 36; and virtue,
16, 37
Emerson, Ralph Waldo, 168
enargeia, 20
Enbridge Gas, 46, 47
episteme (realm of truth and philosophy), 145
ethos, 5, 6, 58, 153–4
Ewanchuk, Steven Brian, 21, 97,
100–1, 105. See also *R. v. Ewanchuk*

Farrer v. the United States, 131
Fischer, Michael, 165, 166, 167, 168
Fish, Stanley, 148, 161–3
focalization, 91, 94
force, as element of crime, 130, 131,
133
formative vocabularies, 158
forms, theory of, 144–5
Fraser, Catherine, Chief Justice: on
consent, 108, 109, 110, 111–12,
113–14; dissent on *Ewanchuk*
case, 105, 108–9, 112–13; polemic

with McClung, 112–15; reliance
on scholarship, 114–15; views of
responsibility of judges, 114

Gaonkar, Dilip Parameshwar, 146,
147, 148
Genette, Gerard, 29, 90
Gewirtz, Paul, 3, 5, 89
Globe and Mail, 9, 118
Gorgias (Plato), 146

Harbottle, James, 75, 76, 78, 80
Harrison v. Carswell, 93
Hazel v. State, 130, 137, 138–9, 141
Hinz v. Berry, 20, 39
Holmes, Oliver Wendell, 9, 33–4, 35
Hook, Harry, 92
human story, 26–7, 28, 31–2. *See also*
narratives; storytelling
Hume, David, 74

imbecile, definition of, 36
interpretations, 160, 162
interpretive communities, 148–9

Jakobson, Roman, 17
judges: omniscient point of view, 91;
pragmatism of, 72–3; rhetorical
choices of, 58
judgments: characteristic of, 15,
89–90, 117; conditions for lasting
impact of, 25; construction of, 71,
153; as dialogue, 117; focalization
and verbalization in, 91; impact
of human and legal stories on,
31; language of, 13–14, 96–7; legal
world created by, 14; as narratives,
8, 16, 26; strategies of writers of,
58; use of imagery and figuration
in, 22

judicial discourse, 17
judicial opinion, 18, 18n4
judicial rhetoric, 57
judicial self-fashioning, 10, 153
judicial writing: analogies in, 11–12; as form of rhetoric, 5; function of language in, 7; importance of legal thinking in, 71; strategies of persuasion, 5–6. *See also* legal writing

Katz v. US, 153
knowledge, 15, 147, 160, 161
Kolodny, Annette, 157

Lambert, John Douglas, Justice: appeal to *pathos*, 82; on casual standards, 85; on cause tests, 84; decision on *R. v. Nette*, 87; on facts found by jury in *Nette* case, 81–2; language of, 85–6; legal principles derived from *Harbottle* case, 84; views of, 85; writing style of, 81, 82
language: as dialogue, 13; function of, 16; intensity of concentration on, 17, 17n3; of judgments, 13–14; in judicial discourse, role of, 14; of law, 13; literary function of, 17, 18; ordinary and actual use of, 167–8; philosophy of, 164–5; reality and, 159, 168; as social activity, 95–6
language-game, 164, 167
Laskin, Bora, Justice, 93, 94
law: as branch of rhetoric, 5, 15, 58; communal nature of, 6–7; facts and, 79; interpretations of stories in, 6; language of, 96–7; linguistic practices of, 151; literary as a constitutive dimension of, 31;

as literature, 4, 5; meaning of, 3; multiplicity of reading in, 7; role of narrative in, 3–4; as system of rules, 151; value of storytelling in, 75
Law's Empire (Dworkin), 90
lawyers, evolution of craft of, 18n5
legal reasoning, 155
legal story, 27, 28
legal writing: logic function in, 155n1; parts of, 36; problem of decorum in, 39; style and content, 38. *See also* judicial writing
Leonard, Elmore, 39, 48
Levinson, Sanford, 32
L'Heureux-Dubé, Claire, Justice: on Bill C-49, 117; *vs.* McClung, 21n6, 116; reference to scholarly texts, 116; on role of judges, 116; ruling on *Ewanchuk* case, 98, 115–16; on sexual consent, 115; sources of, 115; on violence against women, 115
Lincoln, Abraham, 18n5
literary function, 17, 17n2, 21
literary scepticism, 165
Lloyd's Bank v. Bundy, 9, 40
logic, 80, 153, 155
logos, 5, 58
Lord Denning. *See* Denning, Alfred Thompson

Major, John C., Justice, 97, 115
Makin, Kirk, 39
manslaughter, *vs.* murder, 82, 88
McClung, John W., Justice: attack on political correctness, 26n8; on consent, 113; criticism of, 116–17; decision on *Ewanchuk* case, 21, 21n6, 23, 24; inappropriate comments

of, 117–18; intended audience of, 26; language of, 25, 25n7, 26; letter to *National Post*, 106–7; literary devices used by, 24, 25; media attention to, 118; opinion on *Ewanchuk* case, 97, 98, 105–8, 113; polemic with Fraser, 112–15; on sexual assault, 23; stereotypic mindset of, 7, 22; writing and rhetoric of, 7, 23

McClung, Nellie, 112
McEachern, Allan, Justice, 87
McKeon, Richard, 161
McLachlin, Beverley, Justice, 117
mens rea for sexual assault, 111–12
metaphor, definition and function of, 152
Miller v. Jackson, 53–5
Moore, John, Justice, 103, 112
Mount, Nick, 26n8
murder: definition of first degree, 83; first degree *vs.* second degree, 82, 84–5; *vs.* manslaughter, 82; standard of causation for second degree, 84
Murphy, Joseph F., Chief Judge, 120, 136, 137

Narrative Discourse (Genette), 90
narratives: bias of, 13; of civil order, 27n10; creation of images through legal, 7; in law, role of, 3–4, 26n9, 89; in legal decision-making, 12–13, 154–5; narrators and, 94; nature of, 29, 37; persuasive power of, 120; problem of interpretation of, 14; rhetorical force of, 150; of trial, 27n11. *See also* human story; storytelling
narrative theory, 89
narrative thinking, 27

narratology, 12–13
National Post, 106
negligence, 65–6
Nicomachean Ethics (Aristotle), 149
Nietzsche, Friedrich, 160
nihilism, 148
nomos (normative universe), 3
Noonan, John T., Judge, 72
Nussbaum, Martha, 33n12

*Ontario (Ministry of Labour) v.
    Enbridge Gas Distribution Inc.*, 46–9
opening statements, 151
Osterlind v. Hill, 58–9

Palsgraf, Helen, 10, 11, 61, 69, 70
Palsgraf v. Long Island Railroad:
    Andrews's interpretation of, 10, 60–1, 65, 69, 71, 152; appeal at New York's highest court, 60; brief, 59–60; Cardozo's interpretation of, 10, 60, 61, 71, 151–2; Denning's opinion on, 70–1; issue of liability, 71; judgments on, 60–1, 70–1; omission of scientific considerations, 71; proximate cause, 71; social perspective, 72; use of analogy in judgments, 62–3, 64, 152
paralipsis, 23
pathos, 5, 20, 58, 146, 153
Perell, Paul, Justice, 16n1, 154
Perelman, Chaim, 156
persuasion: concept of, 18–19; as cornerstone of rhetoric, 156; cost of, 32
Petty Trespasses Act, 93
Phaedrus (Plato), 145
Philosophical Investigations (Wittgenstein), 164
phronesis (practical thought), 15

Plato: Aristotle and, 15, 143, 150; in European philosophical tradition, 145; on rhetoric, 145–6; theory of forms of, 144–5; view of rhetoric, 147
pluralism, 157
Poethics (Richard Weisberg), 8, 31
Porter, Jason, 50, 51, 52
Posner, Richard: on judicial writing, 10n1; on poetic description of facts, 8; on school of legal scholarship, 32; on style, 9–10, 10n2, 31, 49, 62; on unnecessary details in judicial opinions, 18
postmodernity, 160
postmodern rhetor, 163
Precision Utility, 46, 47
proximate cause: concept of, 11, 66–7, 69; consequences of, 65

railroad accidents, 72
rape: definition of common law, 137; definition of crime of second degree, 132; overturned convictions of, 141; pamphlet of Department of Justice on, 135–6; resistance to, 133–4; statistics of, 135; taboos and myths of, 135; unreported incidents of, 134
reality: distortion of, 28; language and, 168; symbolism of, 159
reason, *vs.* rhetoric, 162
Regina v. Barnsley, 92
relativism, 161
rhetoric: as art, 146–7, 158; contingency of, 148, 160; definition of, 5, 144; devices of, 73; discourses of, 158; instrumental approach to, 161; law as branch of, 58; narrative examples in classical, 150; in

opening statements, 151; as part of judicial decision-making, 72, 80; persuasion in, 150, 156; Plato on, 145–6; popular perception of, 144; postmodernist, 161–2, 163; power of, 146; probable reasoning and, 150; *vs.* reason, 162; strategies of, 37; terministic screen of, 159–60; three parts of discourse of, 6
rhetorical realism, 90n1, 158, 161, 164, 168
rhetorical reasoning, 155
rhetorical screen, 159–60
Rhetoric of Motives, A (Burke), 27n10
Rodell, Fred, 38
Ross, Shawn, 75, 76, 78
Rusk v. State: brief, 14, 119; conflicting discourses of, 119–20; encounters of victim and defendant, 122–3, 124, 128, 129; personality of victim, 129–30, 138; rape complaint, 136; report to police, 129; Rusk's testimony, 137; testimony of defendant's friends, 137; victim's testimony, 121–2, 125
R. v. Ewanchuk: argument of the Crown, 102; argument of the Defence, 102–3; Chief Justice Fraser in dissent, 108–12; decision of Supreme Court on, 115–17; McClung's judgment, 21–2, 23; McClung *vs.* Fraser, 112–15; media and public attention to, 106–7, 117–18; Moore's judgment, 103–4; question of sexual assault, 97–8; rhetoric of judgments in, 14, 97; testimonies, 99–102; trial transcript, 98
R. v. Farrant, 83
R. v. Hallet, 86

R. v. Harbottle: brief, 80; comparison with *R. v. Nette*, 83–4; Cory's conclusion on, 75, 76–9; facts as basis for persuasion, 86–7; impact of appellant's testimony, 118; Lambert's decision on, 87; moral criteria in, 83; standard of causation for second degree murder, 81, 85; statement of appellant, 75–6

R. v. Meiler, 84

R. v. Nette: brief, 79, 80–1; comparison with *R. v. Harbottle*, 83–4; dismissal of appeal, 81; jury verdict, 80, 82; limits of logic in, 80; recommendations of Supreme Court, 88

R. v. Osolin, 115

R. v. Simon: brief, 51–2; characteristic of, 50; fault element in, 50; judgment on, 51, 52; style of, 53

scepticism, 72, 165, 166, 167, 168

Scheppele, Kim Lane, 72

sexual assault: attempt to reform law of, 25; definition of, 111; scenarios of, 141–2; scholarly works on, 114; stereotypic attitudes to, 141–2

Sexual Consent (Archard), 115

Simon, Allister, 50

Simons, David, 124

Simpson, O.J., 8, 27

Smithers v. The Queen: brief, 87–8; decision on, 79; Lambert on, 85–6; standard of causation in, 81

Society of Black Lawyers, 55

sophists, 145

Stanley Cavell and Literary Skepticism (Fischer), 165

sterilization of mentally disabled women, 34

Stewart, Potter, Justice, 95

stories, 16, 16n1, 26–7, 29

storytelling: characteristic of, 5; in courtroom, competition in, 154; in law, 6, 26n9; in legal decision-making, 142–3; in literature, 6; as persuasion, 75, 154

strategies of reading, 159

Strode, Aubrey E., 34, 36

style: call for pure and formalist, 10, 10n2; as integral part of writing, 9; of legal writing, 38; omniscient, 91; variety of, 38; virtue and, 9

Supreme Court of Australia, 86

Supreme Court of Canada: decision on *Harrison v. Carswell*, 93; decision on *R. v. Ewanchuk*, 21–2; decision on *R. v. Nette*, 79, 87; on distinction between first and second degree murder, 84–5

temporizing of essence, 27n10

terministic screens, 159

terminology, 159

text, features and structure of, 162

Thompson, Charles Awdry, Judge: chauvinism of, 131; on consent, 131; on force as element of crime, 130; on "heavy caress," 131–2; manner of portraying victims of rape, 131–2; opinion on *Hazel v. State*, 130–1, 132; opinion on *Rusk v. State*, 14, 121, 122, 124, 125–6, 129; responsibilities as appellant judge, 126; selection and interpretation of facts by, 121, 122–3, 128; vs. Wilner, 121, 128; writing for the majority in *Rusk v. State*, 119

threats to safety, 132, 133

train accidents, 72

truth, expression and interpretation of, 145, 161

Veblen, Thorstein, 160
verbalization, 91, 94
Virginia statute on prevention of transmission of insanity and imbecility, 35
Volosinov, V., 96

Walters, Jesse R., 30
Warren, Earl Burger, Chief Justice, 32
Warren Bitulithic Limited, 46
Watt, David, Justice: characteristic of writing of, 9, 39; judgment on *Ontario v. Enbridge Gas*, 46–8; judgment on *R. v. Simon*, 49, 50–2; personalization of victims by, 48; style of, 10, 46–7, 48, 49, 52–3; use of irrelevant facts by, 49; vocabulary of, 47
Weisberg, Richard, 8, 9, 16, 32, 35, 58n1
Weisberg, Robert, 4, 18n5, 31
Wess, Robert, 90, 158, 161
White, James Boyd: on analogy and disanalogy, 17; on judicial decision-making, 89–90; on *Katz v. US*, 153; on law and literature, 4, 6; on narratives in legal cases, 154; on persuasiveness, 16; on relations between ethics and aesthetics, 9, 33
Whitehead, Alfred North, 145
Whitehead, I.P., 34
Williams, Glanville, 85
Wilner, Alan M., Judge: on consent, 129, 133, 134; on crime of rape, 119–20, 132, 133–4, 135; legal analysis of *Hazel v. State*, 132–3; on myths and taboos around rape, 135; opinion on *Rusk v. State*, 14, 121–3, 124, 127–8, 129, 130; rhetorical strategy of, 123; on Rusk conviction, 120; on social perspective of rape, 130; *vs.* Thompson, 121, 128; on threats to safety, 133; on use of force, 133; on victim's state of mind in *Rusk* case, 136
Winegan v. State, 131
wisdom, conception of prudential, 149
Wittgenstein, Ludwig, 151, 158, 164
Writing Reasons (Berry), 44, 92

Zamora v. State, 141

Lightning Source UK Ltd.
Milton Keynes UK
UKOW04n2319150715

255240UK00002B/8/P

9 781442 637085